50 COOL STORIES 3000 HOT WORDS
Master VOCABULARY in 50 Days

Avinash Inamdar

What this book does for you ?

- ➢ Improves Vocabulary
- ➢ Improves General Awareness
- ➢ Improves Reading Skills
- ➢ Teaches Contextual Usage
- ➢ Helps in Essay Writing
- ➢ Inputs for GD/PI
- ➢ Improves Business Awareness
- ➢ Updates on Current Trends/Issues

- **Head Office :** B-32, Shivalik Main Road, Malviya Nagar, New Delhi-110017
- **Sales Office :** B-48, Shivalik Main Road, Malviya Nagar, New Delhi-110017
  Tel. : 011-26691021 / 26691713

Typeset by Disha DTP Team

DISHA PUBLICATION

ALL RIGHTS RESERVED

For further information about the books from DISHA,

Log on to **www.dishapublication.com** or email to **info@dishapublication.com**

How Useful Is This Book For You?

Ever wonder why being good at English vocabulary is a key to success in your career and social life? In academic exams, competitive exams, interviews and group discussions, a good skill of English vocabulary is necessary. Learning to improve English vocabulary constitutes words, form of words, usage of words etc. With the skills of English vocabulary, you can improve your English, speak in the correct way and use the language like a master.

50 Cool Stories 3000 Hot Words is not a book on the vocabulary building in the traditional sense; it represents a great deal more on a technique of expressing ideas and concepts than do most books. The book contains around **3000 words, idioms and phrasal verbs** that are used in day to day contexts using our unique approach to building vocabulary skills. **50 Cool Stories 3000 Hot Words** uses interesting themes to show how to use words effectively. There are chapters that discuss science, technology, economy, politics; talking about various professions, describing actions and so on. It takes a usage of the word based approach to vocabulary building and traces the replacement of the words being used.

There are a number of features in the book that will help you to navigate from idea to idea. All of the topics give information on **how to improve vocabulary, how to improve general awareness and reading skills.** The purpose of this book is to stimulate interest on a topic that has been a public interest. It assures to improve your confidence, job skills and educational performance.

With this book, you will be able to:

- Expand your vocabulary

- Speak with style

- Write with élan

- Make a better impression at competitive exams, interviews and group discussions

- Use the right words for formal occasions and social events

We hope that **50 Cool Stories 3000 Hot Words** will help those who aspire to learn and practise words, idioms, phrasal verbs that will in turn help them speak and write naturally in English and encourage them to find out more about English language.

– Author

DISHA'S MBA Books At a Glance

Index

STORY 1   I'm Gonna Whup Whoever Stole my Bike!   1

STORY 2   Abolish the Scissors   4

STORY 3   Skirts for Boys, Trousers for Girls   7

STORY 4   Could India Have been an NSG member already?   10

STORY 5   GST Bill- All hurdles cleared?   13

STORY 6   Targeting individual over Sexual Orientation   16

STORY 7   Who can Stop Trump?   19

STORY 8   Face Extreme Whether Conditions in India   22

STORY 9   Education is the Weapon That Can Change the World   25

STORY 10   "Should Educational Qualification Be Made Mandatory for Politicians?"   28

STORY 11   Terraforming   31

STORY 12   The Asian Skyscraper Mania   35

STORY 13   Where Adult Fear to Tread   40

STORY 14   Peer Pressure   45

STORY 15   Vocal Wisdom   49

STORY 16   Pseudonyms   53

STORY 17   The 10 Percent Brain Myth   57

STORY 18   Baby, You Can Take My Heart (I am Getting a Transplant !)   61

STORY 19   Whats on and Whats Off?   67

STORY 20   The Second World War   71

STORY 21   The Reality Circus   75

STORY 22   Is the Keyboard Mightier than the Pen?   80

STORY 23   Smartness is a many Splendored Thing   86

STORY 24	The Battle of Brands	90
STORY 25	Flying in Red Ink	95
STORY 26	Home Smart Home	102
STORY 27	The Shakespeare Controversy	107
STORY 28	Are 3D Movies worth it?	112
STORY 29	Prisoners of Cyberia	117
STORY 30	The Gifts of War	121
STORY 31	Celebrating their Way to the Banks	125
STORY 32	The Glass Ceiling	130
STORY 33	Technology Leapfrogging	135
STORY 34	Shopaholism	140
STORY 35	The Killer Sports	145
STORY 36	Stereotypes	151
STORY 37	Lean and Mean I'm Polythene	157
STORY 38	The Statistical Liar	161
STORY 39	The Cold War	167
STORY 40	Are Newspapers also an Endangered Species?	174
STORY 41	Politically Correct	179
STORY 42	Are We Getting Taller?	184
STORY 43	Peculiar Social Customs	188
STORY 44	What is Hypnosis?	193
STORY 45	Idiot Box Turns Brainy Beauty	198
STORY 46	Canine Commando	202
STORY 47	The Homemaker Entrepreneur	208
STORY 48	China, The Second Super Power	212
STORY 49	Extinction of Species	217
STORY 50	Going to the Movies	221
GLOSSARY		225

DISHA'S General Knowledge Books At a Glance

I'M GONNA WHUP WHOEVER STOLE MY BIKE!

Cassius Clay Sr. gave his son a new red-and-white bike in 1954, which was soon stolen. The 12-year-old, Cassius Clay pledged 'I'm gonna whup whoever stole my bike!" A policeman who was looking into the theft told young Cassius Clay that he better learn how to fight before he challenged anyone. After a brief training with Joe Martin, an instructor, Cassius won his **debut** match in a three-round decision. Young Cassius Clay dedicated himself to boxing with an **unrivalled** fervour. According to Joe Martin, Clay set himself apart by two things: He was '**sassy**', and he outworked all the other boys.

Muhammad Ali or Cassius Clay Jr. was born in 1942 in America into a middle-class family. This black American was an **endowment** to his poor parents, his father a sign painter and mother a part-time cook and cleaner. Who knew one day he would be known as the greatest heavyweight champion of the 20th century! He won 56 matches and lost merely 5 in his 21 year professional career. Among those 56 matches 37 were perfect knockouts. A three-time world heavyweight champion in 1964, 1974 and 1978 died on 3rd June, 2016 in Scottsdale, Arizona. He said that he always wanted to be 'someone', someone who was more than a boxer.

Ali's career in boxing **set out** at the local police station, where **serendipitously** he met Joe Martin. Joe Martin was an officer as well as an instructor. Here he was to file a complaint but maybe God had planned Joe to become his first trainer in the field of boxing!

After he won against Sonny Liston, he converted to the Nation of Islam. He felt that the right time was yet to come to speak about his conversion. Finally, a right day came when he revealed about his conversion to Islam publicly.

Ali was an outspoken person. He spoke **candidly** on issues of race, religion politics etc. He spoke against the terrorist attack of 11 September, 2001. This outspokenness of his came into being due to the fact that he was a **bystander** of how black people in his own nation were treated. He was brought up in an environment where blacks were slaved and it was a disgrace for him to watch them at an early stage. He couldn't see his own people die like this every single day.

So when the armed forces invited him to fight the Vietnam War, he **repudiated**. He never wanted to join hands with those people who were actually his alleged **perpetrators**. He believed in peace and equality. Subsequently, he became a **contentious** figure. Later on, he was sent in for trial and therefore, he was away from boxing from March 1967 to October 1970.

Apart from being a great boxer, Ali was also a great human being. George Foreman rightly called Ali "the greatest human being". He was a devoted humanitarian and provided 232 million meals to the **destitute** in his nation and outside, wherever he got a chance to play. Even after retirement his charitable works didn't come to a halt. He has contributed to Make- A-Wish Foundation, Special Olympics and lately to Muhammad Ali Parkinson's Center.

He was and will remain a true inspiration for many. He was a leader for African Americans, Muslims and boxers. His fans included renowned names such as Elvis Bertrand, Russell and Nelson Mandela. He exhibited **improbable** courage despite physical disability in 1984. He was suffering from a respiratory disease and was declared dead at the age of 87 this year.

It is usually very rare to find a **concoction** like Ali who tasted success both on and off the field. One of his famous quotes is "Float like a butterfly, sting like a bee."

Muhammad Ali **consecrated** his life to his **incredible** work. Unlike others, for example, film or sports stars who live all for fame and money but good works, he always did what he thought was right to do at that moment. His mentality was quite different from selfish and money-minded people of this world. He was a focused person and knew what he was doing.

His ultimate mission was to fight for the injustices of black and poor people and rescue them from their cages. Another of his famous quote is "Service to others is the rent you pay for room here on Earth." He has undoubtedly and definitely lived up to what he has quoted, which proves that he was a man of his words. He will be **immortalised** always as an **exemplar** of great mankind that was once on this Earth.

Bystander
Contextual Meaning(s) : noun; somebody who observes but is not involved in something
Synonyms : eyewitness, spectator

Candidly
Contextual Meaning(s) : adverb; characterized by openness, and sincerity of expression, unreservedly, straightforward
Synonyms : honestly, frankly

Concoction
Contextual Meaning(s) : noun; a new and unusual mixture
Synonyms : mixture, blend

Debut
Contextual Meaning(s) : noun; the act of starting something for the first time
Synonyms : introductory, launching

Destitute
Contextual Meaning(s) : adjective; lacking all money, resources, and possessions necessary for subsistence
Other Meaning(s) : lacking something, lacking a particular quality, e.g.; destitute of ideas
Synonyms : poor, impoverished

Endowment
Contextual Meaning(s) : noun; a natural ability or quality
Synonyms : gift, talent

Exemplar
Contextual Meaning(s) : noun; an ideal example of something, worthy of something being copied or imitated
Synonyms : example, model

Immortalize
Contextual Meaning(s) : verb; make famous forever
Synonyms : remembered, commemorate

Improbable
Contextual Meaning(s) : adjective; not likely to be true or to occur or to have occurred
Synonyms : doubtful, unbelievable

Marvellous
Contextual Meaning(s) : adjective; amazingly impressive, extraordinarily wonderful, e.g.; a marvellous example of Baroque architecture
Synonyms : wonderful, amazing

Perpetrators
Contextual Meaning(s) : noun; Someone who perpetrates wrongdoing
Synonyms : culprit, wrongdoer

Repudiate
Contextual Meaning(s) : verb; cast off, to refuse to acknowledge as belonging or pertaining to oneself
Synonyms : disown, renounce

Sassy
Contextual Meaning(s) : adjective; Improperly forward or bold
Synonyms : overbold, smart

Set out
Contextual Meaning(s) : verb; take the first step or steps in carrying out an action
Synonyms : commence, begin

Serendipitously
Contextual Meaning(s) : adverb; in a serendipitous manner; fortunately; by lucky chance
Synonyms : accidentally, fortunately

Unrivalled
Contextual Meaning(s) : adjective; eminent beyond or above comparison
Synonyms : matchless, nonpareil

ABOLISH THE SCISSORS?

"Censorship is when a work of art expressing an idea which does not fall under current convention is seized, cut up, withdrawn, impounded, ignored, maligned, or otherwise made inaccessible to its audience."

— Ritu Menon, for Women's World Organisation for Rights, Literature, and Development

Cinema in India emerged in the 1890s and soon came to Bombay. Around that time, there was already some regulation of dramatic performances. We had the Dramatic Performances Act of 1876 and India also got press controls. Around the First World War, British decided that cinema would need its own laws. The British government was much more worried about cinema sending out messages of freedom and independence rather than about moralistic matters

Post Independence autonomy of regional censors was abolished and they were brought under the **purview** of Bombay Board of Film Censors. After implementing the Cinematograph Act, 1952, the board was unified and reconstituted, as the Central Board of Film Censors. Cinematograph (Certification) Rules were revised in 1983 and since then the Central Board of Film Censors became known as the Central Board of Film Certification. All Indian films are certified under CBFC. It is a statutory body under the Ministry of Information and Broadcasting and its headquarters lies in Mumbai.

Currently films are certified under 4 heads, namely- U, UA, A and S. U stands for unrestricted public exhibition, UA stands for unrestricted public exhibition- but with a word of caution that parental *discretion* required for children below 12 years, A stands for restricted to adults and S stands for restricted to any special class of persons.

Recently, Udta Punjab controversy was in the headlines and in other social media. The film speaks about crucial and social issue of drug abuse and related crimes in Punjab. The controversy broke in when the Chairperson of CBFC tried to stop the release of the film and demanded to extract the word Punjab from their title and suggested 89 cuts. From then on, a debate started *brewing* **up** between the makers of the film and the Chairperson, Pahlaj Nihalani. Now it is clear that the censors are trying to *bleep out* things and a certain kind of *ultra-conservativeness* is being imposed. But is that really possible in this day and age, especially with technology that can make censorship *redundant*?

There was a huge controversy in connection with the kissing scene in Dhoom 2 resulting in people burning movie's posters and obstructing people from entering the cinema halls to watch the film. Vishwaroopam, a Tamil film was blocked by the Tamil Nadu government after a protest from the Muslim Community. The Vishwa Hindu Parishad protested against the women modelling dresses bearing images of Hindu Gods. A Fatwa was brought against all girls rock band saying it was Un-Islamic. Cartoonist and activist, Aseem Trivedi, was sent to jail on the grounds of *sedition* for publishing a series of cartoons highlighting corruption in India. Taking into account the above incidents, it seems that it's not actually the government censoring but rather the self employed **moral police** doing the job.

As it stands, the Ministry of Information and Broadcasting's decision to form a three-member expert committee under veteran Shyam Benegal to **revamp** the Central Board of Film Certification (CBFC) has been a good move by the government.

The big question that arises now is whether censorship should be abolished or not? Many argue that we should follow the US model, an industry body that *automates*, rather than a government-appointed set up. When it comes to artistic freedom, allow a creative person to think freely without official intervention but at the same time, what you are creating is mass media. It becomes a part of mainstream *discourse*. What you produce has the *potency* to influence the public. Therefore, some amount of censorship is *pertinent*.

- ✍ **Automates**

  Contextual Meaning(s) : verb; make or become automatic
  Synonyms : automatize

- ✍ **Brewing up**

  Contextual Meaning(s) : verb; to form a plan, or arrange in the mind
  Synonyms : devise

- ✍ **Bleep out**

  Contextual Meaning(s) : verb; remove offensive material from a broadcast
  Synonyms : bowdlerize

- ✍ **Discourse**

  Contextual Meaning(s) : noun; serious discussion about something between people or groups
  Synonyms : discussion

- ✍ **Discretion**

  Contextual Meaning(s) : noun; the freedom or authority to judge something or make a decision about it, e.g. Tipping is left to the customer's discretion.
  Synonyms : judgment

- ✍ **Moral police**

  Contextual Meaning(s) : noun; based on what somebody's conscience suggests is right or wrong, rather than on what rules or the law says should be done

- ✍ **Potency**

  Contextual Meaning(s) : noun; a capacity for growth or development
  Synonyms : effectiveness

- ✍ **Pertinent**

  Contextual Meaning(s) : adjective; relevant to the matter being considered
  Synonyms : applicable, appropriate

- ✍ **Purview**

  Contextual Meaning(s) : noun; The range of interest or activity that can be anticipated
  Synonyms : ambit, domain

- ✍ **Revamp**

  Contextual Meaning(s) : verb; to improve the condition or structure of something, alter something for better
  Synonyms : refurbish

- ✍ **Redundant**

  Contextual Meaning(s) : adjective; not or no longer needed or wanted
  Synonyms : superfluous

- ✍ **Sedition**

  Contextual Meaning(s) : noun; actions or words intended to provoke or incite rebellion against government authority
  Synonyms : troublemaking

- ✍ **Ultra-conservativeness**

  Contextual Meaning(s) : noun; exceeding or going beyond all other of the same kind
  Synonyms : extreme

SKIRTS FOR BOYS, TROUSERS FOR GIRLS

Around 80 schools in the UK have come up with a unique idea that suggests 'gender neutral' uniforms, allowing boys to wear skirts and girls don trousers according to their choices. The **overture** is aimed at Britain's new government-funded drive for educational institutions to be more sensitive to 'trans' children. The schools have either avoided references to girls and boys in their dress codes or have rewrite their uniform policy and children as young as five can dress in the uniform in which they feel most comfortable.

The decision comes in the wake of a new UK government-funded drive for schools to be more sensitive to 'trans' children who are questioning their gender identity. To support this, the uniform policy is supposed to be gender neutral which means that all children are expected to wear school uniform, the rules for boys and girls are the same and they should not be insisted that they wear specific items of clothing.

Transgender people may be termed as those who identify as transsexual are usually people who are born with typical male or female **anatomies** but feel as though they've been born into the 'wrong body.' For example, a transgender or transsexual person may have typical female anatomy but feels like a male and seek to become male by taking hormones or electing to have sex reassignment surgeries.

People who have intersex conditions possess anatomy that is not considered typically male or female. A number of people with intersex conditions come to medical attention because they are noticed to be having something **aberrant** about their bodies. On the other hand, people who are transgendered have an internal experience of gender identity that is different from most people.

However, transgender and transsexual people should not be confused with people with intersex conditions because they see two groups of people who would like to choose their own gender identity. Sometimes, those choices require hormonal treatments and/or surgery. These are similarities. Despite all these similarities, these two groups should not be and cannot be thought of as one. The reality is that a majority of people with intersex conditions identify as male or female rather than transgender or transsexual. Thus, where all people who identify as transgender or transsexual experience problems with their gender identity, only a small portion of intersex people experience these problems.

Transgender people come to know about their transgender identity in a variety of ways and may become aware of it at any age. Some can **discern** their transgender identities and feelings back to their earliest memories. They may have an **obscure** feeling of 'not fitting in' with people of their assigned sex or specific wishes to be something other than their assigned sex. Others may become **cognizant** of their transgender identities or gender-nonconforming attitudes and behaviours during *juvenescence* or much later in life. Some transgender people, transsexuals in particular, experience intense dissatisfaction with their sex assigned at birth, physical sex characteristics, or the gender role associated with that sex. These individuals often seek gender-affirming treatments.

Parents may be worried about a child who appears to be gender-nonconforming for various reasons. Some children are quite distressful about their assigned sex at birth or the gender roles they are expected to follow. Some children face difficult social interactions with peers and adults because of their gender expression. Parents may pay attention when what they believed to be a 'phase' does not pass. Parents of gender-nonconforming children have to work with schools and other institutions to address their children's particular needs and ensure their children's safety. It would be helpful to consult with experts and professionals who are familiar with gender issues in children to decide how to best address these concerns. Forcing the child to act in a more gender-conforming way won't work. Peer support from other parents of gender-nonconforming children may also be helpful.

Anti-discrimination laws in most countries do not protect transgender people from discrimination based on gender identity or gender expression. As a result, they face discrimination in nearly every *facet* of their lives. They experience a great deal of discrimination in employment, education, health care, housing, legal systems, and even in their families. They are the targets of hate crimes and the victims of subtle discrimination—which includes everything from glances or glares of **disavowal** or discomfort to *invasive* questions about their body parts.

🐞 **Anatomies**
Contextual Meaning(s) : noun; the human body
Synonyms : figure, shape

🐞 **Aberrant**
Contextual Meanings(s) : adjective; deviating from what is normal or desirable
Synonyms : unusual, abnormal

🐞 **Cognizant**
Contextual Meaning(s) : adjective; (sometimes followed by 'of') having or showing knowledge or understanding or realization or perception
Synonyms : aware

🐞 **Discern**
Contextual Meaning(s) : verb; perceive, recognize, or understand
Synonyms : recognize

🐞 **Disavowal**
Contextual Meaning(s) : noun; a disowning
Synonyms : disapproval, denial

🐞 **Facet**
Contextual Meaning(s): noun; a distinct feature or element in a problem
Synonyms: aspect

🐞 **Invasive**
Contextual Meaning(s) : adjective; involving an intrusion or infringement, e.g. of somebody's privacy or rights
Synonyms : intruding

🐞 **Juvenescence**
Contextual Meaning(s) : noun; the act or process of growing from childhood to youth
Synonyms : adolescence, youthfulness

🐞 **Overture**
Contextual Meaning(s) : noun; a tentative suggestion designed to elicit the reactions of others
Synonyms : move, act

India's failure to clinch a membership in the Nuclear Suppliers Group (NSG) failed as China blocked **consensus** at the elite group which controls transfer of nuclear technology in the world. China will not discuss India's membership bid into the elite group until India first signs the Nuclear Non-Proliferation Treaty, as it is **requisite** and a major criteria set up by the NSG. Nuclear Non-Proliferation Treaty (NPT) is the 'cornerstone' of the international non-proliferation regime, though NPT issue had been addressed in 2008 itself, when India got the country-specific **waiver**.

India has been seeking NSG membership since 2008 and is being backed by US, Switzerland and Mexico for its membership of NSG only due to the commendable efforts by Narendra Modi government. On the other hand, it is being opposed by China, New Zealand, South Africa and Pakistan on the basis that a country which is a non signatory of NPT, CTBT etc shouldn't be inducted into NSG. China has been arguing that if India is to be granted a seat in NSG, then all other South Asian countries like Pakistan which were non-signatory of NPT should also be granted a seat. NSG consists of a group of nuclear supplier countries that seek to prevent nuclear proliferation by controlling the export of materials, equipment and technology that can be used to manufacture nuclear weapons.

Pakistan is **rebutting** India's claim merely because it doesn't want India to possess high end technologies in the nuclear field. It also fears that if India becomes a member it could prevent it from becoming a member just like how China is currently down voting India.

Now, while India is trying its best to **garner** other countries' support to back its Nuclear Suppliers Group (NSG) bid, a book has come into open claiming that Jawaharlal Nehru had the opportunity to get the membership but he rejected it. The author, former foreign secretary Maharajakrishna Rasgotra writes that US president John F Kennedy had offered India a chance to develop and **detonate** a nuclear device much before China's test in 1964. But, Nehru rejected the offer. The writer further says if Nehru had accepted the offer at that time, India would not have to yearn to enter into the Nuclear Suppliers Group today. Rasgotra argues that we would not only have tested the nuclear device first in Asia before China, but it would have **deterred** China from launching its war of 1962 and even warned Pakistan for its war in 1965. According to the book, Nehru discussed the matter with Dr Homi Bhabha and GP Parthasarathy, and rejected the offer.

If all these claims are any indication, it is great irony that India's all these aspirations to become a NSG member were eminently realisable in the past. The big question is that: was it offered to India on a platter but the then prime minister Jawaharlal Nehru refused them on what appears in **retrospect**, **dubious** grounds? The Nehru critics argue that the Nehruvian thoughts that overwhelmingly dominated our **intelligentsia** and political class never questioned Nehru's foreign policy decisions; but things have changed now. The majority of Indians do not know that but for Nehru, India would have been a permanent member of the UNSC, a legitimate nuclear power and a leading global power in the 1950s itself.

However, on the flip side, despite Nehru being a vocal proponent of non-alignment, India always kept the nuclear option and he was keen that India pursue nuclear research and keep its options open for future deployment in war. There is also evidence to suggest that Homi Bhabha was once just a year from testing a nuclear device during Nehru's times. But, it is also true that Nehru deterred Bhabha to hold the programme in **abeyance**.

Just assuming, without taking credible evidence into account, that nukes were offered on a platter to Nehru, the Nehru critics, of course, make the mistake of arguing that getting a membership of NSG would have been the shortest route to super powerdom and global **hegemony**.

🖎 **Abeyance**

Contextual Meaning(s): noun; temporary inactivity or non operation, e.g. a law that has been in abeyance for some time
Synonyms : suspension, stand-down

🖎 **Consensus**

Contextual Meaning(s) : noun; general or widespread agreement among all the members of a group, e.g. after hours of deliberation, they finally reached a consensus.
Synonyms : agreement, consent

🖎 **Dubious**

Contextual Meaning(s) : adjective; not sure about an outcome or conclusion,
Synonyms : doubtful, questionable

🖎 **Detonate**

Contextual Meaning(s) : verb; to make something explode
Synonyms : set off, discharge

🖎 **Deterred**

Contextual Meaning(s) : verb; to prevent or discourage from acting, as by means of fear or doubt, e.g. threats that did not deter her from speaking out.
Synonyms : dissuade

🖎 **Garner**

Contextual meaning(s) : verb; to earn or acquire something by effort
Synonyms : acquire, gain

🖎 **Hegemony**

Contextual Meaning(s) : noun; control or dominating influence by one person or group, especially by one political group over society or one nation over others
Synonyms : supremacy, domination

🖎 **Intelligentsia**

Contextual Meaning(s) : noun, the most intelligent, intellectual, or highly educated members of a society or community, especially those who are interested in the arts, literature, philosophy, and politics.
Synonyms : literati, intellectual

🖎 **Requisite**

Contextual Meaning(s) : adjective; absolutely essential
Synonyms : mandatory

🖎 **Rebutting**

Contextual Meaning(s) : verb; to refute by evidence or argument, e.g. He spent most of his speech rebutting criticisms.
Synonyms : confute, disprove

🖎 **Retrospect**

Contextual meaning(s) : noun; thinking about or reviewing the past, especially from a new perspective or with new information
Synonyms : thoughtfulness

🖎 **Waiver**

Contextual Meaning(s) : noun; the voluntary relinquishment, expressly or by implication, of some claim or right
Synonyms : relinquishment

GST or the Goods and Services tax Bill reforms came into existence when India attained freedom in 1947. Since then, it has been in the limelight, up till now in 2016. However, since free India, ages have passed to bring it into force. It was supposed to get passed by this monsoon session of the Parliament, expected to pass on 1st April of the year but once again got blocked.

Initially, the UPA government, then reigning in 2009, became the first government to discuss and propose the GST Bill, though it failed to get it approved. Thereafter, in December 2014, the NDA government following the footsteps of the UPA government, made *meager* changes to the Bill introduced, which was further introduced in the Lok Sabha. And, finally on 6th May, 2016, it received green signal from the first house of the Parliament.

GST Bill if once passed would **supersede** the **plethora** of Indirect Taxes imposed with a single centralised tax. Mainly, it streamlines the process of taxation by categorizing all such taxes under one roof to make it easy and effective in the long run.

Clearance of the Bill would eventually be leading to economic integration of India. The major role of the Bill will be to transform India into a uniform market by weeding out all fiscal barriers. First and foremost, the single tax so to impose will act as a base and help in the removal of the Indirect tax system in our country. The current Indirect tax system includes overlapping taxes by the Centre and the State separately.

Stating about the framework of GST, it will be duly structured- Central GST and State GST as well as it will be **proffering** equal empowerment to the Centre and State. GST will provide a **podium** both to the Central and State GST. Both the Centre and the State will be in **dominion** of powers to legislate and administer in their respective fields.

Taxes such as excise duty, service tax, Central sales tax, VAT, **octroi** all are **subsumed** by the GST underneath a single umbrella. Basically, GST will be divided under 3 sub-heads namely Central, State and integrated.

After going through the minute details of the Bill it won't be **fictitious** to say that GST Bill must have crossed many barriers **intruding** in its way to its implementation. But as of now, the prime hurdle it has to face is get majority of 2/3rd from the Lok Sabha and the Rajya Sabha together and 50 percent of the state assemblies as well.

The issues raised by the opposition parties may be taken into consideration for making the bill more effective. Congress is demanding reforms in the key areas of the bill. Mainly there are 3 concerns of the party. Firstly, a cap on the GST rate at 18 per cent; secondly, deletion of the provision which allows imposition of 1 per cent tax by additional levy, and an independent dispute resolution mechanism.

The impact of the bill holds many advantages. It will open a number of gateways for the economy in the near future. It is instrumental in the growth of GDP leading up to a rise of 2 percent. By breaking the Indirect tax system, it offers multiple solutions to multinationals and other Companies who wouldn't be burdened to pay innumerable taxes as it would be replaced by one and only tax.

Along with the benefits to be incurred, risk of bill failure also must not be ignored and taken into account. The disadvantages of the bill should be anticipated in advance although they aren't many.

One such drawback of the bill is fear of losing its powers. Some states are afraid of losing their fiscal powers at hand. To their relief, Constitutional amendment bill has promised to give compensation packages for 3 years if any revenue loss is incurred.

Another disadvantage is profit earned on export of petroleum products. For escaping from this, states should continue levying sales or VAT tax on petroleum products except on imports and inter-state.

GST Bill has not covered all the hurdles yet but is close to the motive behind its formation. To some extent, it has cleared some obstacles and that's quite clear from the fact that it has been passed by the Lok Sabha. With its enforcement, the levels of fiscal deficit in the economy will lower and India will gain $15 billion a year because function of the bill will be to promote exports, create employment opportunities and boost growth.

Word – Watch

🖎 **Dominion**

Contextual Meaning(s) : noun; somebody's area of influence or control
Synonyms : possession, control

🖎 **Fictitious**

Contextual Meaning(s) : adjective; not true or genuine, and intended to deceive, e.g. He gave a fictitious name when confronted
Synonyms : false, fake

🖎 **Instigating**

Contextual Meaning(s) : verb; to start or begin
Synonyms : introducing

🖎 **Intruding**

Contextual Meaning(s) : verb; enter uninvited
Synonyms : interrupting, interfering

🖎 **Meager**

Contextual Meaning(s) : adjective; small changes
Synonyms : little, slight

🖎 **Octroi**

Contextual Meaning(s) : noun; former local tax levied on goods entering a town or city
Synonyms : entry tax, local tax

🖎 **Plethora**

Contextual Meaning(s) : noun; a very large amount of something or number of things, especially an excessive amount
Synonyms : excess, surplus

🖎 **Proffering**

Contextual Meaning(s) : verb; to offer something for consideration to somebody, e.g. proffer a suggestion
Synonyms : offer, proposal

🖎 **Podium**

Contextual Meaning(s) : noun; a small raised platform
Synonyms : base, platform

🖎 **Pivotal**

Contextual Meaning(s) : adjective; vitally important, especially in determining the outcome, progress or success of something
Synonyms : crucial, critical

🖎 **Subsumed**

Contextual Meaning(s) : verb; to include or incorporate something into a larger order, category or classification
Synonyms : encompass, include

🖎 **Supersede**

Contextual Meaning(s) : verb; take the place of, put in place of
Synonyms : replace, oust

TARGETING INDIVIDUALS OVER SEXUAL ORIENTATION

Remember the rainbow-coloured flags and wigs that were flashed a few years back? Well, not long ago, though! Yes, we are talking about the LGBT protests of 2013 in India. Many protesters and human rights activists took to the roads of New Delhi in the winter season of December. They were protesting against the Supreme Court banning and criminalizing gay sex.

In a country like ours, where even love marriage in different castes is considered a huge taboo, to speak on the term sexuality is all the more a heavy term to be digested. Our society doesn't favour the same sex love or rather finds it sinful to be frank on topics such as sexuality.

Sexual orientation **ofttimes** has been misunderstood. It is more than a person's preference for sexual relationship with a particular sex. It also involves emotional aspect to it. On 12th June, Orlando witnessed the most horrifying massacre ever in the history of America. As many as 49 lives were brutally eliminated and 53 were injured in a gay night club, Pulse, situated in Florida. After mass killing, at the end, he was killed by the officers in charge during the **rampage**.

Omar Mateen, a 29-year gay fellow who was **unengaged**, killed 49 people in the club where around 320 people were alive before his presence. He was **despondent** with his present state of arranged marriage, in which he was shoved into by his father. Mateen was seeking **contentment** in the form of love and embracement. In search of love and being accepted as he was, he continually relied on gay dating apps and websites. Here he met a man named Miguel with whom he had sexual relationship for a short duration of 2 months. They had met 15 to 20 times in a hotel in Florida.

The place of mass bloodshed was often his and several other Latin men s' destination. Mateen had sexual relations with two Puerto Ricon men. Later on, he got to know that one of them was HIV positive. It was for this reason he **loathed** Latin men and ultimately took revenge for what one of them did with him.

According to some reports, Mateen had links with the ISIS but no clues have been found until now. There is no lucidity of him being a terrorist though.

The fact that led to this **flagrant** act was that, deep inside he was scarred and was **tormented** by sexual identity issues of which he wasn't aware but simply failed to accept or believe the prevailing truth that stood in front of him. His father was in a state of shock when numerable news channels raised questions on his son's sexuality. He denied his son was gay and never saw any implications of being so.

As sexual orientation and gender identity are sensitive issues, people shy away from discussing it in public. But we have to speak out because lives are at stake, and because it is our moral obligation to protect the rights of everyone, everywhere. These lesbian, gay, bisexual and transgender (LGBT) people of all ages and in all regions of the world are exposed to **egregious** violations of their human rights. They are discriminated against in schools, in the labour market, and in hospitals, mistreated and disowned by their own families. They are picked for physical attack – beaten, sexually assaulted, tortured and even killed. In many countries, laws against cross dressing are used to punish transgender people on the basis of their gender identity and expression.

In recent times, a number of countries have made a determined effort to strengthen human rights protection for LGBT people. A variety of new laws has been adopted – including laws banning discrimination, penalizing homophobic and **transphobic** hate crimes, granting recognition of same-sex relationships, and making it easier for transgender individuals to get official recognition that shows their preferred gender. Various programmes have been formulated for police, prison staff, teachers, social workers and other personnel, and anti-bullying initiatives have been taken in many schools.

As men and women of conscience, we have to reject discrimination in general, and in particular discrimination based on sexual orientation and gender identity. While protecting LGBT people from discrimination, we don't need a new set of LGBT-specific rights, nor do we require the new international human rights standards. All the legal obligations of States to safeguard the human rights of LGBT people are there. All people, irrespective of sex, sexual orientation or gender identity, are entitled to enjoy the protections provided for by international human rights law.

It is very disappointing when one encounters the challenges that LGBT youths must face in order to establish their own identity. Who can one turn to when they see a society that does not **foster** multicultural understanding for LGBT populations? For this, the role of the mental health practitioner is most important. It is vital that they be educated, trained, and meet the needs to work with diverse populations such as LGBT youths. In recent times, though, there has been much improvement about tolerance towards LGBT, and guidelines are there to help meet the needs of LGBT youths, society is still far from eliminating oppression and discrimination against the community. Anyways, there is a ray of hope.

✈ **Contentment**
Contextual Meaning(s) : noun; a feeling of calm and satisfaction
Synonyms : satisfaction

✈ **Despondent**
Contextual Meaning(s) : adjective; extremely unhappy and discouraged
Synonyms : unhappy

✈ **Egregious**
Contextual Meaning(s) : adjective; extraordinary in some bad way; glaring; flagrant
Synonyms: gross, outrageous, notorious, shocking

✈ **Flagrant**
Contextual Meaning(s) : adjective; contrary to the standards of conduct or morality
Synonyms : shocking, dreadful

✈ **Foster**
Contextual Meaning(s) : verb; promote the growth of
Synonyms : nurture

✈ **Loathed**
Contextual Meaning(s) : verb; to dislike somebody or something intensely
Synonyms : hate

✈ **Ofttimes**
Contextual Meaning(s) : adverb; many times at short intervals
Synonyms : frequently, often times

✈ **Rampage**
Contextual Meaning(s) : noun; Violently angry and destructive behaviour
Synonyms : run riot

✈ **Transphobia**
Contextual Meaning(s) : noun; unreasoning hostility, aversion, etc., toward transgender people.

✈ **Tormented**
Contextual Meaning(s) : adjective; experiencing intense pain especially mental pain
Synonyms : disturbed, perturbed

✈ **Tainted**
Contextual Meaning(s) : adjective; something undesirable or dangerous
Synonyms : fouled, spoiled

✈ **Unengaged**
Contextual Meaning(s) : adjective; not in action or at work
Other Meaning(s) : not promised in marriage
Synonyms : unemployed, idle

✈ **Vengeful**
Contextual Meaning(s) : adjective; having or showing a strong desire for revenge
Synonyms : revengeful, unforgiving

WHO CAN STOP TRUMP?

Donald Trump and Hillary Clinton both have secured their party's nomination for the presidential race and the clash between the two candidates is set to be **atrocious**. The fact is that Trump has triumphed in Republican Party primaries because the Republican Party is incapable of mounting effective **resistance** to him, not because effective resistance is impossible. Their strategies have failed because highlighting his real weaknesses cuts against too much of what the GOP base believes.

To stop Trump, his opponent is going to be a Democrat — realistically, Hillary Clinton though in principle Bernie Sanders or someone else would work. A Democrat will happily hammer Trump over his weaknesses and bury a candidate who's already held in very low regard by the mass public. Clinton is running on the cause of making the rich pay more, while Trump is promising an enormous unpopular tax cut for himself.

The election for the President of the United States (POTUS) occurs every four years on Election Day, held on the first Tuesday after the first Monday in November. The 2016 Presidential election will be held on November 8, 2016.

Clinton had held a lengthy double-digit lead over Trump, who was once a Republican outsider. This had vanished but looks to be opening up again after she secured a pledge to work together from her **Democrat** rival, Senator Bernie Sanders.

"I would build a great wall, and nobody builds walls better than me, believe me, and I'll build them very inexpensively, I will build a great, great wall on our southern border. And I will have Mexico pay for that wall. Mark my words." – This statement made by Donald Trump during his Presidential Campaign Announcement Speech shows that Trump is a badly **flawed** candidate. Some of the major problems with Trump are that he is a racist, his business record is unimpressive and ethically **dodgy** and last but not the least his policy ideas are terrible. The Republicans haven't been able to **condemn** him effectively in the context of a Republican Party primary because most Republicans don't think white racism is a problem. The **hitch** with Trump is not that his policy positions on immigration, ISIS, health care, Social Security, or whatever don't stand up to a moment of casual **scrutiny**. The trouble with Trump is that he is, by temperament, by experience, and by character, utterly unqualified to be president of the United States. He is a **buffoon**. That's why his campaign is a joke, not the merits or otherwise of his alleged policies. All he brings to the table is a lot of money and a talent for publicity.

Donald Trump appears to be backing away from one of his signature and most controversial proposals—banning Muslims from entering the U.S.—as polls show him falling slightly behind Hillary Clinton.

Since Mr. Trump essentially **clinched** the GOP presidential nomination in May, amid widespread popularity of his proposed ban among primary voters, he has gradually moved away from a blanket religious ban and toward a more **nuanced** policy targeting countries with a record of terrorism.

Republicans haven't stopped Trump so far, and it's why they won't be able to stop him in the future. To beat him, Republicans either need to replace their voters or adjust GOP ideological **orthodoxy**. They can't do the former and won't do the **latter**, so they have lost. Democrats are not constrained in these ways, so they can — and likely will — stop Trump and keep him out of the White House. Therefore, republicans and democrats are seeking an answer to the question of who can still stop the **brash** Donald Trump and the best conclusion they have come to is Hillary Clinton.

🖎 **Atrocious**

Contextual Meaning(s) : adjective; extremely unpleasant to the sense or feelings
Synonyms : repuls

🖎 **Brash**

Contextual Meaning(s) : adjective; self-assertive in an aggressive or rude way
Synonyms : cheeky, nervy

🖎 **Buffoon**

Contextual Meaning(s) : noun; somebody behaving in a silly way
Synonyms : clown, comedian

🖎 **Condemn**

Contextual Meaning(s) : Verb; to say in a strong and definite way that someone or something is bad or wrong.
Synonyms: Castigate, Criticize

🖎 **Clinched**

Contextual Meaning(s) : Verb; to confirm or settle a contract.
Synonyms: conclude, secure

🖎 **Democrat**

Contextual Meaning(s) : Noun; a person who believes in or supports democracy.
Synonyms : egalitarian, leveler

🖎 **Dodgy**

Contextual Meaning(s) : adjective; of doubtful quality or legality
Synonyms : tricky

🖎 **Flawed**

Contextual Meaning(s) : Adjective; having some fundamental weakness or imperfection.
Synonyms: faulty, unsound

🖎 **Hitch**

Contextual Meaning(s) : noun; an obstacle in the way of progress, e.g. There's been a slight technical hitch.
Synonyms : problem

🖎 **Latter**

Contextual Meaning(s) : Adjective; Denoting the second mentioned of two people or thing.
Synonyms : Last mentioned

🖎 **Nauance**

Contextual Meaning(s) : Noun; a very slight difference in appearance or meaning.
Synonyms : variation, gradation

🖎 **Orthodoxy**

Contextual Meaning(s): Noun; authorized or generally accepted theory.
Synonyms: creed, doctrine

🖎 **Resistance**

Contextual Meaning(s) : Noun; to refuse to accept or comply with something.
Synonyms: defiance, opposition

🖎 **Scrutiny**

Contextual Meaning(s) : noun; close, careful, and thorough examination or inspection
Synonyms : examination

India is extremely **susceptible** to the impact of climate events. It has witnessed **cogent** changes in mean and extreme climate during the period of 1951-2013, according to the analysis based on IMD data. As we have seen mean annual air temperature has increased in many regions of the country while **prominent** increase was observed in the number of hot days, night-time temperature, and growing degree days during the period of 1951-2013.

Climate change has contributed to extreme weather events such as droughts, floods and heatwaves in India. Floods and drought are more often than not two sides of the same coin. In certain areas, they damage soil, water systems and ecosystems in repeating cycles that **exacerbate** each other's impact. During the dry season, any rain passes straight through what are often degraded soils, leaving crops to **wither** in the sun. So, farmers rely on wells that tap underground reservoirs. But this resource is quickly **depleted** because most monsoon rainfall runs uncontrollably off the land, without **replenishing** the underlying water.

Today as many as nine states are reeling under drought…India has seen two **consecutive** droughts. On the one hand, several parts of the country are facing water crisis, leading to distress in the rural landscape, on the other, heavy rains and subsequent floods continued to wreak havoc across Madhya Pradesh, Assam, Uttarakhand and Arunachal Pradesh.

Last year, June was struck by heat, **wavering** with 47 degree Celsius temperature. It was recorded hottest in past 62 years and turned out to be the longest heat session of the month. It's not new to the ear that heat strokes have certainly taken lives before and is still counting today.

The monsoon season rainfall became more **erratic** resulting in some of the most severe and widespread droughts during the recent decades (2002, 2009 and 2015). The increased frequency of droughts has led to challenges to food security and water management. With **substantial** increase in the number of hot days and day and night temperatures, India is drying out marked by persistent moisture **deficit** conditions, according to a latest study jointly taken by ASSOCHAM and Skymet Weather Services.

Climate change has a severe impact on Indian agriculture. Rice crop yield decreases with the rise in temperature. For instance, an increase in temperature by

2 degree Centigrade decreases the grain yield by 15 to 17 per cent. It is an **ominous** situation because the paddy and wheat production in Northeast India has already been declining. Short-season crops (vegetables and fruits) are the worst affected by climate changes, particularly during critical periods of their growth.

Fluctuating weather patterns are increasingly manifesting themselves in stronger and more formidable ways. The recent Chennai deluge, El Nino causing back to back droughts and heat records setting new standards every year – all of these are the sign of bigger calamities in the future unless we take them as a serious threat to the environment and to humanity.

Science has progressed substantially in recent years, enhancing more accurate assessment of how much extreme event is driven by climate change and other factors. Because of a focus on heatwaves the pilot countries in South Asia are India and Pakistan.

The climate scientists across the world agree that the main cause for these changes taking place in the weather and weather forecasts is Global Warming. A number of studies published in peer-reviewed scientific journals show that 97 percent climate scientists agree that climate warming trends over the past century are extremely likely due to human activities. Most of the leading scientific organizations worldwide have issued statements endorsing this position.

❧ **Cogent**
Contextual Meaning(s) : adjective; powerfully persuasive
Synonyms : significant

❧ **Consecutive**
Contextual Meaning(s) : Adjective; following each other continuously.
Synonyms: Successive, following

❧ **Depleted**
Contextual Meaning(s) : adjective; use (resources or materials) over time in order to function
Synonyms : consumed

❧ **Deficit**
Contextual Meaning(s) : Noun; deficiency in amount or quality.
Synonyms: shortage, under supply.

❧ **Exacerbate**
Contextual Meaning(s) : verb; make worse
Synonyms : aggravate

❧ **Erratic**
Contextual Meaning(s): adjective; liable to sudden unpredictable change
Synonyms: changeable

❧ **Ominous**
Contextual Meaning(s): adjective; Indicating evil intent or suggesting tragic developments
Synonyms: alarming

❧ **Prominent**
Contextual Meaning(s): Adjective; Something or someone that catches one's attention or is noticeable.
Synonyms : evident, salient

❧ **Replenishing**
Contextual Meaning(s) : verb; fill something that had previously been emptied
Synonyms : refilling

❧ **Susceptible**
Contextual Meaning(s) : adjective; yielding readily to or capable of
Synonyms : vulnerable

❧ **Substantial**
Contextual Meaning(s) : Adjective, of considerable importance, size or worth.
Synonyms: Sizeable, significant

❧ **Wavering**
Contextual Meaning(s) : verb; move or sway in a rising and falling or wavelike pattern
Synonyms : fluctuating

❧ **Wither**
Contextual Meaning(s): verb; lose freshness, vigour, or vitality
Synonyms : fade

EDUCATION IS THE WEAPON THAT CAN CHANGE THE WORLD

"Education is the most powerful weapon which you can use to change the world."- Nelson Mandela

Education plays an important role in transforming the lives of people. It does not just concern with academic learning and does not restrict itself to textbooks, but extends itself to include the application of values, knowledge and skills that have been acquired by the individual over the years. Education can bring changes in the world in two ways, i.e. through the empowerment of individuals and the generation of knowledge. Byproducts of education, in the form of empowerment and knowledge generation, are the most **compelling** weapons that can change the world in different and **potent** ways.

Education can bridge the socio-economic divide that is present in our society, as it equips the people with necessary skills and abilities that would help them to strive for themselves and to provide themselves with the basic necessities of life. In addition, education can be used as a tool to eradicate poverty. Education that targets marginalized and poor populations will bring change to many of the systemic factors that have contributed to the delay in poor communities' development and can prevent the **diffusion** of poverty between generations.

Education can bring changes in the health profile of an individual, family, society, nation and mankind all over the world. Researchers found that there is a 50% chance of an educated mother to protect herself and her children from illnesses if she is educated and it is more likely that her child could survive past age five. Education works as a **pathfinder** to awaken people and make them more aware of the causes of various diseases.

According to the World Bank report on civil war, it is estimated that the risk of war **dwindled** considerably with an increase in education. This is because education **inculcates** the practice of independent thinking that leads to the creation of new ideas. Independent thinkers do not blindly follow the beliefs of others and draw their own conclusion on issues related to the world. Any problem being faced by the world can be resolved practically and logically with the help of these individuals.

Education has made a huge difference to the lives of disabled people. It equips them with increased levels of confidence and problem solving abilities. By being a part of an educational institution, children learn to understand the differences and similarities between people in the real world. They learn to respect and appreciate diversity as they interact with students of **diverging** abilities and cultures.

India, being a **patriarchal** society, is still plagued by a number of issues. The practices of female foeticide, female infanticide, child marriage, dowry, and child trafficking still exist. Female children are looked down upon due to the inferior status that has been attached to them since centuries. One of the few ways to **eradicate** these practices is educate the masses and make them more literate.

Education also has a positive impact on women empowerment as it equips the female population with an increased level of confidence and rationality that helps them to fulfil a number of economic, social and cultural responsibilities which can in turn bridge the gender gap, along with the socio-economic **hierarchy** that persists in society. Through education, women can respond effectively to opportunities and challenge the traditional roles that have been assigned to them. An educated woman can contribute towards the betterment of society by challenging the mal-traditions targeting women.

Education also has a similar impact in the realm of climate change and environmental degradation. It can deliver adequate scientific facts concerning these issues. It equips the younger generations with skills that will help in combating climate change while instilling the philosophy of sustainable development. Education has the power to show the youth of the world that they have wider responsibilities and are entitled to make decisions regarding the environment in which they have to live.

Education is the most powerful weapon that can change the world and make it a better place. Every nation will reach its **pinnacle** when education and equality of opportunity is provided to all. It equips the youth with employable skills that can help them in shaping their lives. Besides, it has transformed the lives of women and disabled people, all around the world, by empowering them and educating them about their rights; hence, education is the tool that can make everything possible and correct all the wrongs that plagued the world.

> **Compelling**
> *Contextual Meaning(s)* : adjective; tending to persuade by forcefulness of argument
> *Synonyms* : powerful

> **Dwindled**
> *Contextual Meaning(s)* : verb; become smaller or lose substance
> *Synonyms* : reduced

> **Diffusion**
> *Contextual Meaning(s)* : noun; the spreading of something more widely
> *Synonyms* : transmission

> **Diverging**
> *Contextual Meaning(s)* : adjective; tending to move apart in different directions
> *Synonyms* : differing

> **Eradicate**
> *Contextual Meaning(s)* : Verb; to put an end to or destroy completely.
> *Synonyms* : remove, eliminate.

> **Hierarchy**
> *Contextual Meaning(s)*: Noun; an organisation or society where members are ranked according to authority or status.
> *Synonyms*: ranking, social order

> **Inculcates**
> *Contextual Meaning(s)*: Verb; to instil an idea or habit by persistent instruction.
> *Synonyms*: instil, ingrain

> **Potent**
> *Contextual Meaning(s)* : adjective; having great power, influence, or effect
> *Synonyms* : effective

> **Pathfinder**
> *Contextual Meaning(s)* : noun; someone who can find paths through unexplored territory
> *Synonyms* : guide

> **Patriarchal**
> *Contextual Meaning(s)* : adjective; characteristic of a form of social organization in which the male is the family head and title is traced through the male line
> *Synonyms* : paternal

> **Pinnacle**
> *Contextual Meaning(s)* : noun; the highest level or degree attainable; the highest stage of development
> *Synonyms* : zenith

"SHOULD EDUCATIONAL QUALIFICATION BE MADE MANDATORY FOR POLITICIANS?"

"Corruption in education leads to some people getting highly educated and then these people support the uneducated to rule over the illiterate masses."

– Amit Abraham

Since India's independence, the country has seen extremely educated as well as uneducated leaders. This has stirred a huge debate as to whether education should be deemed a necessary precondition for politicians. In India, there is no minimum educational qualification required to become a minister; but, there is a minimum educational requirement to become a peon. A string of past events prove that even the well educated politicians use their education to **gratify** their selfish desires.

There have been a number of politicians involved in scams and corruption. Huge funds with the government have always been **meddled** with. Higher educational skills do not guarantee the presence of moral and ethical values in politicians; it is just a statement of how literate they are as they can use the same expertise to carry out their illegal activities.

The emphasis on the importance of education is often contradicted when the educated leaders and politicians get involved in a number of scams and controversies related to the government's finances. Political corruption exists in many forms and at all levels of the government. The nation has witnessed many such acts of corruption in the form of tax evasion, forcing the electorate to vote for a particular candidate, accumulation of black money with politicians and funding of electoral campaigns. There have been a number of scams like the common wealth games scam, Indian coal allocation scam and fodder scam that witnessed the **embezzlement** of funds worth thousands of crores. Hence, to make education the ONLY basis for electing leaders is also wrong.

Having a certain degree does not guarantee that someone will be a good leader. Being inflexible in terms of who contests elections and who doesn't is also the murder of the political system. With a literacy rate of 74.04% and a ranking of 105 out of the 127 countries in UNESCO's 'Education for all development Index (EDI)', putting an educational qualification as the minimum basic requirement would mean depriving a number of deserving candidates from availing this opportunity, who might end up being better leaders as compared to the educated politicians who have spent a bigger part of their lives locked up in classrooms and have been away from the happenings of the world around them. A good leader is the one who understands the needs of the society and does his best to make life easier for the country's citizens.

It is, however, important to ensure that the candidate chosen must be educated in the field of Public Administration and certain basic philosophies. He/she must be aware of the needs of a multicultural and diverse society to ensure that the socio-economic hierarchy that is present in society is abolished. An educated person can help better in the development process of our country and in changing its status to that of a developed country.

An educated politician won't be **hoodwinked** easily by their counterparts like the **bureaucrats**. They will apply an analytical approach when confronted by any issue being faced by the public. Educated politicians can be better policy makers and executers and can guide and control bureaucrats intelligently for the welfare of the nation. Educated politicians can prove to be better administrators, statesmen, foreign ministers, international political negotiators, etc.

There is a need to set a basic minimum education criterion in order to avoid **incongruous** legislations and drain of wealth which are two very important aspects in the development of a nation. It is also important that the candidate is not solely judged by the degree that they have earned. A well rounded leader is the one who possesses the required positive will power, intelligence, **efficiency**, vision, creativity and also has a dynamic and charismatic personality for development of society and the nation.

Just like possessing certain skills makes you a more deserving candidate for a job, acquiring educational qualifications will only help a person to grow as an individual. Education will also help them to identify their strengths and weaknesses as an individual. Therefore, the role of education must not be **despised** altogether.

However, a politician must not be **discerned** solely on how much education they have received because in the end, the will power of a politician pushes them to work. We live in a country which has not yet achieved cent per cent literacy and to impose an educational qualification to contest elections would mean depriving a huge fraction of the nation from achieving its political rights and this would in turn mean the violation of the essence of democracy.

🗳 **Bureaucrat**

Contextual Meaning(s) : Noun; a person who is among the people who run is among the people who run a government organization.
Synonyms: administrator, official

🗳 **Despised**

Contextual Meaning(s): verb; look down on with disdain
Synonyms: disregarded

🗳 *Discerned*

Contextual Meaning(s): verb; See or hear differences; identify a particular part or parts of a whole; detect with difficulty
Synonyms: judged

🗳 *Embezzlement*

Contextual Meaning(s): noun; the sum of money that is misappropriated
Synonyms : misappropriation

🗳 *Evasion*

Contextual Meaning(s) : Noun; the act of avoiding something that you do not want to deal with.
Synonyms: dodging, elusion

🗳 *Efficiency*

Contextual Meaning(s) : Noun; the state or quality of being efficient.
Synonyms : productivity, readiness

🗳 *Gratify*

Contextual Meaning(s) : verb; yield (to); give satisfaction to
Synonyms : satisfy

🗳 *Hoodwinked*

Contextual Meaning(s): verb; Influence by slyness
Synonyms: misguided

🗳 **Incongruous**

Contextual Meaning(s): adjective; Lacking in harmony, compatibility or appropriateness
Synonyms: senseless

🗳 **Meddled**

Contextual Meaning(s) : verb; interfere unwantedly
Synonyms : tampered

🗳 *Scam*

Contextual Meaning(s) : Noun a dishonest scheme or a fraud.
Synonyms : suindle, fraud.

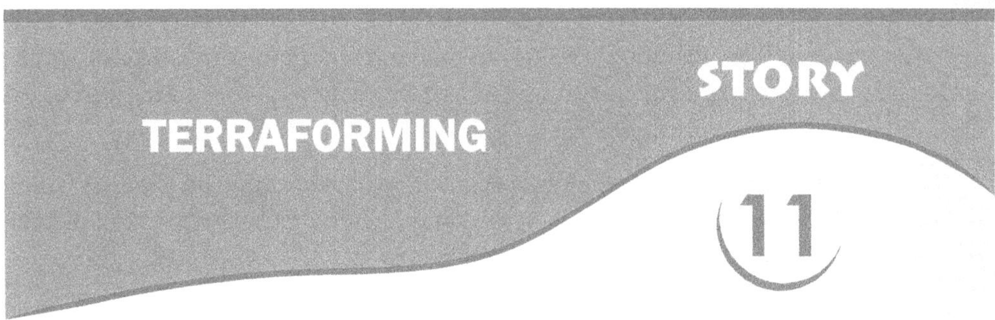

Terraforming is the process of transforming a hostile environment into one **apposite** for a particular variety of life either human or alien.

The term was coined by Jack Williamson in a science-fiction story ("Collision Orbit") published in 1942 in *Astounding Science Fiction*, but the concept may **predate** this work.

Since Mars is the most Earth-like planet, it is the best **claimant** for terraforming. Once, just the subject of science fiction novels, it is now becoming a **viable** research area. The famous astronomer and Pulitzer prize winner, Carl Sagan, says that there is **monumental** promise in the search for ancient life on Mars. If life was once sustainable on Mars, it is important to know what **decimated** the population and caused Mars to evolve into the **gelid** and **comatose** planet it is today. With this knowledge, we can terraform Mars by reversing the process.

NASA scientists believe that amongst all reachable planets, it is technologically possible at the present time to at least **conceptualise** of producing considerable global climate changes on Mars, allowing humans to live there. Successfully terraforming the planet Mars ,could ultimately help solve the problem of overpopulation on earth, help to preserve our species, and could lead to new sources of minerals and energy.

But this will be an **onerous** task. Raising Mars's atmospheric pressure and surface temperature , are the two biggest challenges, followed by producing sufficient quantities of water there.

The temperature of Mars must be raised by a minimum of 60 degrees from the existing temperature. One approach is to heat portions of the surface of Mars with giant orbiting mylar mirrors spanning 125 km. in diameter. Some 200,000 tons of **mylar** would be required to build these solar mirrors, and they would have to be constructed in space, using power from nuclear reactors.

The atmospheric pressure on Mars is far below the level at which people can survive without pressure suits. Martian atmosphere can be pressurized to life-sustaining levels by populating it with enough CO_2 or other green housing gases. The planet's atmosphere must be populated with enough breathable air and sufficient densities of oxygen, and a portion of the planet will need to be populated with adequate quantities of accessible water.

An approach is to **blare** an ammonia-containing asteroid toward Mars, which upon impact would create enough energy to melt a trillion tons of its frozen water, resulting in a warmer atmosphere, and would cover about a quarter of the surface of Mars with about 1 meter deep water.

The successful terraforming of Mars could lead to its replication on similar planets elsewhere in the galaxy. However, using existing technologies, energy required for terraforming Mars for us will take about 1,000 years!

Besides, the economic **wherewithal** required to do so are far beyond that which any government or society is willing to allocate to the purpose. The long time scales and **intricacies** of terraforming are other reason this may not see **fruition**. Other unanswered questions relate to the ethics, logistics, economics, politics, and methodology of altering the environment of an **extraterrestrial** world.

Now consider the **antithesis** : An alien civilization, a thousand years more advanced than us. They may be **gigantic** creatures, and we may appear **lilliputians** to them. Else they may be much more sophisticated than us and **deconstruct** us as **barbarians.** In either case , we would be deemed unworthy of sharing living space with them and as such fit for **extirpation** by them, just the way we try to kill mosquitoes!

These aliens then plant an atmospheric converter (a kind of machine) at an **arcane** location on planet earth. This releases a **catalyst** that mixes with our air and converts it into an atmosphere that's alien-friendly but **fatal** for us. Maybe it could convert all our oxygen to Methane , this would be enough to **deracinate** us **earthlings**, but let their **ilk** flourish !

Likewise, there are terraforming theories that may be applied to our own planet in an attempt to **expiate** the environmental damage done by pollution and deforestation and improve its ecology for mankind to survive here long. One popular project that has been explored is the planetary engineering of our deserts to make them inhabitable. Shimizu Corporation's Desert Aqua-Net is one popularly discussed project. This futuristic project involves building a series of canals and lakes in the Sahara Desert. The canals run water from the oceans to the lakes, and each of the lakes has a man-made island at its center with large forests of eucalyptus trees. People could migrate and lead a comfortable life in this otherwise **desiccated** land. The eucalyptus forests could effectively cool the planet and offset the production of CO_2 caused by the burning of fossil fuels besides all other so called developmental activities.

If achieved, our own terraforming here on earth could lead to engineered climate change and **arable** soil expansion, ease overpopulation, and lead to new sources of food and renewable natural resources such as trees. However, any of these fantastic projects can only take place once technologies such as nuclear fusion and long-distance manned spaceflight come to fruition. But no harm in dreaming , because everything is considered impossible till someone does it, said Nelson Mandela !

Antithesis
Contextual Meaning(s) : Noun; the juxtaposition of contrasting words or ideas to give a feeling of balance; exact opposite
Synonyms : oppositeness

Apposite
Contextual Meaning(s) : Adjective; being of striking appropriateness and pertinence
Synonyms : appropriate, pertinent

Arcane
Contextual Meaning(s) : Adjective; requiring secret or mysterious knowledge
Synonyms : mysterious

Arable
Contextual Meaning(s) : Noun; land that is fit for planting crops
Other Meaning(s) : Adjective; describes the land that can be cultivated for growing crops
Synonyms : land suitable for cultivation

Barbarians
Contextual Meaning(s) : Noun; uncultured or uncivilized people
Synonyms : savages

Blare
Contextual Meaning(s) : Verb; to make a loud harsh noise, e.g. speakers blaring rock music Synonyms : blast, boom

Catalyst
Contextual Meaning(s) : Noun; noun something that causes an important event to happen;
Other Meaning(s) : (chemistry) a substance that initiates or accelerates a chemical reaction without itself being affected
Synonyms : accelerator

Comatose
Contextual Meaning(s) : Adjective; in a state of deep and usually prolonged unconsciousness; unable to respond to external stimuli; relating to or associated with a coma
Synonyms : unconscious

Claimant
Contextual Meaning(s) : Noun; person trying for position, person desiring a job
Synonyms : applicant, suitor, candidate

Conceptualise
Contextual Meaning(s) : Verb; to form a concept
Synonyms : conceive

Decimated
Contextual Meaning(s) : Verb; destroyed completely
Synonyms : razed

Deconstruct
Contextual Meaning(s) : Verb; interpret (a text or an artwork) or understand
Synonyms : interpret

Deracinate
Contextual Meaning(s) : Verb; pull up as if by the roots; destroy
Other Meaning(s) : move (people) forcibly from their homeland into a new and foreign environment
Synonyms : uproot, , displace

Desiccated
Contextual Meaning(s) : Adjective; thoroughly dried out;
Other Meaning(s) : lacking vitality or spirit; lifeless; preserved by removing natural moisture
Synonyms : arid

Expiate
Contextual Meaning(s) : Verb; make amends for
Synonyms : atone

Extirpation
Contextual Meaning(s) : Noun; the act of pulling up or out; uprooting; cutting off from existence;
Other Meaning(s) : surgical removal of a body part or tissue
Synonyms : excision, ablation, cutting out

- **Extraterrestrial**

  Contextual Meaning(s) : Adjective; existing or coming from somewhere outside Earth and its atmosphere

  Other Meaning(s) : Noun; alien, a living being that comes from outside Earth, especially in science fiction

  Synonyms : outside Earth, outer space

- **Earthlings**

  Contextual Meaning(s) : Noun; especially in science fiction, a human being opposed to an extraterrestrial or supernatural being

  Other Meaning(s) : worldling, somebody who concentrates on everyday matters

  Synonyms : human being, inhabitant of earth

- **Fatal**

  Contextual Meaning(s) : Adjective; bringing death; having extremely unfortunate or dire consequences; bringing ruin

  Other Meaning(s) : controlled or decreed by fate; predetermined; having momentous consequences; of decisive importance; (of events)

  Synonyms : mortal

- **Fruition**

  Contextual Meaning(s) : Noun; enjoyment derived from use or possession; the condition of bearing fruit; something that is made real or concrete

  Synonyms : realization

- **Gelid**

  Contextual Meaning(s) : Adjective; extremely cold

  Synonyms : glacial, icy, polar

- **Gigantic**

  Contextual Meaning(s) : Adjective; so exceedingly large or extensive as to suggest a giant or mammoth

  Synonyms : gargantuan

- **ilk**

  Contextual Meaning(s) : Noun; a kind of person

  Synonyms : type

- **lilliputians**

  Contextual Meaning(s) : Noun; people who are tiny

  Other Meaning(s) : inhabitants of fictional place "lilliput"

  Synonyms : pigmies

- **Intricacies**

  Contextual Meaning(s) : Noun; the character of something that has many aspects or parts arranged together in a particularly complex or artful way, e.g. a carving of incredible intricacy

  Synonyms : complexity, details

- **Monumental**

  Contextual Meaning(s) : Adjective; of outstanding significance; relating or belonging to or serving as a monument;

  Other Meaning(s) : imposing in size or bulk or solidity

  Synonyms : massive, monolithic

- **Mylar**

  Contextual Meaning(s) : Noun; a trademark for a thin strong polyester film

  Synonyms : trademark

- **Onerous**

  Contextual Meaning(s) : Adjective; not easily borne; wearing

  Synonyms : burdensome, taxing

- **Predate**

  Contextual Meaning(s) : Verb; establish something as being earlier relative to something else; be earlier in time; go back further;

  Other Meaning(s) : prey on or hunt for; come before

  Synonyms : antedate, precede,

- **Viable**

  Contextual Meaning(s) : Adjective: capable of life or normal growth and development; capable of being done with means at hand and circumstances as they are

  Synonyms : feasible, workable

- **Wherewithal**

  Contextual Meaning(s) : Noun; the necessary means (especially financial means)

  Synonyms : resources

The rush to build bigger, more elegant skyscrapers was essentially an American **infatuation** through the 20th Century, shaping the distinctive skylines of two great cities, New York and Chicago. The 102-story Empire State Building, 385 m tall was built in Manhattan, New York. It stood as the tallest building in the world from its completion until 1972. In 1974, Chicago's Sears Tower (442 meters) took its place, which reined for 25 years.

A major turning point in the evolution of skyscraper construction occurred in the late 1990s, in what then seemed a surprising location: Kuala Lumpur. The completion of the Petronas Towers put Malaysia and most importantly Asia on the map. Designed by architect Cesar Pelli, the **iconic** twin towers were **proclaimed** the world's tallest buildings. But the **euphoria** was rather short lived because in 2004, Taiwan's **soaring** skyscraper, Taipei 101 came on line, tickling the clouds at 509 meters.

It too had to **concede** its top position within 5 years, as the monstrous 168 floor Burj Khalifa, Dubai, a tower complex reaching 800 meters in height, opened in 2009. Its architect was Adrian Smith, who has designed some of the world's most **noted** skyscrapers including, Jin Mao Tower, Trump International Hotel and Tower, as well as the proposed 1,000 m (3,300 ft) Kingdom Tower at Jeddah, Saudi Arabia. The last mentioned building may in a few years occupy the **numero uno** standing in this **rarefied** space.

During the late 70s the Americans put a full-stop to the activity of building ultra tall buildings; they started learning *the art of living* from Indian **anchorites**. They probably now wanted to just lift their souls ! But the eastern hemisphere literally started waking up to a *good morning* from the world at windows 500 metres above earth. Having done decades of high thinking they decided it was time to live high, too !

Middle east is likely to be the biggest tower maker for some time to come. In a historical sense, it's part of the grand cycle of human construction. Building big, began here, when humans started piling up stone blocks to construct the pyramids.

Nowadays, engineers and architects agree there is a statement of power with each new **erection**. "The **exposure** that comes from building the super-tall towers is undeniable," says Adrian Smith, the distinguished architect. Yet he adds that big buildings can also generate value in establishing new destinations, as is happening in Dubai and other neighboring Gulf states.

The other big change is the pace of **one-upmanship**. Previously, tall buildings were rarer, reining supreme for decades at a time. Now, with a dozen super skyscrapers rising simultaneously, the **frantic** pursuit of **bragging** rights means a tall building might be **eclipsed** within a few years.

You could easily move into one of these buildings and never find a need to leave. These buildings include everything from grocery stores and retail outlets to fitness centers with swimming pools.

Asian developers are utilizing this high-rise housing model for one specific reason: Land is scarce. Most Asian economies lack the vast **terra firma** that the West finds so readily abundant.

Take Singapore, for example :it's roughly only 3.5 times the size of Washington, D.C., with an economy greater than New Zealand's and a growth rate double that of the United States.

Hong Kong is another example: it's only six times the size of Washington D.C., but has an annual GDP on par with Argentina and Portugal.

The point is land is, and always will be, the most valuable asset in places like Hong Kong, Shanghai, Tokyo, Taipei and Singapore. These Asian cities lack the land for urban **sprawl** in places like Chicago, Washington, Houston, Los Angeles, Melbourne and Atlanta.

Not to be outdone by the other asian tigers, China's Shanghai city has erected enough high-rises, since 1990, to fill a big **chunk** of Manhattan. The 88-story Jin Mao Tower, with its distinctive **tiered pagoda** design, is the tallest building in China, rising to 421 meters. Or at least it will be, until the 492-m. Shanghai World Financial Center is completed in 2008.

India Tower at Mumbai will be 720 metres high ,have 125 floors, and is slated to be completed by 2016,when it may become world's second tallest tower.

The Petronas Towers may no longer be the tallest building in the world, but it changed Malaysia and the perception of Kuala Lumpur. A world-class building can also raise the bar for other buildings in the city, be it malls, office blocks, or hotels.

Seoul and other major cities across Korea will see a new skyline as the construction of 12 skyscrapers with over 100 stories is underway at this moment.

It appears as if these creature made of steel and cement grow a bit taller every day, **steeped** in their **astral** dreams. The mega corporates, who often buy space in these towers, obviously want to see their logos hanging as high as possible! One ambitious plan calls for a 200-story high-rise on the edge of Hong Kong's Victoria Harbor.

Just as the completion of the Petronas shifted tall-building construction to Asia last decade, the Burj signals the emergence of the Gulf region as a fertile ground for the next generation of mega-skyscrapers. The Burj towers above the rest, yet scores more high-rises are shooting up across the United Arab Emirates and nearby.

Of the skyscrapers which are currently under construction, most will **dwarf** today's top ten countdown, according to the Council on Tall Buildings and Urban Habitat. Stimulated by an **exponentially** growing population and, therefore, thriving economy, Asia has contributed more soaring buildings to the world's Super tall list than all other continents combined. Very soon the model will shift from current 400 meters skyscraper genre to a higher level.

After the 9/11 **calamity**, America's existing 21,000 high-rises have realized the **vulnerability** to hazards like terror attacks, fires, **stampedes** and earthquakes. Understandably skyscrapers are being now built there rather **gingerly.**

And the gigantic towers world over are being provided with sophisticated security systems, regular **evacuation** drills and even a "lifeboat" capsule that can eject out of the building and land to safety using giant parachutes !

Critics of the super tall **furor** point out that very high buildings rarely, if ever, make financial sense in terms of conventional accounting. They are only constructed if there is too much capital chasing too few productive ideas - hence developers come up with imaginative ways to justify overbuilding .The building will be a status symbol, it will therefore command a 50% premium over other office buildings. Skyscraper construction is characterized by bursts of intense activity , lot of capital, and excessive **optimism**. But by the time those skyscrapers are finished, the economy would have slipped into recession. They are therefore the visible evidence of a finance driven property bubble, destined to burst .

And with China and the Gulf pushing sky wards over the next several years, history's boom and bust cycle suggests their economies may crash back to the ground sometime near the end of this decade!

Cynics seem to be always a few meters taller than the tallest !

🖎 **Anchorites**
Contextual Meaning(s) : Noun; people retired from society for religious reasons
Synonyms : hermits

🖎 **Astral**
Contextual Meaning(s) : Adjective; being or relating to or resembling or emanating from stars
Synonyms : stellar

🖎 **Bragging**
Contextual Meaning(s) : Adjective; exhibiting self-importance;
Other Meaning(s) : noun an instance of boastful talk
Synonyms : boasting

🖎 **Calamity**
Contextual Meaning(s) : Noun; an event resulting in great loss and misfortune
Synonyms : disaster

🖎 **Chunk**
Contextual Meaning(s) : Noun; a substantial amount; a compact mass;
Other Meaning(s) : verb group or chunk ther in a certain order or place side by side; put together indiscriminately
Synonyms : lump, clump

🖎 **Concede**
Contextual Meaning(s) : Verb; eventually becoming ready admit, make a clean breast of; acknowledge defeat; give over;
Other Meaning(s) : surrender or relinquish to the physical control another
Synonyms : yield

🖎 **Cynics**
Contextual Meaning(s) : Noun; people who doubt everything
Synonyms : faultfinders

🖎 **Dwarf**
Contextual Meaning(s) : Verb; make appear small by comparison
Other Meaning(s) : noun a person who is markedly small; a legendary creature resembling a tiny old man; lives in the depths of the earth and guards buried treasure; verb check the growth of;
Synonyms : overshadow

🖎 **Eclipsed**
Contextual Meaning(s) : Verb; hidden something behind itself, grown bigger than something else.
Synonyms : occulted

🖎 **Erection**
Contextual Meaning(s) : Noun; a structure that has been erected; the act of building or putting up
Synonyms : building

🖎 **Exponentially**
Contextual Meaning(s) : Adverb; In an exponential manner
Synonyms : rapidly

🖎 **Euphoria**
Contextual Meaning(s) : Noun; a feeling of great (usually exaggerated) elation
Synonyms : ecstasy

🖎 **Evacuation**
Contextual Meaning(s) : Noun; the act of evacuating; leaving a place in an orderly fashion; especially for protection;
Other Meaning(s) : removal of contents of some container
Synonyms : emptying

🖎 **Expansive**
Contextual Meaning(s) : Adjective; spacious[capable of or finding to expand in size
Other Meaning(s) : adjective friendly and open and willing to talk; marked by exaggerated feelings of euphoria and delusions of
Synonyms : wide

🖎 **Exposure**
Contextual Meaning(s) : Noun; publicity or visibility to people
Other Meaning(s) : vulnerability, revealing of a secret
Synonyms : publicity

🖎 **Frantic**
Contextual Meaning(s) : Adjective; excessively agitated; marked by uncontrolled excitement or emotion
Synonyms : rabid

- **Furor**
  Contextual Meaning(s) : Noun; a sudden outburst of interest followed with exaggerated zeal
  Other Meaning(s) : a sudden outburst of anger
  Synonyms : rage

- **Gingerly**
  Contextual Meaning(s) : Adjective; with extreme care or delicacy;
  Synonyms : charily

- **Iconic**
  Contextual Meaning(s) : Adjective; relating to or having the characteristics of an icon
  Synonyms : symbolic

- **Infatuation**
  Contextual Meaning(s) : Noun; foolish and usually extravagant passion or love or admiration; temporary love of an adolescent
  Other Meaning(s) : noun an object of extravagant short-lived passion;
  Synonyms : crush

- **Noted**
  Contextual Meaning(s) : Adjective; worthy of notice or attention; widely known and esteemed
  Synonyms : renowned

- **Numero Uno**
  Contextual Meaning(s) : Adjective; one that is first in rank, order, or importance
  Synonyms : Number one

- **One-upmanship**
  Contextual Meaning(s) : Noun; the practice of keeping one jump ahead of a friend or competitor
  Synonyms : outdoing

- **Optimism**
  Contextual Meaning(s) : Noun; tendency to expect best, the tendency to believe, expect, or hope that things will turn out well
  Synonyms : hopefulness, confidence

- **Proclaimed**
  Contextual Meaning(s) : Adjective; declared publicly; made widely known
  Synonyms : announced

- **Rarefied**
  Contextual Meaning(s) : Adjective; reserved for an elite group; of high moral or intellectual value; elevated in nature or style;
  Other Meaning(s) : having low density
  Synonyms : lofty

- **Soaring**
  Contextual Meaning(s) : Adjective; ascending to a level markedly higher than the usual; moving to great heights with little apparent effort; of imposing eight; especially standing out above others;
  Other Meaning(s) : noun the activity of flying a glider
  Synonyms : towering

- **Sprawl**
  Contextual Meaning(s) : Noun; an aggregation or continuous network of urban communities;
  Other Meaning(s) : noun an ungainly posture with arms and legs spread about;
  Synonyms : conurbation

- **Stampedes**
  Contextual Meaning(s) : Adjective; a headlong rush of people fleeing in panic
  Synonyms : panic

- **Steeped**
  Contextual Meaning(s) : Verb; let sit in a liquid to extract a flavour or to cleanse.
  Synonyms : soaked, drenched

- **Terra firma**
  Contextual Meaning(s) : Noun; a light coloured highland or mountainous area of the Moon of a planet
  Synonyms : Highland area of moon or planet

- **Tiered pagoda**
  Contextual Meaning(s) : Noun; a pagoda is a tiered tower with multiple eaves, built in traditions originating in historic South Asia and further developed in East Asia
  Synonyms : layers of tower

- **Vulnerability**
  Contextual Meaning(s) : Noun; exposure to injury or attack;
  Synonyms : susceptibility

Language -with all of its magnificent complexities- is one of the greatest gifts we give our children. Yet, we so often treat our verbal communication with children in a **flippant** way. There is a **delusion** that children learn language passively; this needs to be **disabused** .The adult must have a strong emotional link with the child as imitation is the first step that child takes towards speech. It must brings pleasant feelings which function as positive **reinforcement**. How much easier this learning process can then become for children when adults are active participants ?

The child's brain is learning and changing more during language **acquisition** in the first six years of life than during any other **cognitive** ability.

There is no genetic code that leads a child to speak English or Spanish or Japanese. Language is learned through environment. We are born with the capacity to make 40 sounds and our brain learns to make associations between sounds and objects, actions, or ideas. The combination of these capabilities allows the creation of language. Sounds come to have meaning. The **babbling** sound "ma - ma - ma" of the infant becomes mama, and then mother. In the first years of life children listen, practice, and learn. The amusing sounds of a young **toddler** practicing language -in seemingly meaningless **gabble**, is really their modeling of the whatever they see in us.

In many parts of the world, young children pick up four or five **motley** languages with no awareness that they're talking different languages. It's just: This is the way you talk to your aunt, this is the way you talk to your father, this is the way your neighbor understands and so on and so forth. It's just like **mouthing** both English and Japanese because that's the **lingua** your father and mother spoke, respectively.

One of the most **pertinent** discoveries in biology in the last 50 years is that the brains of all young animals, including children, go through critical periods when they are particularly **malleable** to learning or **mapping** different forms of information.

The primary **postulation** goes back to Eric Lenneberg, who founded the current trends in biology of language. His thesis which was pretty much everyone's was that language development was like other forms of growth and development. Almost invariably, growth and development has what's called a critical period. There's a particular period of **maturation** in which, with external **stimulation** of the appropriate kind, the capacity will pretty suddenly develop and mature. **Predating** that and later than that, it's either harder or impossible.

This is similar to the critical period of human maturation during which the visual system develops binocular vision under normal circumstances—but under **deprivation**, it won't. At roughly 4 months of age, under normal stimulation, binocular vision will develop.

In experiments with animals, say cats and monkeys, it's been shown that if they're deprived of stimulation if e.g., a kitten doesn't get patterned visual stimuli in the first several weeks of life its capacity to develop vision dies and the **neural** basis for it actually **degenerates**. But if pattern stimulation does appear at that time, then the kitten will develop normal vision.

That's a **pointed** example of a critical period. After age 10, learning new words becomes progressively harder until, as adults, it is exceedingly difficult. **Puberty** may be the end of the critical learning age. There are numerous examples of **feral** children who found learning human languages **recondite**. The older you get, the more you use your native language and the more it comes to dominate your linguistic map. You still have brain **litheness**, but your mother tongue rules. Your brain trains itself to not be **advertent** to foreign sounds, and the space in your head dedicated to language gets rather crowded almost like a "Write only" hard disk!

The exciting news about "critical-period **lissomeness**" is that it may be possible to reopen it so that adults can pick up languages the way children do. In experiments with rats, Dr. Michael Merzenich has reopened their critical-period **plasticity** by artificially turning on and keeping on their **nucleus basilis** using **microelectrodes** and an electric current. Someday, may be the same thing will be done with humans, using micro injections of certain drugs or chemicals. Just imagine, spending some time with Swahili speaking folks, you'll be able to learn Swahili and speak it without your mother-tongue accent!

There are experts who **demur** at this theory in that they believe learning a second language, in particular, is easier during 10-14 years, because by then the child has mastered the grammar of his first language and can use similar rule for the second unlike a toddler. Its always possible that his early environment may be that of an odd **dialect**, and a **reorientation** may be required of him to use the rules of the languages **scrupulously**.

Both theories agree that children have a neurological advantage in learning languages, and that after puberty one may find the idea of learning new languages rather **vapid**. Some adults are **receptive** to any changes they don't want to give themselves a further chance in life and remain **stagnant**. So silence in homes or in classrooms may not be golden after all!

To be fair, there are exceptions. There are grown ups who display an amazing flair for picking up new languages. These are usually people who have managed to keep the kids inside them alive !

✍ Acquisition

Contextual Meaning(s) : Noun; the act of contracting or assuming or acquiring possession of something; something acquired; an ability that has been acquired by training; the cognitive process of acquiring skill or knowledge
Synonyms : attainment

✍ Advertent

Contextual Meaning(s) : Adjective; giving attention
Synonyms : attentive

✍ Amenable

Contextual Meaning(s) : Adjective; disposed or willing to comply; liable to answer to a higher authority; open to being acted upon in a certain way; readily reacting to suggestions and influences
Synonyms : responsive

✍ Babbling

Contextual Meaning(s) : Noun; gibberish resembling the sounds of a baby
Other Meaning(s) : adjective continuous low murmuring sound; as especially of water; talking idly or incoherently;
Synonyms : jabbering

✍ Contemporary

Contextual Meaning(s) : Adjective; belonging to the present time; characteristic of the present; occurring in the same period of time; noun a person of nearly the same age as another
Synonyms : contemporaneous

✍ Cognitive

Contextual Meaning(s) : adjective; Of or being or relating to or involving cognition
Synonyms : intellectual, mental

✍ Degenerates

Contextual Meaning(s) : Verb; becomes bad or foul
Synonyms : deteriorate

✍ Delusion

Contextual Meaning(s) : Noun; the act of deluding; deception by creating illusory ideas; a mistaken or unfounded opinion or idea; (psychology) an erroneous belief that is held in the face of evidence to the contrary
Synonyms : misconception

✍ Demur

Contextual Meaning(s) : Verb; take exception to; enter a demurrer
Other Meaning(s) : noun (law) a formal objection to an opponent's pleadings;
Synonyms : disagree

✍ Deprivation

Contextual Meaning(s) : Noun; act of depriving someone of food or money or rights; the disadvantage that results from losing something; a state of extreme poverty
Synonyms : privation, neediness

✍ Dialect

Contextual Meaning(s) : Noun; the usage or vocabulary that is characteristic of a specific group of people
Synonyms : idiom

✍ Disabused

Contextual Meaning(s) : Adjective; freed of a mistaken or misguided notion
Synonyms : correct

✍ Feral

Contextual Meaning(s) : Adjective; wild and menacing
Synonyms : feline, savage

✍ Flippant

Contextual Meaning(s) : Adjective; showing inappropriate levity
Synonyms : dismissive

✍ Grabble

Contextual Meaning(s) : Verb; to talk reapidly and unintellingibly
Synonyms: jabber, babble

- ***Intricacy***
  Contextual Meaning(s) : Noun; marked by elaborately complex detail
  Synonyms : involution

- ***Lingua***
  Contextual Meaning(s) : Noun; language
  Other Meaning(s) : Noun; a mobile mass of muscular tissue covered with mucous membrane and located in the oral cavity
  Synonyms : tongue

- ***Lissomeness***
  Contextual Meaning(s) : Noun; the gracefulness of a person or animal that is flexible and supple
  Synonyms : nimbleness, agility

- ***Litheness***
  Contextual Meaning(s) : Noun; the gracefulness of a person or animal that is flexible and supple
  Synonyms : suppleness

- ***Malleable***
  Contextual Meaning(s) : Adjective; capable of being taught, managed, shaped or bent.
  Synonyms : pliable

- ***Maturation***
  Contextual Meaning(s) : Noun; coming to full development; becoming mature;
  Other Meaning(s) : (medicine) the formation of morbific matter in an abscess or a vesicle and the discharge of pus; (biology) the process of an individual organism growing organically; a purely biological unfolding of vents involved in an organism changing gradually from a simple to a more complex level
  Synonyms : ripening suppuration

- ***Motley***
  Contextual Meaning(s) : Adjective; consisting of a haphazard assortment of different kinds (even to the point of incongruity);
  Other Meaning(s) : adjective having sections or patches colored differently and usually brightly; noun a multicolored woolen fabric woven of mixed threads in 14th to 17th century England; a garment made of motley (especially a court jester's costume); a collection containing a variety of sorts of things; verb make motley; color with different colors; make something more diverse and varied
  Synonyms : smorgasbord, potpourri

- ***Mouthing***
  Contextual Meaning(s) : noun; something said that is hypocritical or meaningless
  Synonyms : voice, speech

- ***Mapping***
  Contextual Meaning(s) : noun; sketching or planning
  Synonyms : outline, plan

- ***Mouthing***
  Contextual Meaning(s) : Verb; speaking
  Synonyms : uttering

- ***Microelectrodes***
  Contextual Meaning(s) : noun; an electrode with a very small tip for use in brain studies. The device can be inserted without membrane damage into nervous tissue to record the bioelectrical activity of a simple neuron.
  Synonyms : micas, micate

- ***Neural***
  Contextual Meaning(s) : adjective; of or relating to a nerve or the nervous system
  Synonyms : neuronal, neuronic

- ***Nucleus Basilis***
  Contextual Meaning(s) : noun; the positively charged central region of an atom, consisting of protons and neutrons and containing most of the mass
  Synonyms : important element

- ***Perishes***
  Contextual Meaning(s) : Noun; becomes foul
  Synonyms : decays

- ***Pertinent***
  Contextual Meaning(s) : Adjective; having precise or logical relevance to the matter at hand; being of striking appropriateness and pertinence
  Synonyms : appropriate

- ***Pointed***
  Contextual Meaning(s) : Adjective; direct and obvious, or reference; often unpleasant; having a point
  Synonyms : targeted

- ***Postulation***
  Contextual Meaning(s) : Noun; (logic) a declaration of something self-evident; something that can be assumed as the basis for argument; a formal message requesting something that is submitted to an authority
  Synonyms : supposition

- ***Predating***
  Contextual Meaning(s) : Noun; occupying earlier in time
  Synonyms : antedating

- ***Puberty***
  Contextual Meaning(s) : Noun; the time of life when sex glands become functional
  Synonyms : pubescence

- ***Plasticity***
  Contextual Meaning(s) : noun; the condition of being soft and capable of being moulded
  Synonyms : smoothness, flexibility

- ***Recondite***
  Contextual Meaning(s) : Adjective; difficult to penetrate; incomprehensible to one of ordinary understanding or knowledge
  Synonyms : esoteric

- ***Reinforcement***
  Contextual Meaning(s) : Noun; information that makes more forcible or convincing; an act performed to strengthen approved behavior; a device designed to provide additional strength; (psychology) a stimulus that strengthens or weakens the behavior that reduced it
  Other Meaning(s) : a military operation (often involving new supplies of men and materiel) to strengthen a military force or aid in the performance of its mission;
  Synonyms : strengthener

- ***Reorientation***
  Contextual Meaning(s) : verb; to change the direction or management of something, to deal with a new situation
  Synonyms : change, turnabout

- ***Receptive***
  Contextual Meaning(s) : adjective; ready and willing to accept something such as new ideas
  Synonyms : open, amenable

- ***Scrupulously***
  Contextual Meaning(s) : Adverb; with extreme conscientiousness
  Synonyms : conscientiously, religiously

- ***Stimulation***
  Contextual Meaning(s) : Noun; the act of arousing an organism to action; any stimulating information or event; acts to arouse action; physiology) the effect of a stimulus (on nerves or organs etc.);
  Synonyms : arousal

- ***Semantics***
  Contextual Meaning(s) : Noun; the study of language Meanings
  Synonyms : linguistics

- ***Stagnant***
  Contextual Meaning(s) : adjective; not developing or making progress
  Synonyms : sluggish, inactive

- ***Toddler***
  Contextual Meaning(s) : Noun; a young child
  Synonyms : yearling, bambino

- ***Vapid***
  Contextual Meaning(s) : Adjective; lacking significance or liveliness or spirit or zest; lacking taste or flavor or tang
  Synonyms : bland, tasteless

PEER PRESSURE

There is an ice-cream store at the corner. Its mid-afternoon and the owner anxiously looks at the clock.

He is waiting for the gang of school kids who will come and buy all his stock. Even though some of them are getting overweight, they will come. He is sure that he will not be disappointed, because he's got an **infallible** sales plan. Its called peer pressure ! And its quite **condign** that many of these kids turn irreversibly **obese** !

A child sees another child carrying a balloon and immediately makes the same demand of his parents. A preteen **importunes** his dad for a fancy bike like his friend rides. This is all **nascent** peer pressure in human beings. This **snowballs** and develops gradually with age. And in case of several people this habit continues till old age.

The change that "peer pressure" goes through is in the kind of things one aspires for. During childhood kids **covet** chocolates and toys that their friends possess. In the teens if the outspoken types like certain type of music, movies, gadgets, clothes or, books, the rest of the herd also follows.

If they don't follow, they may be branded **renegades** and **ostracized**.

In the **twilight** of life a man may seek comfort and support of his grown up children and the pleasure of watching his grandchildren play. However his hapless **coevals** who don't have this opportunity may feel miserable by constant comparison.

However, it's always the "teenager" who comes to mind whenever this word is spoken. Peer pressure is one thing that all teens have in common.

Common negative activities associated with peer pressure are drugs, sex, **truancy**, **delinquency**, and theft.

Listening to country music when your classmates are tuned to hip-hop may be **sacrilegious**. You can't escape the mob mentality; it is **ubiquitous**. Mob-mentality is also true in case of students pursuing higher studies. For instance now days even a science graduate pursues on MBA.

No matter what your personality type be, how aloof you may be or how together you feel, sooner or later you will have to face peer pressure. In study after study, peer pressure is associated (in adolescents of all ethnic and racial backgrounds) with at-risk behaviors such as cigarette smoking, truancy, drug use, fighting, shoplifting, and daredevil stunts.

Nine-year-old Sarah wore a new shirt to school once then **repudiated** it because her friends made fun of it. Jeff, at sixteen, works out three hours a day, since he **begrudges** his friend's "perfect" body. When one of his friends at the gym offers him some **anabolic** steroids, he accepts, though he knows it's **insalubrious** in the long run. Equally **amenable** to peer pressure is the girl who develops **anorexia** or another eating disorder in an effort to have the "perfect" female body.

Meanwhile, Jeff's forty-year-old father just took out a loan he couldn't afford to buy a new BMW because most of his neighbors drive luxury cars, and he didn't want them to think he is too **indigent** to afford it. No one is **imperviable** to peer-pressure.

When ugly situations arise and peer pressure kicks in to high gear it is very easy to get caught up in the moment and forget that you will have to live with the choices you make. If you give in and do something that is contrary to your character or core value system it will cause you distress later and you will be **contrite** about it one day.

When peer pressure rears its **despicable** head, try to focus on how you feel about what is happening rather than get **dithery**, caught up in the crowd. Always stand up for what you think is right.

Some people may not like it when you go against the group but doing the right thing is rewarding. Peer pressure only works if you let it. If you refuse to let it **browbeat** you, it loses its power. The secret is to be assertive without becoming preachy or **sanctimonious**. Stand your ground but refrain from standing on a **pulpit**.

Always remember , the ice-cream store ; you don't have to buy from *peer pressure* **disguised** as a super salesman.

🖎 **Amenable**
Contextual Meaning(s) : Adjective; disposed or willing to comply; liable to answer to a higher authority; open to being acted upon in a certain way; readily reacting to suggestions and influences
Synonyms : conformable

🖎 **Anorexia**
Contextual Meaning(s) : Noun; a prolonged disorder of eating due to loss of appetite
Synonyms : eating disorder

🖎 **Anabolic**
Contextual Meaning(s): Adjective; characterized by, or promoting constructive metabolism e.g. some athletes take anabolic steroids to increase muscle size temporarily
Synonyms : energy-storing

🖎 **Begrudges**
Contextual Meaning(s) : Verb; envies or be jealous of
Synonyms : envies

🖎 **Browbeat**
Contextual Meaning(s) : Verb; discourage or frighten with threats or a domineering manner; intimidate; be bossy towards
Synonyms : bullyrag, hector

🖎 **Burgeons**
Contextual Meaning(s) : Verb; Swells or grows in size or effect.
Synonyms : evolves

🖎 **Coevals**
Contextual Meaning(s) : Noun; all the people living at the same time or of approximately the same age
Synonyms : contemporaries

🖎 **Condign**
Contextual Meaning(s) : Adjective; fitting or appropriate and deserved; used especially of punishment.
Synonyms : deserving, merited

🖎 **Contrite**
Contextual Meaning(s) : Adjective; feeling regret for a fault or offence; feeling or expressing pain or sorrow for sins or offenses
Synonyms : remorseful

🖎 **Covet**
Contextual Meaning(s) : Verb; wish, long, or crave for (something, especially the property of another person)
Synonyms : envy

🖎 **Delinquency**
Contextual Meaning(s) : Noun; an antisocial misdeed in violation of the law by a minor; a tendency to be negligent and uncaring; *Other Meaning(s) :* nonpayment of a debt when due
Synonyms : dereliction

🖎 **Despicable**
Contextual Meaning(s) : Adjective; morally reprehensible
Synonyms : detestable

🖎 **Dithery**
Contextual Meaning(s) : Adjective; characterized by lack of decision and firmness.
Synonyms : indecisive

🖎 **Disguised**
Contextual meaning(s): Verb; to change the appearance or guise of so as to conceal identity or mislead, as means of deceptive garb
Synonyms : misled, masked, veiled, hidden

🖎 **Impervious**
Contextual Meaning(s) : Adjective; not admitting of passage or capable of being affected
Synonyms : imperviable

🖎 **Importunes**
Contextual Meaning(s) : Verb; Pleads or requests earnestly
Synonyms : beseeches

Indigent

Contextual Meaning(s) : *Adjective; poor enough to need help from others*
Synonyms : impoverished, necessitous

Infallible

Contextual Meaning(s) : *Adjective; incapable of failure or error.*
Synonyms : unerring, foolproof

Insalubrious

Contextual Meaning(s) : *Adjective; detrimental to health*
Synonyms : unhealthful, unhealthy

Imperviable

Contextual Meaning(s) : *Adjective; not admitting of passage or capable of being affected; " a material impervious to water" ; " someone impervious to argument"*
Synonyms : impervious

Nascent

Contextual Meaning(s) : *Adjective; being born or beginning*
Synonyms : incipient

Ostracized

Contextual Meaning(s) : *Verb; removed from society due to some misconduct.*
Synonyms : excommunicate

Obese

Contextual Meaning(s) : *Adjective; excessively fat*
Synonyms : corpulent, rotund

Pulpit

Contextual Meaning(s) : *Noun; a platform raised above the surrounding level to give prominence to the person on it*
Synonyms : dais, podium, rostrum

Renegades

Contextual Meaning(s) : *Adjective; outlaws or deserters.*
Synonyms : deserters, apostates.

Repudiated

Contextual Meaning(s) : *Adjective; thing any denied or disowned*
Synonyms : disowned

Sacrilegious

Contextual Meaning(s) : *Adjective; grossly irreverent toward what is held to be sacred*
Synonyms : profane

Sanctimonious

Contextual Meaning(s) : *Adjective; excessively or hypocritically pious*
Synonyms : pietistic, pharisaic, self-righteous

Snowballs

Contextual Meaning(s) : *Verb; increase or accumulate at a rapidly accelerating rate*
Other Meaning(s) : *Noun; snow pressed into a ball for throwing (playfully); ball of crushed ice with fruit syrup; ball of ice cream covered with coconut and usually chocolate sauce; plant having heads of fragrant white trumpet-shaped flowers; grows in sandy arid regions*
Synonyms : expand

Truancy

Contextual Meaning(s) : *Noun; failure to attend (especially school)*
Synonyms : hooky

Twilight

Contextual Meaning(s) : *Noun; old age*
Other Meaning(s) : *adjective lighted by or as if by twilight; noun the diffused light from the sky when the sun is below the horizon but its rays are refracted by the atmosphere of the earth; a condition of decline following successes; the time of day immediately following sunset*
Synonyms : dusk, nightfall

Ubiquitous

Contextual Meaning(s) : *Adjective; being present everywhere at once*
Synonyms : omnipresent

The idea that living organisms function according to the laws of physics, and could in principle be **simulated** by means of mechanical constructions, is a scientific hypothesis. In the early seventeenth century, Descartes presented the thesis that animals are, in fact machines.

Three hundred years on, science and technology has come a long way. But ever since the robot HAL 9000 spoke its first words in the movie "2001: A Space Odyssey" four decades ago, most people have known computers can speak. And when Stephen Hawking started using a voice synthesizer in the 1980s, we saw that humans could use computers to voice their thoughts. Stephen hawking uses a synthesized voice due to medical challenges and his audience is never disappointed ; they come to listen to his thoughts. But if you had a computer **impersonating,** say George Clooney's voice, you would be very **disenchanted**, because you came to listen to the way he speaks, his rich **timbre, intonation, modulation** and expressions. And this is an area where technology is still **embryonic.**

Given how far we've come in generating completely photo-realistic artificial images in CGI, one would have thought that creating or imitating voices would have been a **breeze**, and yet it's clear that the opposite seems to be the case. Even generating a **credible** artificial voice of a particular person, from scratch has proven to be an extremely difficult task. Those that are even moderately convincing are actually generated from sampling real voices. The market forces that propelled the CGI revolution really had to do with producing images that couldn't be brought to an impressive **fruition** if produced otherwise, that is by actually shooting them with a camera. But if you really wanted to have a scene with Humphrey Bogart's voice you could find somebody to mimic it almost certainly as convincingly as you could by generating it by way of computer. Thus the time and the resources required for **propelling** this technology forward may not be deemed **tenable**.

But some individual's have had an extraordinary desire to replicate their voice artificially. When film critic Roger Ebert, who lost his voice following complications from thyroid cancer in 2006, **unveiled** a **prototype** of his newly synthesized voice on "The Oprah Winfrey Show" a year ago, and again this March at the TED conference in Long Beach, reports described it as "miraculous," "experimental" and "amazing."

It was ultimately by sampling a gigantic volume of the "target" person's voice and then manipulating this database by the computer, that a realistic artificial speech could be developed.

"Someone who's desirous of artificially generating his own voice because of medical reasons or otherwise can record his speech in advance," says Carnegie Mellon's Black.

For this, the individual receives a transcript of about 10,000 prompts to be read aloud and recorded on the computer. The prompts need to **encapsulate** all speech sounds necessary for the English language today — including rarer sounds like "oy," a soft "j" or sounds that appear in words of foreign origin (nasal vowels, for example). Also, each sound needs to appear in multiple language environments — for example, the t-sound in cat, stop, button, etc. — and in both function and content words. The software records and labels these sounds based on the original transcript and **coalesces** them into new words as needed.

In the late 1990s, for example, Black worked with a Japanese company to synthesize Bill Clinton's voice from available data, and when CereProc synthesized President Bush's voice several years ago, they used found data from his presidential speeches.

So if you **envisage** a time when you could type in a sentence and then choose from a menu any favorite person of yours say Sean Connery or Amitabh Bachchan, hoping to **embellish** the line using his **baritone**- well, this scenario is still miles away.

- ***Baritone***
Contextual Meaning(s) : Adjective; lower in range than tenor and higher than bass; noun the second lowest brass wind instrument; the second lowest male singing voice; a male singer
Synonyms : voice

- ***Breeze***
Contextual Meaning(s) : Noun; any undertaking that is easy to do;
Synonyms : cinch

- ***Coalesces***
Contextual Meaning(s) : Verb; fusess or causes to grow together; mixes together different elements
Synonyms : blends

- ***Credible***
Contextual Meaning(s) : Adjective; appearing to merit belief or acceptance; capable of being believed; a common but incorrect usage where credulous' would be appropriate
Synonyms : believable

- ***Disenchanted***
Contextual Meaning(s) : Adjective; freed from a strong magical influence.
Synonyms : crestfallen

- ***Embellish***
Contextual Meaning(s) : Verb; make more beautiful; add details to; make more attractive by adding ornament, colour, etc.; be beautiful to look at
Synonyms : fancify, grace, deck

- ***Embryonic***
Contextual Meaning(s) : Adjective; in an early stage of development;
Other Meaning(s) : of an organism prior to birth or hatching
Synonyms : budding

- ***Encapsulate***
Contextual Meaning(s) : Verb; put in a short or concise form; reduce in volume;
Other Meaning(s) : enclose in a capsule or other small container
Synonyms : capsulise

- ***Envisage***
Contextual Meaning(s) : Verb; form a mental image of something that is not present or that is not the case
Synonyms : visualize

- ***Fruition***
Contextual Meaning(s) : Noun; something that is made real or concrete
Other Meaning(s) : Noun; enjoyment derived from use or possession; the condition of bearing fruit;
Synonyms : realization

- ***Impersonate***
Contextual Meaning(s) : Verb; deceiving by pretending to be some other person
Synonyms : pose

- ***Intonation***
Contextual Meaning(s) : Noun; the production of musical tones (by voice or instrument); especially the exactitude of the pitch relations; the act of singing in a monotonous tone; singing by a soloist of the opening piece of plainsong; rise and fall of the voice pitch
Synonyms : cantillation

- ***Modulation***
Contextual Meaning(s) : Noun; the act of modifying or adjusting according to due measure and proportion (as with regard to artistic effect); (electronics) the transmission of a signal by using it to vary a carrier wave; changing the carrier's amplitude or frequency or phase; a manner of speaking in which the loudness or pitch or tone of the voice is modified; rise and fall of the voice pitch; a musical passage moving from one key to another
Synonyms : inflection

🖎 **Proffered**
Contextual Meaning(s) : Verb; Presented
Synonyms : offered

🖎 **Propelling**
Contextual Meaning(s) : Adjective; tending to take toward
Synonyms : driving

🖎 **Prototype**
Contextual Meaning(s) : Noun; the original or model on which something is based or formed; someone or something that serves to illustrate the typical qualities of a class; model
Other Meaning(s) : Verb; to develop a prototype of something
Synonyms : model, sample, trial product

🖎 **Simulated**
Contextual Meaning(s) : Adjective; reproduced or made to resemble; imitative in character; not genuine or real; being an imitation of the genuine article
Synonyms : imitated

🖎 **Singular**
Contextual Meaning(s) : Noun; the single one of its kind; beyond or deviating from the usual or expected; unusual or striking;
Other Meaning(s) : adjective being a single and separate person or thing; grammatical number category referring to a single item or unit; composed of one member, set, or kind; noun the form of a word that is used to denote a singleton
Synonyms : unique, curious, remarkable

🖎 **Tenable**
Contextual Meaning(s) : Adjective; based on sound reasoning or evidence
Synonyms : viable

🖎 **Timbre**
Contextual Meaning(s) : Noun; (music) the distinctive property of a complex sound (a voice or noise or musical sound)
Synonyms : tone

🖎 **Unnveiled**
Contextual Meaning(s) : verb; to reveal something that has been hidden or kept secret
Other Meaning(s) : take covering of something, to remove a veil or other covering from something, especially somebody's face or plaque, monument, or artwork during a formal ceremony
Synonyms : uncover, to disclose.

PSEUDONYMS

Writing under pseudonyms or "pen names" is a fine and honored tradition; many of the **stellar** names in literature were "invented," and many of the bestselling authors used and continue to use pseudonyms as well.

Five decades after the Hardy Boys books appeared, Leslie McFarland revealed himself as their writer Franklin W. Dixon. My kid sister, a Nancy Drew fan, felt **deceived** on finding out that Carolyn Keene is not really the author of the *Nancy Drew Mystery Series*. Mildred Wirt Benson, a young journalist, was the original ghostwriter for the them. Horror writer Stephen King also wrote as Richard Bachman for a variety of reasons. Some of them were **obviating** over exposure, writing his darker, more twisted tales and just substantiating that he sold *not* due to his name *but* genuine good work. To his **chagrin**, the Bachman book *Thinner* sold 28,000 copies during its initial run— and then ten times as many when it was revealed that Bachman was, in fact, King!

A lot of writers already have a more or less **thriving** career in a different field, and, well , writing can be a lottery. So they publish their first book under another name wondering if it clicks and when it does, that pseudonym has all the marketing goodwill attached by the time they write their next. If it fails, they lose nothing.

Then there are people who write **fluff** romance novels under one name to earn their daily bread, and serious literature under another, apprehensive that they won't be taken seriously if the readers of the latter find out about the former.

At times writers have the same name as an existing famous author, say John Grisham, Anne Rice, or J. D. Salinger, then the publisher may ask to "change" it to avoid confusion. Sometimes you can get away with a variation on your name -- for example, by writing as S. S. King when your name is actually Sidney Sheldon King!

Often, **collaborative** authors will invent a pseudonym to convey the impression that a book was written by a single author. For example, Robert Silverberg and Randall Garrett collaborated under the name "Robert Randall." Similarly Emma Darcy, a famous Harlequin Mills and Boon author is actually a husband and wife team, Wendy and Frank Brennan !

Authors writing for competing publications are known to use different names for different magazines, say Varun Khanna becomes Samar Singh for another magazine and Abdul Rizvi for a third one.

Celebrated novelist Dean Koontz's early novels brought in very little money, so he wrote several ones each year. When an unknown author writes that much, publishers urge him to use a pen name, since they feel **prolific** authors will not be taken **earnestly**. Dean wrote under 11 pseudonyms from David Axton to Aaron Wolfe, **encompassing** genres from psychological thrillers to Romance mystery. Finally he killed all his pen names and re-released all his novels under his own name, now famous and made a fortune.

Some writers adopted a pen name because they had a history of failure, and went on to write best-sellers under a different name.!

People writing in a genre that has "expectations" about its authors may also be forced to use a more **congruous** name with the genre. When was the last time you saw a romance novel by "Jake Hammersmith" or a hard-core thriller by "Felicity Valentine"?

One reason authors use pen names is to mask the fact that they are writing in the "wrong" gender for their field. In 1968 a new star burst upon the science fiction scene, James Tiptree Jr. The stories were literate, brilliant, **piquant** … but no one knew who he was or how he got to be so damned good. As **speculation** bristled, people **contended** that one thing was clear from his distinctive style- A lady would be too **timorous** for this; Tiptree was surely a man.

Finally it was disclosed that Tiptree was a former CIA intelligence agent and doctor of experimental psychology, a woman named Alice Sheldon !

Joanne Rowling's publishers **exhorted** her to use only initials 'J.K.' for the publication of her Harry Potter novels with fear that the target audience of young boys would **balk** at having to read something written by a woman !

It's true that George Eliot and Charlotte Bronte used male pen names so that their work could be published at all.

Mary Ann Evans became George Eliot, and

Charlotte Bronte initially published "Jane Eyre" as a male called Curer Bell.

Some great authors were forced to use a false name to avoid the **indignation** of their employers or coworkers. In 1969, the Edgar Award for best mystery novel was won by Jeffrey Hudson … a Harvard Medical School intern whose real name was Michael Crichton ! He, of course, went on to be the writer of phenomenal stories like " Jurassic Park" and others. Two decades earlier, a young writer and Ph.D. candidate worried that his chemistry **dissertation** might be rejected because of a humorous essay published under his real name, despite asking his publisher to use a pseudonym. Fortunately, he was too talented -- as both writer and scientist -- to be turned down, and so he became "Doctor" Isaac Asimov.

Some had this fear of charges of **slander** or **libel** because they were revealing secrets of relatives, friends, coworkers, or corporate employers.

Keep in mind when using a pseudonym that it will not protect you from any legal action in case its deemed a **transgression**. A pseudonym has no existence as a "legal" entity; no matter what name you put on your work, the ultimate responsibility for that work always rests on you.

Balk

Contextual Meaning(s) : Verb; refuse to comply

Other Meaning(s) : noun an illegal pitching motion while runners are on base; the area on a billiard table behind the balkline; one of several parallel sloping beams that support a roof; something immaterial that interferes with or delays action or progress;

Synonyms : resist, jib

Celebrated

Contextual Meaning(s) : Adjective; having an illustrious past; widely known and esteemed

Synonyms : notable, renowned

Chagrin

Contextual Meaning(s) : Noun; strong feelings of embarrassment;

Other Meaning(s) : verb cause to feel shame; hurt the pride of

Synonyms : humiliation, mortification

Collaborative

Contextual Meaning(s) : Adjective; accomplished by team work.

Synonyms : cooperative

Congruous

Contextual Meaning(s) : Adjective; suitable or appropriate together; corresponding in character or kind

Synonyms : appropriate, matching

Contended

Contextual Meaning(s) : Verb; fought over or disputed

Synonyms : argued

Deceived

Contextual Meaning(s) : Verb; cheated or lied (to someone)

Synonyms : cheated, tricked

Dissertation

Contextual Meaning(s) : Noun; a treatise advancing a new point of view resulting from research; usually a requirement for an advanced academic degree

Synonyms : thesis

Earnestly

Contextual Meaning(s) : Adverb; in a serious manner

Synonyms : seriously

Encompassing

Contextual Meaning(s) : Adjective; closely encircling; broad in scope or content

Synonyms : covering, including

Exhorted

Contextual Meaning(s) : Verb; strongly urged or inspired

Synonyms : motivated, forced

Fluff

Contextual Meaning(s) : Noun; any light downy material; something of little value or significance;

Other Meaning(s) : verb ruffle (one's hair) by combing towards the ends towards the scalp, for a full effect; erect or fluff up; make a mess of, destroy or ruin

Synonyms : frivolity

Indignation

Contextual Meaning(s) : Noun; a feeling of righteous anger

Synonyms : outrage

Libel

Contextual Meaning(s) : Noun; the written statement of a plaintiff explaining the cause of action (the defamation) and any relief he seeks; a false and malicious publication printed for the purpose of defaming a living person; verb print slanderous statements against

Synonyms : calumny, slander

- ✍ **Obviating**
  Contextual Meaning(s) : Adjective; made impossible
  Synonyms : preclusive

- ✍ **Obviating**
  Contextual Meaning(s) : verb; prevent the occurrence of; prevent from happening
  Synonyms : debarring

- ✍ **Piquant**
  Contextual Meaning(s) : Adjective; engagingly stimulating or provocative; having an agreeably pungent taste; attracting or delighting
  Synonyms : salty, savory

- ✍ **Prolific**
  Contextual Meaning(s) : Adjective; bearing in abundance especially offspring; intellectually productive
  Synonyms : fertile, fecund

- ✍ **Slander**
  Contextual Meaning(s) : Noun; words falsely spoken that damage the reputation of another; an abusive attack on a person's character or good name;
  Other Meaning(s) : verb charge falsely or with malicious intent; attack the good name and reputation of someone
  Synonyms : aspersion, defamation, denigration

- ✍ **Speculation**
  Contextual Meaning(s) : Noun; a hypothesis that has been formed by speculating or conjecturing (usually with little hard evidence); continuous and profound contemplation or musing on a subject or series of subjects of a deep or abstruse nature; a message expressing an opinion based on incomplete evidence
  Other Meaning(s) : an investment that is very risky but could yield great profits;
  Synonyms : conjecture surmise

- ✍ **Stellar**
  Contextual Meaning(s) : Adjective; being or relating to or resembling or emanating from stars; indicating the most important performer or role
  Synonyms : astral, leading

- ✍ **Substantiate**
  Contextual Meaning(s) : Verb; solidify, firm, or strengthen; establish or strengthen as with new evidence or facts; make real or concrete;
  Other Meaning(s) : give reality or substance to; represent in bodily form
  Synonyms : confirming, corroborating

- ✍ **Thriving**
  Contextual Meaning(s) : Adjective; very lively and profitable
  Other Meaning(s) : having or showing vigorous vegetal or animal life;
  Synonyms : flourishing, booming

- ✍ **Timorous**
  Contextual Meaning(s) : Adjective; timid by nature or revealing timidity
  Synonyms : fearful, trepid

- ✍ **Transgression**
  Contextual Meaning(s) : Noun; the action of going beyond or overstepping some boundary or limit; the act of transgressing; the violation of a law or a duty or moral principle;
  Other Meaning(s) : the spreading of the sea over land as evidenced by the deposition of marine strata over terrestrial strata
  Synonyms : breach, overstepping, violation

THE 10 PERCENT BRAIN MYTH

The idea that we only use a very small percentage of our brain is a **myth**. The popular media and some very influential thinkers have **endorsed** this **misconception**. Statements that humans only use a fraction of their brains have been wrongly attributed to physicist Albert Einstein and anthropologist Margaret Mead. The **canard** then became famous through Dale Carnegie's best-seller "How to Stop Worrying and Start Living" and through **psychic** superstar Uri Geller, who explained his "spoon magic" by **asserting** better usage of the brain. A generation of "positive thinking" gurus have talked about the brain's untapped potential and gradually "10 percent of our potential" **morphed** into "10 percent of our brain."

The advertising industry is equally guilty of using the idea to sell their products. This **innuendo** is found in connection with certain new-age brain **jogging** products, which promise the access to huge unused brain areas- but the ones to actually gain most from these products are their sellers!

The 10-percent brain usage **legend** is one of those hopeful **shibboleths** that refuses to die simply because it would be so nice if it were true. I'm sure none of us would turn down a mighty **increment** in brainpower if it were attainable, and a stream of **factitious** schemes and devices continues to be advanced by **quacks** who trade on the myth.

Always on the lookout for a "feel-good" story, the media have also played their part in keeping the myth alive. A study of self-improvement products by a panel of the prestigious National Research Council, *Enhancing Human Performance*, surveyed a collection of the less far-fetched offerings of the "brain booster" genre and came to the conclusion that there is no reliable substitute for one's practice and **sedulousness** when it comes to getting ahead in life.

This unwelcome news has done little, however, to **dissuade** millions who are comforted by the prospect that the shortcut to all their unfulfilled dreams lies in the fact that they just haven't quite found the secret to tap this vast, **allegedly** unused cerebral **reservoir**. According to the believers of this myth, if we used more of our brain, then we could perform super memory **feats** and have other fantastic mental abilities - maybe we could even move objects with a single thought, just like Yuri Geller. Or achieve thought transmission, extremely high intelligence, as well as **telekinesis**.

Why would a neuroscientist disbelieve that 90 percent of the average brain lies **perpetually fallow**? First of all, it is obvious that the brain, like all our other organs, has been shaped by natural selection.

While the brain only weighs 2% of the total body weight, it uses 20% of the whole energy. Thus brain tissue is metabolically expensive both to grow and to run, and it seems absurd to think that evolution would have permitted **squandering** of resources to build and maintain such a massively under utilized organ. In simpler terms, from an evolutionary point of view, it is unlikely that larger brains would have developed if there was not an advantage to man from them.

Arguments against the myth are fueled by a lot of evidence from clinical neurology. Losing far less than 90 percent of the brain to accident or disease has horrific consequences. What is more, observing the effects of head injury reveals that there does not seem to be any area of the brain that can be destroyed by strokes, head trauma, or any other manner, without leaving the patient with some kind of functional deficit. Likewise, electrical stimulation of points in the brain during neurosurgery has failed so far to uncover any **dormant** areas where no percept, emotion or movement is **elicited** by applying tiny currents. Remember, this can be done with conscious patients under local anesthetic because the brain itself has no pain receptors !

Even during sleep, no brain area is completely inactive. On the contrary, lack of activity in certain brain regions would be indicative of a serious malfunction.

All told, the foregoing arguments suggest that there is no cerebral spare tire waiting to be mounted in service of one's grade point average, job advancement, or one's invention of Time Machine.

Imagine the following horror scenario: a masked man holds his gun onto your forehead and menaces: "Give me your money or I will shoot!" According to the 10% myth, you would **placidly** refuse his order, as the chance that the bullet hits a brain area, which you actually use, lies only at 10%. But reality is different: Nobody would risk such an injury. No brain region can be damaged without leaving a person with mental or physical deficits.

But there are stories about people who lived for years with a bullet in their brain or who completely recover from a stroke. The fact that these people are able to lead a more or less normal life is due to an extraordinary capacity of the brain: its plasticity. The brain is extremely good in compensation. Other nerve cells are able to take over the tasks of damaged nerve cells, like in a soccer game: If one player gets the red card, the other players take over his role and **recompense** his absence. But the entire team of eleven has to be there and contribute actively in order to win. Ditto with the brain!

🖎 **Allegedly**
Contextual Meaning(s) : Adverb; according to what has been said against someone or something
Synonyms : supposedly

🖎 **Ample**
Contextual Meaning(s) : Adjective; affording an abundant supply; more than enough in size or scope or capacity; fairly large
Synonyms : copious, plenteous,

🖎 **Asserting**
Contextual Meaning(s) : Adjective; relating to the use of or having the nature of a declaration
Synonyms : declarative, declaratory

🖎 **Assortment**
Contextual Meaning(s) : Noun; a collection containing a variety of sorts of things; the act of distributing things into classes or categories of the same type
Synonyms : potpourri, motley,

🖎 **Calamitous**
Contextual Meaning(s) : Adjective; (of events) having extremely unfortunate or dire consequences; bringing ruin
Synonyms : black, disastrous

🖎 **Canard**
Contextual Meaning(s) : Noun; a deliberately misleading tale
Synonyms : rumour

🖎 **Dissuade**
Contextual Meaning(s) : Verb; turn away from by persuasion
Synonyms : deters

🖎 **Dormant**
Contextual Meaning(s) : Adjective; inactive but capable of becoming active; in a condition of biological rest or suspended animation
Other Meaning(s) : of e.g. volcanos; not erupting and not extinct;
Synonyms : inactive, hibernating, torpid

🖎 **Elicited**
Contextual Meaning(s) : Adjective; called forth from a latent or potential state by stimulation
Synonyms : evoked

🖎 **Endorsed**
Contextual Meaning(s) : Adjective; formally supported especially by public statement
Synonyms : approved

🖎 **Factitious**
Contextual Meaning(s) : Adjective; not produced by natural forces or artitiual or unreal
Synonyms : fake, unauthentic

🖎 **Fallow**
Contextual Meaning(s) : Adjective; undeveloped but potentially useful;
Other Meaning(s) : left unplowed and unseeded during a growing season; noun cultivated land that is not seeded for one or more growing seasons
Synonyms : uncultivated, barren

🖎 **Feats**
Contextual Meaning(s) : Noun; a noteworthy or extraordinary act or achievement, usually displaying boldness, skill
Other Meaning(s) : noun; accomplishments
Synonyms : a specialized skill, profession

🖎 **Increment**
Contextual Meaning(s) : Noun; the amount by which something increases; a process of becoming larger or longer or more numerous or more important
Synonyms : increase, growth

🖎 **Innuendo**
Contextual Meaning(s) : Noun; an indirect (and usually malicious) implication
Synonyms : insinuation

🖎 **Jogging**
Contextual Meaning(s) : Verb; serve to stimulate
Other Meaning(s) : noun running at a jog trot as a form of cardiopulmonary exercise
Synonyms : activating

🖎 **Legend**

Contextual Meaning(s) : Noun; a story about mythical or supernatural beings or events;

Other Meaning(s) : brief description accompanying an illustration

Synonyms : fable, caption

🖎 **Myth**

Contextual Meaning(s) : Noun; a traditional story accepted as historically true; serves to explain the world view of a people

Synonyms : legend

🖎 **Misconception**

Contextual Meaning(s) : noun; a mistaken idea or view resulting from a misunderstanding of something

Synonyms : misunderstanding, mistaken belief

🖎 **Morphed**

Contextual Meaning(s) : verb; to cause something to change its outward appearance completely and instantaneously, or undergo this process

Synonyms : alter, modify

🖎 **Placidly**

Contextual Meaning(s) : Adverb; in a placid and good-natured manner; in a quiet and tranquil manner

Synonyms : calmly, quietly

🖎 **Preposterous**

Contextual Meaning(s) : Adjective; incongruous; inviting ridicule

Synonyms : derisory, nonsensical

🖎 **Psychic**

Contextual Meaning(s) : Noun; a person apparently sensitive to things beyond the natural range of perception

Other Meaning(s) : adjective; outside the sphere of physical science; affecting or influenced by the human mind;

Synonyms : clairvoyant

🖎 **Perpetually**

Contextual Meaning(s) : adverb; forever, or for a very long time, repeatedly at very short intervals, and so appearing to be continuous

Synonyms : everlastingly, eternally

🖎 **Quacks**

Contextual Meaning(s) : Noun; unqualified persons pretending to be physicians.

Other Meaning(s) : Adjective; medically unqualified people; verb- the sound made by a duck.

Synonyms : charlatan, mountebank

🖎 **Recompense**

Contextual Meaning(s) : Verb; compensate; make amends for; pay compensation for

Other Meaning(s) : noun the act of compensating for service or loss or injury; payment or reward (as for service rendered); verb make payment to;

Synonyms : compensation, compensate, indemnify

🖎 **Reservoir**

Contextual Meaning(s) : Noun; a supply or source of something.

Synonyms: Stock, hoard, store.

🖎 **Sedulousness**

Contextual Meaning(s) : Noun; the quality of being constantly diligent and attentive

Synonyms : diligence

🖎 **Shibboleths**

Contextual Meaning(s) : Noun; slogans or a cathourds or mottored

Synonyms : slogans, catchwords

🖎 **Squandering**

Contextual Meaning(s) : Noun; spending resources lavishly and wastefully

Synonyms : wasting

🖎 **Telekinesis**

Contextual Meaning(s) : an alleged psychic ability allowing a person to influence a physical system without physical interaction

Synonyms : Psychokinesis

Poets, writers, singers and artists of all genres have **romanticized** the human *heart* as the symbol of love. Its supposed to be the **sanctum** of our most treasured feelings, memories and sentiments; it aches when somebody hurts you, it pounds when you are nervous, it **flutters** when your beloved is near and it breaks when some loved one leaves you. It's in the title of songs, movies, books and its almond shape represents it in emoticons, greeting cards, sketches and all forms of communication.

But there is a problem with all these traditions and colorful heart metaphors. Something that all the neuroscientists, cardiologists and other medical **wizards** have been telling us all the while. The heart is just a ten-ounce muscle; a biological machine that pumps around 5 litres of blood to all parts of the body. A vital function, an **occlusion** of which would certainly be **fatal**. But that's the primary function of the heart. Its not really the centre of our emotions or feelings, its actually quite *heartless*! That leaves the Brain as the nucleus of every sentiment, **whim**, fancy and obsession . Unfortunately its shape is rather **knotty** and the color is a dull grey; it wont make an ideal icon for a **besotted** valentine .

So when Toni Braxton sings *Unbreak my heart* ,or Black Eyed Peas sing *Don't Phunk With My Heart* they are just following what the entire breed of artistes have been doing for generations- confusing *heart* for *brain*.

Researchers have long back discovered the center of "emotions" in the brain. "A region at the front of the brain's right hemisphere, the pre frontal cortex, plays a critical role in how the human brain processes emotions," says a 2001 University of Iowa report. Scientists monitored single brain cells—neurons—in the right pre frontal **cortex** and found that these cells responded remarkably rapidly to unpleasant images, which included pictures of **mutilation** and scenes of war. Happy or neutral pictures did not cause the same rapid response from the neurons.

Mothers, when seeing pictures of their own babies compared to seeing someone else's baby or no image at all, showed greater activity in the orbito frontal cortex - a brain region in the lower part of the frontal lobe that's involved in decoding the emotional value of a pleasant stimulus .

The heart is a rather straightforward structure to study, though it has a **labyrinthine** structure of nerves, valves and chambers, its working is no more complex than an engine; medical science has grasped its biomechanics quite well. We are able to transplant hearts, make artificial hearts, perform heart surgeries almost risk free and medically diagnose its malfunctions thoroughly.

Conversely, lets try and understand the complexity of the human brain. The human brain weighs only three pounds but is estimated to have about 100 billion cells. It is hard to get a handle on a number that large (or connections that small). Let's try to get an understanding of this complexity by comparing it with something humans have created, the entire phone system for the planet. If we took all the phones in the world and all the wires (there are over four billion people on the planet), the number of connections and the trillions of messages per day would *not* equal the complexity or activity of a single human brain .

One of the reasons, mankind started associating emotions with the heart could be the physical sensations it **emanates** as we encounter different situations. When frightened; we can feel it thumping, when anxious; we can feel it **flapping** when we are excited, it beats faster. And its most steady when we feel **tranquil**. It is interesting to note that the heart starts beating in the unborn fetus even before the brain has been formed. Thus the **apologists** for the sentimental heart do have a point. In contrast, the brain seemingly transmits almost no sensation other than the good old headache or the **atrocious migraine**.

There is a distinct possibility that the **manipulative** product marketers have also found using the *heart* as a tool, a much more attractive proposition rather than using the *brain*. Just try replacing the word heart with brain in any advertising campaign : How about *brain warming* instead of *heartwarming* ? Or *brain felt* instead of *heartfelt*? Would *brain break* or *heartbreak* sound better ? Won't *from the bottom of the brain* sound mindless? Would a box of chocolates, a bunch of red roses and a *brain* shaped cake look good together — especially when trying to **court** someone?

So the *heart* hijacked the role of the *emotion manager* of our body in our collective conscious; the entire human race has lived under the illusion ever after. Thankfully, researchers and scientists have lately come up with more pointed knowledge about the brain. Daniel Goleman has credited the brain has having an emotional intelligence , the **amygdala** has been recognized as the part of the brain which responds to emotions, even the clever marketers now try to *capture the customer's mind* rather than the *heart*.

Alternative therapies have long recognized the need to put a positive influence on our body via soothing the brain's emotional receptors. The color therapy approaches the brain through visual faculty, music therapy uses the auditory senses and the hypnosis has always tried to heal us through the subconscious brain. The brain has and always will be the **citadel** of our feelings.

Heart is always **mercurial**, brave and a bit naive, whereas Brain prefers to think it over, sometimes he tends to be shy and over-intellectual, but he always shows a lot of patience and tolerance for Heart's extravagant behavior. Almost like father and son one would say.

I have enough knowledge by now to **affirm** with confidence that all of my joy, sadness, anger and hope reside totally inside the brain. And I say it with my hand on my heart !

Acquisition
Contextual Meaning(s) : Noun; the act of contracting or assuming or acquiring possession of something; something acquired; an ability that has been acquired by training; the cognitive process of acquiring skill or knowledge
Synonyms : attainment

Advertent
Contextual Meaning(s) : Adjective; giving attention
Synonyms : attentive

Affirm
Contextual Meaning(s) : Verb; to declare or affirm solemnly and formally as true; say yes to
Other Meaning(s) : Verb; establish or strengthen as with new evidence or facts
Synonyms : aver, avow

Amenable
Contextual Meaning(s) : Adjective; disposed or willing to comply; liable to answer to a higher authority; open to being acted upon in a certain way; readily reacting to suggestions and influences
Synonyms : responsive

Apologist
Contextual Meaning(s) : Noun; a person who argues to defend or justify some policy or institution
Synonyms : proponent, advocate

Atrocious
Contextual Meaning(s) : Adjective; provoking horror; exceptionally bad or displeasing; shockingly brutal or cruel
Synonyms : detestable

Amygdale
Contextual Meaning(s) : noun; an almond shaped neural structure in the anterior part of the temporal lobe of cerebrum; intimately connected with hypothalamus and the hippoc campus and the cingulated gyrus; as part of the limbic system it plays an important role in motivation and emotional behaviour

Babbling
Contextual Meaning(s) : Noun; gibberish resembling the sounds of a baby
Other Meaning(s) : adjective continuous low murmuring sound; as especially of water; talking idly or incoherently;
Synonyms : jabbering

Besotted
Contextual Meaning(s) : Adjective; very drunk
Synonyms : inebriated

Citadel
Contextual Meaning(s) : Noun; a stronghold into which people could go for shelter during a battle
Synonyms : fortress

Contemporary
Contextual Meaning(s) : Adjective; belonging to the present time; characteristic of the present; occurring in the same period of time; noun a person of nearly the same age as another
Synonyms : contemporaneous

Court
Contextual Meaning(s) : Verb; engage in social activities leading to marriage; make amorous advances towards; seek someone's favor
Other Meaning(s) : Noun; respectful deference; an area wholly or partly surrounded by walls or buildings; a specially marked horizontal area within which a game is played; a room in which a lawcourt sits; the residence of a sovereign or nobleman; the sovereign and his advisers who are the governing power of a state; the family and retinue of a sovereign or prince; an assembly (including one or more judges) to conduct judicial business;

Australian woman tennis player who won many major championships (born in 1947); a hotel for motorists; provides direct access from rooms to parking area
Synonyms : romance, solicit, woo

Cortex
Contextual meaning(s) : noun; the outer layer of a solid organ or a part of the body, e.g. the outer covering of the kidney or brain cerebral cortex
Synonyms : cerebral mantle, pallium

Degenerates
Contextual Meaning(s) : Verb; becomes bad or foul
Synonyms : deteriorate

Delusion
Contextual Meaning(s) : Noun; the act of deluding; deception by creating illusory ideas; a mistaken or unfounded opinion or idea; (psychology) an erroneous belief that is held in the face of evidence to the contrary
Synonyms : misconception

Demur
Contextual Meaning(s) : Verb; take exception to; enter a demurrer
Other Meaning(s) : noun (law) a formal objection to an opponent's pleadings;
Synonyms : disagree

Deprivation
Contextual Meaning(s) : Noun; act of depriving someone of food or money or rights; the disadvantage that results from losing something; a state of extreme poverty
Synonyms : privation, neediness

Dialect
Contextual Meaning(s) : Noun; the usage or vocabulary that is characteristic of a specific group of people
Synonyms : idiom

Disabused
Contextual Meaning(s) : Adjective; freed of a mistaken or misguided notion
Synonyms : corrected

Emanates
Contextual Meaning(s) : Verb; proceeds or issues forth, as from a source; gives out (breath or an odor)
Synonyms : radiates, emits

Fatal
Contextual Meaning(s) : Adjective bringing death.
Synonyms : lethal, terminal

Feral
Contextual Meaning(s) : Adjective; wild and menacing
Synonyms : ferine, savage

Flapping
Contextual Meaning(s) : Noun; the motion made by fluttering up and down
Synonyms : beating

Flippant
Contextual Meaning(s) : Adjective; showing inappropriate levity
Synonyms : dismissive

Flutters
Contextual Meaning(s) : verb; to beat rapidly because of nervousness or excitement
Synonyms : palpitate, thump

Intricacy
Contextual Meaning(s) : Noun; marked by elaborately complex detail
Synonyms : involution

Knotty
Contextual Meaning(s) : Adjective; tangled in knots or snarls; making great mental demands; hard to comprehend or solve or believe; highly complex or intricate
Other Meaning(s) : used of old persons or old trees; covered with knobs or knots
Synonyms : complex

Labyrinthine
Contextual Meaning(s) : Adjective; resembling a labyrinth in form or complexity
Other Meaning(s) : relating to or affecting or originating in the inner ear
Synonyms : serpentine

✉ **Lingua**

Contextual Meaning(s) : Noun; language
Other Meaning(s) : Noun; a mobile mass of muscular tissue covered with mucous membrane and located in the oral cavity
Synonyms : tongue

✉ **Lissomeness**

Contextual Meaning(s) : Noun; the gracefulness of a person or animal that is flexible and supple
Synonyms : nimbleness, agility

✉ **Litheness**

Contextual Meaning(s) : Noun; the gracefulness of a person or animal that is flexible and supple
Synonyms : suppleness

✉ **Manipulative**

Contextual Meaning(s) : Adjective; skillful in influencing or controlling others to your own advantage
Synonyms : scheming

✉ **Maturation**

Contextual Meaning(s) : Noun; coming to full development; becoming mature;
Other Meaning(s) : (medicine) the formation of morbific matter in an abscess or a vesicle and the discharge of pus; (biology) the process of an individual organism growing organically; a purely biological unfolding of vents involved in an organism changing gradually from a simple to a more complex level
Synonyms : ripening suppuration

✉ **Mercurial**

Contextual Meaning(s) : liable to sudden unpredictable change
Other Meaning(s) : Adjective; relating to or containing or caused by mercury; relating to or having characteristics (eloquence, shrewdness, swiftness, thievishness) attributed to the god Mercury; relating to or under the (astrological) influence of the planet Mercury;
Synonyms : temperamental

✉ **Motley**

Contextual Meaning(s) : Adjective; consisting of a haphazard assortment of different kinds (even to the point of incongruity);
Other Meaning(s) : adjective having sections or patches colored differently and usually brightly; noun a multicolored woolen fabric woven of mixed threads in 14th to 17th century England; a garment made of motley (especially a court jester's costume); a collection containing a variety of sorts of things; verb make motley; color with different colors; make something more diverse and varied
Synonyms : smorgasbord, potpourri

✉ **Migraine**

Contextual Meaning(s) : noun; a recurrent, throbbing, very painful headache, often affecting one side of the head and sometimes accompanied by vomiting or by distinct warning signs, including visual disturbances
Synonyms : headache, megrim

✉ **Occlusion**

Contextual Meaning(s) : Verb; blocking the path or passage
Synonyms : obstructing

✉ **Semantics**

Contextual Meaning(s) : Noun; the study of language Meanings
Synonyms : smorgasbord, potpourri

✉ **Mouthing**

Contextual Meaning(s) : Verb; speaking
Synonyms : uttering

✉ **Mutilation**

Contextual Meaning(s) : Noun; an injury that causes disfigurement or deprivation of a body part.
Synonyms : injury

✉ **Perishes**

Contextual Meaning(s) : Noun; becomes foul
Synonyms : decays

- **Pertinent**
  Contextual Meaning(s) : Adjective; having precise or logical relevance to the matter at hand; being of striking appropriateness and pertinence
  Synonyms : appropriate

- **Pointed**
  Contextual Meaning(s) : Adjective; direct and obvious in Meaning(s) or reference; often unpleasant; having a point
  Synonyms : targeted

- **Postulation**
  Contextual Meaning(s) : Noun; (logic) a declaration of something self-evident; something that can be assumed as the basis for argument; a formal message requesting something that is submitted to an authority
  Synonyms : supposition

- **Predating**
  Contextual Meaning(s) : Noun; coming earlier in time
  Synonyms : antedating

- **Puberty**
  Contextual Meaning(s) : Noun; the time of life when sex glands become functional
  Synonyms : pubescence

- **Recondite**
  Contextual Meaning(s) : Adjective; difficult to penetrate; incomprehensible to one of ordinary understanding or knowledge
  Synonyms : esoteric

- **Reinforcement**
  Contextual Meaning(s) : Noun; information that makes more forcible or convincing; an act performed to strengthen approved behavior; a device designed to provide additional strength; (psychology) a stimulus that strengthens or weakens the behavior that produce it
  Synonyms : strengthener

- **Romanticized**
  Contextual Meaning(s) : verb; to think or express something in an amorous, idealistic, or sentimental way
  Synonyms : idealize

- **Sanctum**
  Contextual Meaning(s) : Noun; a place of inviolable privacy; a sacred place of pilgrimage
  Synonyms : holy-place

- **Scrupulously**
  Contextual Meaning(s) : Adverb; with extreme conscientiousness
  Synonyms : conscientiously, religiously

- **Stimulation**
  Contextual Meaning(s) : Noun; the act of arousing an organism to action; any stimulating information or event; acts to arouse action; physiology) the effect of a stimulus (on nerves or organs etc.);
  Synonyms : arousal

- **Toddler**
  Contextual Meaning(s) : Noun; a young child
  Synonyms : yearling, bambino

- **Tranquil**
  Contextual Meaning(s) : Adjective; not agitated; without losing self-possession
  Synonyms : serene, placid, calm

- **Vapid**
  Contextual Meaning(s) : Adjective; lacking significance or liveliness or spirit or zest; lacking taste or flavor or tang
  Synonyms : bland, tasteless

- **Wizards**
  Contextual Meaning(s) : Noun; someone who is dazzlingly skilled in any field
  Other Meaning(s) : Adjective; possessing or using or characteristic of or appropriate to supernatural powers; one who practices magic or sorcery
  Synonyms : virtuoso, ace

- **Whim**
  Contextual Meaning(s) : noun; a sudden thought, idea, or desire, especially one based on impulse rather than reason or necessity
  Synonyms : impulse, craze

In the past decade, online retail sales have grown by more than 20% annually compared with only 2.9% for retail sales overall

Online shopping allows you to **duck** those holiday mall crowds and checkout lines, **evade** the drive to stores, **sidestep** the **cumbersome** parking process, and escape wasting expensive fuel .It is also **accessible** around the clock and you don't have to dress up .Besides, shopping online allows you to compare products and prices between retailers with a couple of clicks of the mouse, the same would require lots time and energy in the store. Besides, many of us feel **chagrined** at the thought of saying no to that **ingratiating** salesperson.

On the other hand, there are often shipping and handling fees associated with online shopping that don't come with in-store purchases. Prices can be greatly influenced by these logistics. Clearance items and end-of-season **merchandise** hardly ever goes up on a stores web site. Department stores receive new merchandise one season ahead of time and are expected to have it ready for display and sale as soon as possible. Merchandise that is current or from a previous season needs to be sold quickly, and the best way department stores can clear it away is by **tendering** a deep discount. Warehouses, on the other hand, have a great amount of space and so the e-shop has the ability to avoid price **slashing.** Hence no clearance sale is ever organized on an online store. In the end goods are **dearer** on a store's web site, and they are less expensive in the physical store.

If you shop online, you don't get the **exhilaration** of walking in the door with purchases on hand. There always seems to be some **impediment** in receiving your online purchases in the promised time. But, in-store shopping allows that instant joy of owning your product immediately.

Online you can't personally examine or try the product you are buying, like you can, in a store. This is important with innumerous types of products. Let's say you are shopping for fine china or silverware, it will be very difficult to purchase exactly what you want because simply pictures will not an satisfy you . Same goes for automobiles, footwear, furniture, linen…, the list is endless. There are many online shops that sell cake but you have no way to really know if the cake is tasty ,and fresh ! With traditional shopping you get to smell and in some cases even taste the cake.

Neither are product demonstrations available, which one often wishes when buying electronics, machinery or automobiles, though online demo videos are being made available of late. However if the product quality is highly assured because of the brand credibility, people buy it online freely.

Items such as Books, CDs, DVDs, are products which can be bought without a touch and feel experience. These are particularly well-suited for online selling because they are mostly of similar size and weight, allowing the merchant to plan for standard shipping boxes and spend less time and cost in handling and shipping. The buyer is passed on the benefit, too. No wonder these have always been the top sellers year on year. Travel Tickets, Holidays, Concert/Theatre/Festival/ Cinema tickets are also best sellers because they involve no physical delivery besides high discounts can be obtained because of an auction mode selling. Computer hardware, software, toys, video games and office supplies sell easily because of high brand loyalty. Beauty and health products also do well for similar reasons. Men's apparel also are quite saleable online because of a certain **disdain** most men have for traditional shopping !

Finding things online is pretty easy. You just open up a search engine like Google and type in what you are looking for. This is probably the biggest advantage of online shopping vs. traditional shopping. With traditional shopping you will need to search from one shop in the mall to the other looking for what you want, sometimes driving all over town amongst the mass of several different stores. There might also be times when you won't find what you are looking for. With online shopping you will instantly know if you can find what you are looking for, or if you can't, potentially saving you hours looking for what you want.

Security is a concern when it comes to online shopping .There are online **predators** seeking to steal identities, cheat merchants, shoppers and the card companies. The e-stores as well as credit card companies are constantly upgrading the security measures but it is safer to buy through trusted e-stores only.

There is a category where a combination of various modes is used. Say buying or renting property, used automobiles and other equipment, personnel hiring- people do the initial short listing online, fix appointments over the phone and finally buy after one to one negotiation !

Even if one stage of traditional shopping is replaced by online **forays**, society will have a lesser mass of polluting steel moving on the roads, benefiting the environment considerably.

Accessible
Contextual Meaning(s) : Adjective; capable of being reached; easy to get along with or talk to; friendly; easily obtained; capable of being read with comprehension
Synonyms : approachable

Chagrined
Contextual Meaning(s) : Adjective; feeling or caused to feel uneasy and self-conscious
Synonyms : abashed, embarrassed

Cumbersome
Contextual Meaning(s) : Adjective; difficult to handle or use especially because of size or weight; not elegant or graceful in expression
Synonyms : awkward, clumsy

Dearer
Contextual Meaning(s) : Noun; costlier
Synonyms : costlier

Disdain
Contextual Meaning(s) : Noun; a communication that indicates lack of respect by patronizing the recipient; lack of respect accompanied by a feeling of intense dislike; verb reject with contempt; look down on with disdain
Synonyms : contempt, scorn

Duck
Contextual Meaning(s) : Noun; avoid or try to avoid fulfilling, answering, or performing (duties, questions, or issues); dip into a liquid
Other Meaning(s) : noun small wild or domesticated web-footed broad-billed swimming bird usually having a depressed body and short legs; a heavy cotton fabric of plain weave; used for clothing and tents; flesh of a duck (domestic or wild); (cricket) a score of nothing by a batsman; verb to move (the head or body) quickly downwards or away; submerge or plunge suddenly;
Synonyms : dodge, sidestep

Evade
Contextual Meaning(s) : Verb; use cunning or deceit to escape or avoid; practice evasion; avoid or try to avoid fulfilling, answering, or performing (duties, questions, or issues); escape, either physically or mentally
Synonyms : hedge, fudge

Exhilaration
Contextual Meaning(s) : Noun; the feeling of lively and cheerful joy
Synonyms : excitement

Forays
Contextual Meaning(s) : Noun; adventures
Synonyms : adventures

Gratification
Contextual Meaning(s) : Noun; the act or an instance of satisfying; state of being gratified; great satisfaction
Synonyms : satisfaction, delight

Impediment
Contextual Meaning(s) : Noun; any structure that makes progress difficult; something immaterial that interferes with or delays action or progress
Synonyms : obstruction, handicap

Ingratiating
Contextual Meaning(s) : Adjective; calculated to please or gain favor; capable of winning favor
Synonyms : insinuating, ingratiatory

✦ ***Mandated***

Contextual Meaning(s) : Noun; made compulsory
Synonyms : required, authorized

✦ ***Merchandise***

Contextual Meaning(s) : Noun; commodities offered for sale;
Other Meaning(s) : verb engage in the trade of
Synonyms : ware, trade

✦ ***Predators***

Contextual Meaning(s) : Noun; entities looking to hunt & devour
Synonyms : marauders

✦ ***Sidestep***

Contextual Meaning(s) : Verb; avoid or try to avoid fulfilling, answering, or performing (duties, questions, or issues)
Other Meaning(s) : noun a step to one side (as in boxing or dancing);
Synonyms : hedge, fudge

✦ ***Slashing***

Contextual Meaning(s) : cutting
Synonyms : Adjective

✦ ***Tendering***

Contextual Meaning(s) : Verb; offering of service
Synonyms : servicing

In 1929, in what has become known as "the great depression" many people suddenly found their finances **deplorable**, there happened a **disenthrallment** with capitalism in parts of Europe and a rise of doctrines of nationalism and racism. Leading this pack were Germany, Japan and Italy, later called the Axis forces, who developed, a highly militaristic and **belligerent** attitude . In 1933 Adolf Hitler rose to power in Germany at the head of his Nazi party.

Hitler began to rearm Germany, and built a **formidable** war machine by 1936, breaking the Treaty of Versailles. With Hitler's anti-**semetic** policies and aggressive re-armament of Germany ,war was **imminent**. On 1st September 1939 Germany invaded Poland, two days later, France and Britain declared war on Germany, beginning World War II.

On September 17, Soviet troops invaded Poland from the east. Under attack from both sides, Poland fell quickly.

The Second World War would prove to be even more **lethal** and **protracted** than the first war. A global conflict in every sense of the word the war would see an **unexampled** number of casualties and would change the world forever.

After taking Poland, in May 1940 Germany invaded Belgium, the Netherlands and Luxembourg. The same day, King George VI asked Churchill to be prime minister of Britain.

Germany was extremely successful in its early expansions and soon also took Denmark and Norway. Within four weeks of their assault Germany took on France and on 14th of June 1940 Paris was occupied. Soon after Hitler would launch an **assault** against Britain, attempting to gain air superiority in order to clear way for an aquatic invasion from France. But Churchill **rallied** the **beleaguered** people of Britain with **unflagging** strength and **vitality**, even when things looked their **bleakest**. In what has become known as the Battle of Britain the RAF successfully **rebuffed** the German attacks and claimed aerial superiority over England, ending German hopes of invasion.

Churchill established a strong relationship with American president Franklin Roosevelt, who did much to help the British war effort despite America's position of neutrality. When Japan attacked Pearl Harbour in Dec. 1941, the United States officially entered the war .

Turning his attention away from Britain, Hitler looked to invade the communist Soviet Union. After a delay in Yugoslavia and Greece after the Italian's defeat Germany assaulted the Soviet Union with the largest army ever known to man. Over three million Germans took part in the invasion, laying **siege** to Leningrad and getting to within 15 miles of Moscow. The Germans would have to stop for the Russian Winter however, and by Spring 1942 an entire division were trapped in the snow at Stalingrad, eventually leading to their **capitulation**. Hitler had seen what should have been a sure victory turn into a defeat. Russian casualties, too were **astronomical**, they lost around 27 million people, about half of the total casualties in the war.

As Germany were getting frozen out of the Soviet Union ,the Americans, allied with the British and the Soviets would continue to push the German forces back.

On 6th June 1944 the Allies launched an attack onto the beaches of Normandy. The German were deceived into thinking that the Allies would attack Calais and were unprepared for an invasion on the beaches. At a great cost of human life the beach invasion was successful and the Allies were able to push into France. By 1945 the German army was pushed back by the Soviets from the East and the Americans and British from the West. Once the Soviets reached Berlin, Hitler committed suicide and seven days later the Germans surrendered, ending the war in Europe. The USA would end the war with the **infamous** use of nuclear weapons against Japan in Hiroshima and Nagasaki.

After the war the United States and the Soviet Union emerged as the two dominant super-powers, with much of Europe in **ruin** after the bombings in the war. Many top-ranking German officers were convicted of war crimes, at the famous Nuremberg trials. The most **heinous** crimes were committed at Auschwitz concentration camp in Poland, where Germans **immured** millions of Jews and other minorities, starving and eventually murdering them in one of the worst events in human history.

Assault

Contextual Meaning(s) : Noun; a threatened or attempted physical attack by someone who appears to be able to cause bodily harm if not stopped; close fighting during the culmination of a military attack;

Other Meaning(s) : thoroughbred that won the triple crown in 1946; the crime of forcing a woman to submit to sexual intercourse against her will; verb attack in speech or writing; attack someone physically or emotionally; force (someone) to have sex against their will

Synonyms : violation, outrage

Astronomical

Contextual Meaning(s) : adjective; immeasurably numerous, high, or great; e.g. reached astronomical proportions

Other Meaning(s) : adjective; relating to astronomy

Synonyms : sky-high

Beleaguered

Contextual Meaning(s) : Adjective; troubled, worried

Other Meaning(s) : encircled by the enemy army

Synonyms : surrounded, troubled

Belligerent

Contextual Meaning(s) : Adjective; engaged in war; characteristic of an enemy or one eager to fight;

Other Meaning(s) : noun someone who fights (or is fighting)

Synonyms : militant, aggressive

Bleak

Contextual Meaning(s) : Adjective; unpleasantly cold and damp; offering little or no hope; providing no shelter or sustenance

Synonyms : gloomy, dour

Capitulation

Contextual Meaning(s) : Noun; the act of surrendering (under agreed conditions);

Other Meaning(s) : a summary that enumerates the main parts of a topic

Synonyms : fall, surrender

Deplorable

Contextual Meaning(s) : Adjective; bad; unfortunate; of very poor quality or condition; bringing or deserving severe rebuke or censure

Synonyms : lamentable, woeful

Disenthrallment

Contextual Meaning(s) : Noun; the state of losing interest or attraction

Synonyms : disenchantment

Disillusionment

Contextual Meaning(s) : Adjective; a feeling of disappointment

Synonyms : disillusion

Formidable

Contextual Meaning(s) : Adjective; inspiring fear; extremely impressive in strength or excellence

Synonyms : redoubtable, unnerving

Heinous

Contextual Meaning(s) : Adjective; shockingly brutal or cruel

Synonyms : atrocious, flagitious

Imminent

Contextual Meaning(s) : Adjective about to happen.

Synonyms : forthcoming, close

Immured

Contextual Meaning(s) : Adjective; imprisoned, jailed

Synonyms : incarcerated, jailed

Impendent

Contextual Meaning(s) : Adjective; close by in time; about to occur

Synonyms : imminent, impending

- *Infamous*

  Contextual Meaning(s) : Adjective; well known for some bad quality or deed.
  Synonyms : notorious, disreputable

- *Lethal*

  Contextual Meaning(s) : Adjective; of an instrument of certain death
  Synonyms : baleful

- *Protracted*

  Contextual Meaning(s) : Adjective; relatively long in duration; tediously prolonged
  Synonyms : lengthy, prolonged

- *Rallied*

  Contextual Meaning(s) : Verb; bought together to as team to fight for a cause.
  Synonyms : mobilized, gathered

- *Rebuffed*

  Contextual Meaning(s) : Verb; forced to recede.
  Synonyms : snubbed, rejected

- *Ruin*

  Contextual Meaning(s) : Noun; an irrecoverable state of devastation and destruction; destruction achieved by causing something to be wrecked or ruined; failure that results in a loss of position or reputation; *Other Meaning(s)* : a ruined building; an event that results in destruction the process of becoming dilapidated; verb fall into ruin; reduce to ruins; destroy or cause to fail; deprive of virginity; destroy completely; damage irreparably; reduce to bankruptcy
  Synonyms : dilapidation, ramshackle

- *Semitic*

  Contextual Meaning(s) : Adjective; of jewish origin
  Synonyms : jewish

- *Siege*

  Contextual Meaning(s) : Noun; the action of an armed force that surrounds a fortified place and isolates it while continuing to attack
  Synonyms : military-blockade, occupation

- *Unexampled*

  Contextual Meaning(s) : Adjective; having no previous example or precedent or parallel
  Synonyms : unprecedented

- *Unflagging*

  Contextual Meaning(s) : Adjective; unceasing; showing sustained enthusiastic action with unflagging vitality
  Synonyms : indefatigable, tireless

- *Unprecedented*

  Contextual Meaning(s) : Adjective; having no precedent; novel
  Synonyms : unexampled, historic

- *Vitality*

  Contextual Meaning(s) : Noun; an energetic style; the property of being able to survive and grow; *Other Meaning(s)* : (biology) a hypothetical force (not physical or chemical) once thought by Henri Bergson to cause the evolution and development of organisms; a healthy capacity for vigorous activity
  Synonyms : verve, vim

THE REALITY CIRCUS

Every time **wooing** lovers share an **intimate** whisper on "The Bachelor," viewers know there's a crew of 20 sound and light technicians, production assistants and script consultants standing by. It's no secret that the **veracity** of reality TV is **dubious**.

The **precursor** to reality shows can be traced back to the forties with shows like Allen Funt's Candid Camera that captured **blunt** reactions of people to humorous tricks and pranks. TV shows without **stringent** story-lines, soon became increasingly popular with the audience. Ordinary people captured in real-life situations like MTV Bakra seemed to amuse the audience, which was hitherto **pelted** with ultra-dramatic soaps and movies.

Some of these reality shows are talent hunts, game shows, celebrity shows, documentary-style shows, makeover shows, or some of them are just plain **voyeurism personified**. However different their concepts might be, all the reality shows, **intrinsically** run on the same path. They put ordinary people or celebrities in real-life situations and allow peeping toms to enjoy the thrill of watching them!

Every time players strategize on "The Amazing Race," a story editor is there with a clipboard, taking notes. Producers increasingly say that their shows are "gently scripted." That's a phrase that might have **mortified** viewers a few years ago but which is now **quotidian**. How **gullible** viewers become when consuming reality TV?

"Lightly scripted" has become a new **narrative** form, like jazz music is "lightly scripted" and prone to **improvisation**.

Nobody minds an **incendiary**, **inflated** version of the facts if it adds to entertainment pleasure, and viewers, too, have learned how to watch reality TV with a trained suspension of disbelief. Just like, say, live theater. We're all for melodrama that's made to appear **instinctive.**

The producers explain that viewers simply don't care if scenes are manipulated or manufactured. "There's a reason any entertainment programming is so much higher-rated than news programming," they say. Viewers can be **incorrigible escapists**.

After a decade of "Big Boss," we're fluent in the **nuances**, strengths and shortcomings of reality shows. Some pop-culture critics go so far as to say they have evolved into a new art form by itself.

Such **chicanery** is considered minor and wholly different from leaking answers to game show contenders who compete for money.

Public expects a TV game show to be less **manipulated** than celebrity reality show because the **lure** of big money that is promised to any ordinary contestant, they could even be your next door neighbors . In "Kaun Banega Crorepati", the Indian version of *"Who wants to be a Millionaire?"*, contestants are known to have been preparing *industriously for years* .

Often, Reality television allows the audience to be a part of the show. Take for example *The American Idol*, or the Zee TV's singing contest SAREGAMA; these shows allow the audience to choose the winner through a voting system. Although the **integrity** of these voting systems is debated about forever, the interactivity factor definitely fetches the show a lot of fan following.

Renowned producer Mark Burnett ("Survivor," "The Apprentice" and "Are You Smarter than a Fifth Grader?") asked Fox to **abort** the game show "Our Little Genius". This was to be a show about **precocious** kids. The withdrawl followed allegations by one of the little geniuses' parents that crews leaked answers to questions about music history and theory before shooting.

"Undercover Boss," in which a powerful CEO **masquerades** as a low-level employee to observe how his business works, is typical of the **guile**, staged and manipulated to be in the reality genre.

Take the case of the hated Big Boss contender Dolly Bindra. What better way to help viewers feel good about their own behavior ? According to a magazine article, she may have been the victim of reality TV editors. Clashes and ugly **feuds** between the reality stars may be constructed and participants can be projected as incarnations of evil !

However, fans watch in a shared state of denial, as if they don't care if its all **pretentious**, as long as it entertains.

Participants of these shows are given **caveats** beforehand and they have to sign extensive and detailed legal **waivers** that protect the network from any liability if someone gets hurt on the show physically or otherwise.

Viewers need to remind themselves: It's a set up, it's prearranged, it's almost all calculated in the service of drawing viewers and increasing ratings.

Or perhaps they already know.

🖎 **Abort**

Contextual Meaning(s) : Noun; terminate before completion
Synonyms : terminate

🖎 **Blunt**

Contextual Meaning(s) : Verb; make less sharp; make less intense; make less lively, intense, or vigorous; impair in vigor, force, activity, or sensation; make dull or blunt; make numb or insensitive
Other Meaning(s) : Adjective; devoid of any qualifications or disguise or adornment; characterized by directness in manner or speech; without subtlety or evasion; used of a knife or other blade; not sharp; having a broad or rounded end
Synonyms : deaden

🖎 **Caveats**

Contextual Meaning(s) : Noun; A statement that limits or restricts some claim
Synonyms : qualification, caution

🖎 **Chicanery**

Contextual Meaning(s) : Noun; the use of tricks to deceive someone (usually to extract money from them)
Synonyms : trickery, shenanigan

🖎 **Dubious**

Contextual Meaning(s) : Adjective; not convinced; fraught with uncertainty or doubt; open to doubt or suspicion
Synonyms : doubtful

🖎 **Escapists**

Contextual Meaning(s) : noun; a daydreamer, or fantasist who tries to avoid reality
Other Meaning(s) : adjective; providing a means of forgetting about everyday or unpleasant realities for a while
Synonyms : daydreamer, fantasizer

🖎 **Feuds**

Contextual Meaning(s) : Noun; rivalries or quarrels or hostilities between people.
Synonyms : altercations

🖎 **Gullible**

Contextual Meaning(s) : Adjective; easily tricked because of being too trusting; naive and easily deceived or tricked
Synonyms : fleeceable, green

🖎 **Guile**

Contextual Meaning(s) : noun; a cunning, deceitful, or treacherous quality
Synonyms : slyness, astuteness

🖎 **Improvisation**

Contextual Meaning(s) : Noun; an unplanned expedient; a creation spoken or written or composed extemporaneously (without prior preparation); a performance given extempore without planning or preparation
Synonyms : extemporization

🖎 **Incendiary**

Contextual Meaning(s) : Adjective; arousing to action or rebellion;
Synonyms : inflammatory, instigative

🖎 **Incorrigible**

Contextual Meaning(s) : Adjective; impervious to correction by punishment
Synonyms : unreformable

🖎 **Industriously**

Contextual Meaning(s) : Adverb; accomplished with hard work
Synonyms : energetically

🖎 **Inflated**

Contextual Meaning(s) : Adjective; enlarged beyond truth or reasonableness; increased especially to abnormal levels; pretentious (especially with regard to language or ideals)
Synonyms : exaggerated, hyperbolic,

Integrity

Contextual Meaning(s) : Noun; moral soundness; an undivided or unbroken completeness or totality with nothing wanting
Synonyms : unity, wholeness

Intimate

Contextual Meaning(s) : Adjective; marked by close acquaintance, association, or familiarity; a romantics relationship; having mutual interests or affections; of established friendship; innermost or essential;
Other Meaning(s) : thoroughly acquainted through study or experience; having or fostering a warm or friendly and informal atmosphere; noun someone to whom private matters are confided; verb give to understand; imply as a possibility
Synonyms : cozy, inner

Instinctive

Contextual Meaning(s) : Adjective; relating to or prompted by instinct or done without conscious thought.
Synonyms : natural, innate

Intrinsically

Contextual Meaning(s) : Adverb; with respect to something basic nature
Synonyms : basically

Lure

Contextual Meaning(s) : Noun; *qualities that attract by seeming to promise some kind of reward; anything that serves as an enticement;*
Other Meaning(s) : verb provoke someone to do something through (often false or exaggerated) promises or persuasion
Synonyms : enticement

Manipulated

Contextual Meaning(s) : Verb, Influence or control shrewdly or deviously
Synonyms : falsify, misrepresent

Masquerades

Contextual Meaning(s) : Adjective; disguises one self
Synonyms : disguises

Mortified

Contextual Meaning(s) : Adjective; made to feel uncomfortable because of shame or wounded pride;
Other Meaning(s) : Adjective; suffering from tissue death
Synonyms : embarrassed, humiliated,

Narrative

Contextual Meaning(s) : Adjective; consisting of or characterized by the telling of a story;
Other Meaning(s) : noun a message that tells the particulars of an act or occurrence or course of events; presented in writing or drama or cinema or as a radio or television program
Synonyms : story, tale

Nuances

Contextual Meaning(s) : Noun; difference in shades, subtlety distinctions.
Synonyms : shades, fineries

Pelted

Contextual Meaning(s) : Adjective; hurled, thrown or bombarded with intention to harm
Synonyms : bombarded, hit

Precocious

Contextual Meaning(s) : Adjective; appearing or developing early; characterized by or characteristic of exceptionally early development or maturity (especially in mental aptitude)
Synonyms : prodigious

Precursor

Contextual Meaning(s) : Noun; an indication of the approach of something or someone
Other Meaning(s) : noun a person who goes before or announces the coming of another; a substance from which another substance is formed (especially by a metabolic reaction);
Synonyms : forerunner, harbinger, herald

❧ ***Pretentious***

Contextual Meaning(s) : Adjective; making claim to or creating an appearance of (often undeserved) importance or distinction; intended to attract notice and impress others; of a display that is tawdry or vulgar
Synonyms : ostentatious, kitsch

❧ ***Personified***

Contextual Meaning(s) : verb; to be an embodiment or perfect example of something
Synonyms : incarnate, embodied

❧ ***Quotidian***

Contextual Meaning(s) : Adjective; found in the ordinary course of events
Synonyms : routine, unremarkable

❧ ***Stringent***

Contextual Meaning(s) : Adjective; demanding strict attention to rules and procedures
Synonyms : rigorous, tight

❧ ***Veracity***

Contextual Meaning(s) : Noun; unwillingness to tell lies
Synonyms : truthfulness

❧ ***Voyeurism***

Contextual Meaning(s) : Noun; a perversion in which a person receives gratification from witnessing others' private behavior
Synonyms : scopophilia

❧ ***Waivers***

Contextual Meaning(s) : Noun; a written legal statement of forgoing or offering a concession.
Synonyms : concessions

❧ ***Wooing***

Contextual Meaning(s) : Adjective; courting, seeking the affections of the opposite sex.
Other Meaning(s) : noun a man's courting of a woman; seeking the affections of a woman (usually with the hope of marriage)
Synonyms : courting

IS THE KEYBOARD MIGHTIER THAN THE PEN?

In a world that **reveres** technology and has a **yearning** to own the latest and fastest gadget, students are increasingly using these gadgets to take their class notes as well as in their all other communication. And the practice is **dispersive**.

However, life science believes there's a close connection between body and mind, and this body-mind link activates learning. Research shows a **brawny** relationship between brain activity and fine motor skills. An *Indiana University study* recently revealed that the brain **flurry** in children who are taught to form letters by hand is significantly more adult-like than that of children who do not receive this instruction. The brains of the children who were taught handwriting actually showed "a huge **spike**" in activity in the **neural** network associated with reading.

This kind of brain stimulation does not occur during keyboarding. Research from the *University of Washington* found it's because keyboarding involves selecting a whole letter with one stroke. The difference lies in the sequenced movements.

Neurologist Frank Wilson has **meticulously** explored this subject and strongly favors working with the hands in order to develop higher thinking skills. Undoubtedly learning writing by hand should be mandatory for the first time learners, infact till grade 5 use of keyboards must be **abjured**.

Lets now come to bigger kids. Many students type faster than they write. They would obviously be the first ones to **relinquish** pen and paper, the moment the system allows it. Some students can't read their own handwriting, its so **shoddy**; typing **circumvents** their problem.

Also, it spell checks, looks **dandy** and can present a well formatted report quickly.

On the other end of the spectrum, there are many students who learn to take notes in their own personal form of shorthand. Some scribble a couple of words, and draw some lines to connect things which would be **nebulous** to anybody but themselves. They are likely to advocate hand writing all their lives. Then there would be the artistic types who have an **insatiable** desire for hand writing and won't let gadgets **arrogate** their right to write!

But most students would prefer a **hybrid** of the traditional and the digital .Like using their iPad as a notebook with a stylus. Or a touchscreen tablet where notes can be handwritten directly. Some of these devices can translate the pen markings into digital typewritten fonts just with a click. Then there are programs that allow one to view an e-text book and highlight, underline, or write on those documents little notes as one sees fit.

These documents can be swapped with classmates, updated in a revision class, used to write a thesis with minimum duplication, and sent over the net anywhere on the planet.

However, an outcome of a recent Facebook survey was that most students would still like taking their notes by pen and paper. So why exactly are handwritten notes favored over using a laptop?

First and foremost, poll respondents said that they feel more engaged in class material when they're taking notes by hand. When typing notes, it can be easy to get into a groove where your fingers do the typing without even realizing what's being typed. However, taking notes by hand might not feel so robotic and you might remain more focused on the task at hand. Hand written notes act a good source for quick learning and revision.

Another benefit mentioned by students is that handwritten notes present far fewer distractions than using a laptop. With your laptop open, it could **incite** you to check e-mail, get on Facebook or play a few rounds of solitaire during class. Most likely you wouldn't be able to find many distractions in your notebook.

A notebook or binder with all your handwritten notes could also make it easier to refer back to information from a previous lecture. For instance, if your teacher starts talking about a concept from last week's class, you can easily flip back to your notes to refresh your memory or write down **elucidatory** remarks. It might be a bit more **convoluted** to try to find the right file on your computer.

Handwritten notes could even improve your peace of mind. Imagine the **debacle** you'd face if in the middle of class your note taking program shut down without saving what you had been typing. It could prove to be a very **odious** situation. As long as you have paper and a couple pens or pencils, this shouldn't be a concern.

Some professors won't allow students to use their laptops at all during class. Before showing up to class without any paper or writing **implements**, be sure to verify that you are permitted to take notes on your laptop.

The school, **harrowed** by ecological concerns, is making an effort to become as paperless as possible. In some high-schools every kid's laptop is **endowed** to them from the school; here, there is a distinct down fall in the amount of writing. On some days, kids wont even take their binders out or open the backpack, just use their laptops for everything. All handouts and courseware is available on line for them to download.

Pro-digitisation folks have presented **outlandish** problems due to use of pens and pencils : **distracting** noise, harmful **makeshift** weapons and **incredible** mess. In addition, Pens and pencils can be used as a bullying trick amongst kids by use of **sinister** notes that pass from hand to hand across the rows of desks. Kids have free reign to write and **disseminate** messages that use **unsavory** language and **vile** speech. Pencils can be used to play games like Hangman, Tic-Tac-Toe, word searches, crosswords, and now the latest craze: Sudoku.

Both forms of communication, written as well as digital, are critical to the future of our society. We all have our preferences. If you want to tap into the right side of your brain for creative and conceptual ideas, you need to doodle and draw with your hand. Pencil and paper are always accessible anywhere - bedroom, bus-ride or a basketball match.

Handwriting is a must when one is doing 1 on 1 stuff ,like conducting a job interview, or learning from some tutor.

You never know when you'll need to pick up that pencil to write an important message down. You never know that when you write "I miss you" in your own handwriting, you'll actually pass on an important message that may change your life, and someone else's! So I urge you to continue writing, at least till mankind stops making paper and pencil !

🖎 **Abjured**
Contextual Meaning(s) : Verb; to formally reject a former belief.
Synonyms : retract

🖎 **Arrogates**
Contextual Meaning(s) : Verb; to take over something using force without the authority to do so
Synonyms : usurps

🖎 **Brawny**
Contextual Meaning(s) : Adjective; possessing physical strength and weight; rugged and powerful
Synonyms : powerful, sinewy

🖎 **Circumvents**
Contextual Meaning(s) : Verb; to avoid doing something
Synonyms : eludes, skirts

🖎 **Convoluted**
Contextual Meaning(s) : Adjective; rolled or coiled together; highly complex or intricate
Synonyms : Byzantine, tortuous

🖎 **Dandy**
Contextual Meaning(s) : Adjective; very good;
Other Meaning(s) : noun a man who is much concerned with his dress and appearance; a sailing vessel with two masts; a small mizzen is aft of the rudder post
Synonyms : gallant, smashing

🖎 **Debacle**
Contextual Meaning(s) : Noun; a sudden and violent collapse; a sound defeat
Other Meaning(s) : flooding caused by a tumultuous breakup of ice in a river during the spring or summer;
Synonyms : fiasco

🖎 **Dispersive**
Contextual Meaning(s) : Adjective; spreading by diffusion
Synonyms : diffusing, scattering, spreading

🖎 **Disseminate**
Contextual Meaning(s) : Verb; cause to become widely known
Synonyms : circulate, broadcast

🖎 **Distracting**
Contextual Meaning(s) : Verb; causing to stray from the desired direction.
Synonyms : perturbing

🖎 **Elucidatory**
Contextual Meaning(s) : Adjective; making something understandable.
Synonyms : enlightening

🖎 **Endowed**
Contextual Meaning(s) : Adjective; provided or supplied or equipped with (especially as by inheritance or nature)
Other Meaning(s) : Adjective; having received a financial donation form some foundation or trust.
Synonyms : gifted

🖎 **Flurry**
Contextual Meaning(s) : Noun; a rapid active commotion;
Other Meaning(s) : verb move in an agitated or confused manner; cause to feel embarrassment, a light brief snowfall and gust of wind (or something resembling that);
Synonyms : bustle, hustle

🖎 **Harrowed**
Contextual Meaning(s) : Verb; caused discomfort & pain
Synonyms : distressed

☙ *Hybrid*

Contextual Meaning(s) : Noun; composite of mixed origin;

Other Meaning(s) : adjective; produced by crossbreeding; an organism that is the offspring of genetically dissimilar parents or stock; especially offspring produced by breeding plants or animals of different varieties or breeds or species; a word that is composed of parts from different languages (e.g., `monolingual' has a Greek prefix and a Latin root)

Synonyms : crossed

☙ *Implements*

Contextual Meaning(s) : Noun; tools used for any activity

Synonyms : tools

☙ *Incite*

Contextual Meaning(s) : Verb; provoke or stir up; urge on; cause to act; give an incentive for action

Synonyms : instigate

☙ *Incredible*

Contextual Meaning(s) : Adverb; not easy to believe

Synonyms : implausible, unbelievable

☙ *Indispensable*

Contextual Meaning(s) : Adjective; unavoidable; not to be dispensed with; essential; absolutely necessary; vitally necessary

Synonyms : essential

☙ *Insatiable*

Contextual Meaning(s) : Adjective; impossible to satisfy

Synonyms : unquenchable

☙ *Makeshift*

Contextual Meaning(s) : Adjective; done or made using whatever is available;

Other Meaning(s) : noun something contrived to meet an urgent need or emergency

Synonyms : stopgap, improvised

☙ *Mess*

Contextual Meaning(s) : Adjective; dirty and disorderly

Synonyms : disorderliness

☙ *Meticulously*

Contextual Meaning(s) : Adverb; in a neat & proper manner

Synonyms : punctiliously

☙ *Nebulous*

Contextual Meaning(s) : Adjective; lacking definition or definite content; lacking definite form or limits;

Other Meaning(s) : of or relating to or resembling a nebula

Synonyms : vague

☙ *Neural*

Contextual Meaning(s) : Adjective; of or relating to the nervous system

Other Meaning(s) : adjective; of or relating to neurons

Synonyms : nervous

☙ *Odious*

Contextual Meaning(s) : Adjective; unequivocally detestable

Synonyms : detestable, execrable

☙ *Outlandish*

Contextual Meaning(s) : Adjective; conspicuously or grossly unconventional or unusual

Synonyms : bizarre, freakish

☙ *Relinquish*

Contextual Meaning(s) : Verb; turn away from; give up; part with a possession or right; do without or cease to hold or adhere to

Other Meaning(s) : verb relinquish to the power of another; yield to the control of another; release, as from one's grip;

Synonyms : surrender, forgo

✎ **Reveres**

Contextual Meaning(s) : Verb; worships or respects

Synonyms : worships

✎ **Shoddy**

Contextual Meaning(s) : Adjective; of inferior workmanship and material;

Other Meaning(s) : Adjective; designed to deceive or mislead either deliberately or inadvertently; cheap and shoddy; noun reclaimed wool fiber

Synonyms : tawdry

✎ **Sinister**

Contextual Meaning(s) : Adjective; stemming from evil characteristics or forces; wicked or dishonorable

Other Meaning(s) : adjective; on or starting from the wearer's left; threatening or foreshadowing evil or tragic developments;

Synonyms : malicious, dark

✎ **Spike**

Contextual Meaning(s) : Verb; manifest a sharp increase;

Other Meaning(s) : noun sports equipment consisting of a sharp point on the sole of a shoe worn by athletes; a long metal nail; any holding device consisting of a sharp-pointed object; a long sharp-pointed implement (wood or metal); a sharp-pointed projection along the top of a fence or wall; a transient variation in voltage or current; a sharp rise followed by a sharp decline; (botany) an indeterminate inflorescence bearing sessile flowers on an unbranched axis; fruiting spike of a cereal plant especially corn;

Synonyms : surge

✎ **Unsavory**

Contextual Meaning(s) : Adjective; adj. morally offensive; not pleasing in odor or taste

Synonyms : offensive, distasteful

✎ **Upshot**

Contextual Meaning(s) : Noun a phenomenon that follows and is caused by some previous phenomenon

Synonyms : consequence

✎ **Vile**

Contextual Meaning(s) : Adjective; morally reprehensible;

Synonyms : despicable

✎ **Yearning**

Contextual Meaning(s) : Noun prolonged unfulfilled desire or need

Synonyms : longing

SMARTNESS IS A MANY SPLENDORED THING

"Everybody is a genius. But if you judge a fish by its ability to climb a tree, it will live its whole life believing that it is stupid." ~Albert Einstein

I have an intelligence quotient (IQ) of 125, a fact that **alludes** to me being almost a genius. However, I have a confession; I am in a big **quandary** when trying to reach a new location, or even when returning to my base from there. And I know people with an IQ below average who can perform the same task effortlessly. So am I intelligent or dumb ?

Harvard psychologist Howard Gardner's theory of multiple intelligences discerns intelligence down into at least eight different components: logical, linguistic, **spatial**, musical, **kinesthetic**, **naturalist**, intra personal and inter-personal intelligences.

This theory of Multiple Intelligences (MI) is in direct confrontation with the "classical view of intelligence." The latter tests people on reasoning, arithmetical and linguistic logic and builds a score commonly called IQ.

This score has been the generally accepted measure of any person's intelligence for decades. But now scientists believe that people are smart in more areas than math or English, and that these types of intelligences should be recognized and **accorded** their due place.

Originally intended for the **realm** of psychologists ,the multiple intelligence theory, MI has become widespread and very successful among educators at all levels.

These types of intelligence, when recognized in school, boost children's self-esteem by simply calling attention to their talents. Teachers can use this theory in planning lessons by keeping all kinds of intelligences in mind.

Linguistic Intelligence is to be found in ample among Authors, Poets, Writers, Orators, Journalists and TV Anchors. These people have a **profound** understanding of words and a sensitivity to the literal and **figurative** meanings of words. They have **facile** communication style, and an inborn aptitude for grammar.

Logical-Mathematical Intelligence is an ability to understand numbers and logical concepts well, an ability to perceive numerical and logical patterns, and possession of highly developed reasoning and analytical skills.

Musical-Rhythmic Intelligence is defined by an ability to **descry**, recall and express musical forms. Musically intelligent people also have a high sensitivity to rhythm, pitch, meter, **timbre**, or melody. Beethoven, Stevie Wonder and Conductor Arturo Toscanini are **illustrious** examples of musically intelligent people.

Spatially intelligent people have a high ability to understand visual and spatial objects, sensitivity to the relationship between line, color, shape, space, and form. They make great Graphic artists, architects, map-makers . They are also good at repairing machines , understanding geometry, and completing jigsaw puzzles.

Bodily-Kinesthetic intelligence is defined by highly developed coordination, balance, **dexterity**, strength, **agility**, and flexibility of the body. Pilots, Racing drivers, Dancers, football players, and gymnasts **epitomize** bodily-kinesthetic intelligence.

Interpersonal Intelligence is defined by an ability to distinguish and make distinctions in the moods, characteristics, intentions, **temperaments**, motivations, and feelings of other people. Those who have highly developed interpersonal intelligence are successful leaders, bosses, entrepreneurs, and military officers.

People that have **verdant** intra personal intelligence know themselves well. This means a precise knowledge of one's dreams, goals, strengths, limitations, moods, anxieties, desires, and motivations. They aren't forced into **molds**, and they make decisions based on what is right for themselves. They possess a strong sense of identity and purpose. This **facet** of intelligence is what is also labeled as Emotional intelligence by author Daniel Goleman. Several other researchers have also **delved** much further into "emotional intelligence", and believe it plays a major role in a person's overall mental makeup and peace of mind.

However all types of intelligences are somewhat correlated: people who score highly on one test tend to score well on all of them; a **consummate** artist will tend to be an intelligent person. Still its important to understand what one's core competence is; in which of these eight intelligence facets is one most gifted? People who develop their career in a direction which gives them natural advantage over others are **slated** to be successful in work.

Were I to try and be a town planner it would have been a disaster. I am spatially challenged and am **feckless** at reaching a new location without asking for directions a dozen times! Thankfully I realized I have a flair for linguistics and became a **wordsmith** instead!

🔖 **Alludes**

Contextual Meaning(s) : Verb; hint at or indicate
Synonyms : touches

🔖 **Agility**

Contextual Meaning(s) : Noun; the gracefulness of a person or animal that is quick and nimble
Synonyms : lightness, lissomeness, nimbleness

🔖 **Accorded**

Contextual Meaning(s) : Verb; give the right or opportunity or position
Synonyms : granted

🔖 **Consummate**

Contextual Meaning(s) : Adjective; having or revealing supreme mastery or skill; without qualification; used informally as (often pejorative) intensifiers; perfect and complete in every respect; having all necessary qualities; verb make perfect; bring to perfection;
Synonyms : masterful, virtuoso

🔖 **Delved**

Contextual Meaning(s) : Verb; dug into, unearthed
Synonyms : dug

🔖 **Descry**

Contextual Meaning(s) : Noun; verb catch sight of
Synonyms : spot, espy, spy

🔖 **Dexterity**

Contextual Meaning(s) : Noun; adroitness in using the hands or skilled in
Synonyms : sleight

🔖 **Discerps**

Contextual Meaning(s) : Verb; divide into pieces
Synonyms : severs

🔖 **Epitomize**

Contextual Meaning(s) : Verb; embody the essential characteristics of or be a typical example of
Synonyms : typify

🔖 **Facet**

Contextual Meaning(s) : Noun; a distinct feature or element in a problem
Other Meaning(s) : a smooth surface (as of a bone or cut gemstone)
Synonyms : aspect

🔖 **Facile**

Contextual Meaning(s) : Adjective; expressing one self readily, clearly, effectively
Other Meaning(s) : performing adroitly and without effort; arrived at without due care or effort; lacking depth;
Synonyms : eloquent, fluent

🔖 **Feckless**

Contextual Meaning(s) : Adjective; generally incompetent and ineffectual; not fit to assume responsibility
Synonyms : inept

🔖 **Figurative**

Contextual Meaning(s) : Adjective; (used of the Meaning(s) of words or text) not literal; using figures of speech;
Other Meaning(s) : consisting of or forming human or animal figures
Synonyms : non-literal, figural

🔖 **Facets**

Contextual Meaning(s) : noun; a part or possible aspect of something, e.g. an important facet of our work
Other Meaning(s) : verb; to cut facets in something, especially a gemstone
Synonyms : aspect, phase

🔖 **Illustrious**

Contextual Meaning(s) : Adjective; having or conferring glory; widely known and esteemed; having or worthy of pride
Synonyms : famed, glorious, redoubtable

🔖 **Kinesthetic**

Contextual Meaning(s) : adjective; the sense that detects bodily position, weight, or movement of the muscles, tendons, and joints
Synonyms : weight

* **Mold (UK mould)**
Contextual Meaning(s) : noun; to work into a required shape or form, to influence in determining or forming
Synonyms : shape

* **Naturalist**
Contextual Meaning(s) : noun; a student or an expert in natural history, especially botany or zoology. The term is particularly used to describe a field biologist
Synonyms : environmentalist, natural scientist

* **Profound**
Contextual Meaning(s) : Adjective; of the greatest intensity; complete; showing intellectual penetration or emotional depths; from the depths of your being; (of sleep) deep and complete; far-reaching and thoroughgoing in effect especially on the nature of something
Other Meaning(s) : situated at or extending to great depth; too deep to have been sounded or plumbed; coming from deep within one
Synonyms : deep

* **Quandry**
Contextual Meaning(s) : Noun; state of uncertainty or perplexity especially as requiring a choice between equally unfavorable options; a situation from which extrication is difficult especially an unpleasant or trying one
Synonyms : dilemma, predicament

* **Realm**
Contextual Meaning(s) : Noun; a knowledge domain that you are interested in or are communicating about; the domain ruled by a king or queen; a domain in which something is dominant
Synonyms : region

* **Realm**
Contextual Meaning(s) : Verb; designate or schedule

Other Meaning(s) : Noun; (formerly) a writing tablet made of slate; a list of candidates nominated by a political party to run for election to public offices; a fine-grained metamorphic rock that can be split into thin layers; thin layers of rock used for roofing; cover with slate; enter on a list or slate for an election
Synonyms : planned

* **Slated**
Contextual Meaning(s) : Adjective; being in accordance with the prescribed or logical course of events.
Synonyms : anticipated, due

* **Spatial**
Contextual Meaning(s) : adjective; relating to, occupying, or happening in space
Synonyms : relating to space

* **Timbre**
Contextual Meaning(s) : noun; the quality or colour of tone of an instrument or voice, the quality of a speech sound that comes from its tone rather than its pitch or volume
Synonyms : character, quality

* **Temperament**
Contextual Meaning(s) : noun; the combination of mental, physical and emotional traits of a person; natural predisposition
Synonyms : unusual personal attitude

* **Verdant**
Contextual Meaning(s) : Adjective; characterized by abundance or fullness
Synonyms : luxuriant

* **Wordsmith**
Contextual Meaning(s) : Noun; a fluent and prolific writer
Synonyms : author

THE BATTLE OF BRANDS

The term "just google it" has become part of our daily **vernacular**; this is the **epitome** of a brand google's recognition. This year, however, Apple, the Cupertino based company that reinvented the personal computer, transformed the music business with ipod and itunes and created the world's most popular tablet ipad . This finally ended Google's four-year rule as world's top brand-as per most **authentic** brand survcys.

Louis Vuitton was named the world's most valuable luxury brand for the sixth consecutive year, and online retailer Amazon **vanquished** Walmart in the retail category. Thus online buying beat store purchases for the first time in marketing **chronicles**.

The fastest growing brand in the world are led by Facebook and Baidu ("China's google"); these are the brands projected to define the next generation brands. Bank of china, Amazon, AT & T, Marlboro and Docomo are next in line. Some historically famed brands have always retained their exclusivity viz Harley-Davidson, Georgio Armani and Mercedez.

The rise of technology and telecommunications is quite amazing. We started with two or three tech brands in the top ten in 2006. Now they're four out of the top five. It imports how **pivotal** telecom infrastructure has become to people's lives. Millions of people around the world have **leapfrogged** straight to the mobile web because they couldn't afford a computer. If it's mobile banking in Africa, it's farmers checking on the price of crops in local markets; the technological revolution is **ubiquitous.** No wonder tech brands are at the **zenith** of the countdown !

So how is brand value estimated ? A high proportion of a company's earnings is due to **intangibles**. One of the biggest **unpalatable** factors is the brand value. For the top 100 companies, about 30 percent of their total value is **confined** in this **enigma** called brand.

To identify people who are brand loyal, we weed out those who are driven by price and location, so that we're focusing on the proportion of people buying the brand above and beyond convenience. The revenues from these folks gives us Brand Contribution. We use that to determine what portion of a company's total earnings are **fostered** by their brand value. The more this portion, the more is the brand value.

Finally, we want to know if the brand value will prevail in times ahead. If brand has huge potential in BRICs (short hand for Brazil, Russia, India, and China), the **vanguard** of emerging markets, its **poised** for growth during the next two decades.

For some companies, branding is everything. Coca Cola has a **colossal** brand distribution around the world. But without a brand, it's just this brown fizzy liquid. Coca Cola is at one end of the spectrum where brand is everything, and GE is at the other end, where products are sold based on technological specifications and bids. Brand contributes about 20% to GE's total earnings, whereas Coca Cola is nearer to 80%.

A big brand also reduces business risk, since it's more likely to ride out a negative PR story or a **recession**. Last year Toyota fell because of recalls due to manufacturing flaws. This year it recovered faster than expected because it has very strong brand loyalty.

One of the surprises lately has been Baidu, the Chinese search engine, which had the highest possible score in Brand Contribution and had the world's fastest growing brand value after Facebook.

In today's world, brands are everywhere, a familiar part of daily life for most people. But a few brands, such as Coca-Cola, Nike, and McDonald's, have **delineated** themselves . These brands have come to represent something more than a product or service. They are rooted in our culture and our consciousness. They are icons.

Iconic brands inspire an **enduring** form of affection that any marketer would want for his brand. But iconic status, is enjoyed by relatively few brands. Iconic brands are instantly recognizable: the shape of a VW Beetle is unique, Lego bricks are familiar to everyone since childhood, McDonald's arches are **proverbial** in any landscape, Nike's orange positive sign is a signature every child recognizes. A brand with such powerful visual symbol has an **intrinsic** advantage over others, because it is both a signboard as well as an advertisement.

One important **fallout** of developing an iconic brand is the growth of brand communities. Brand communities are largely imagined communities that represent a form of human association because of common brand **adulation**. Brand communities are collections of active loyalists- users of a brand who are determined, **fastidious** and almost passionate. There is an **intrinsic** connection between members and the collective sense of difference from others not in the community.

Branding is the sum total of a company's identity from its name and logo to every piece of communication, internal or external to every encounter every customer or potential customer has with it. Branding is **abstract** yet solid, silent yet **strident**!

Abstract
Contextual Meaning(s) : Noun; a concept or idea not associated with any specific instance; a sketchy summary of the main points of an argument or theory;
Other Meaning(s) : existing only in the mind; separated from embodiment; dealing with a subject in the abstract without practical purpose or intention; not representing or imitating external reality or the objects of nature
Synonyms : amorphous, vague

Adulation
Contextual Meaning(s) : Noun; servile flattery; exaggerated and hypocritical praise
Synonyms : worship, admiration

Authentic
Contextual Meaning(s) : Adjective; not counterfeit or copied; conforming to fact and therefore worthy of belief
Synonyms : unquestionable, veritable

Chronicles
Contextual Meaning(s) : Noun; records or narrative descriptions of past events
Other Meaning(s) : Verb; verb record in chronological order; make a historical record
Synonyms : annals

Colossal
Contextual Meaning(s) : Adjective; so great in size or force or extent as to elicit awe
Synonyms : prodigious, stupendous

Confined
Contextual Meaning(s) : Adjective; enclosed by a confining fence; in captivity
Other Meaning(s) : not free to move about; not invading healthy tissue; deprived of liberty; especially laced under arrest or restraint;
Synonyms : captive, imprisoned, jailed

Conscientious
Contextual Meaning(s) : Adjective; guided by or in accordance with conscience or sense of right and wrong
Other Meaning(s) : characterized by extreme care and great effort;
Synonyms : painstaking, scrupulous

Cues
Contextual Meaning(s) : Verb; hints or signs
Synonyms : indications, prompts

Delineated
Contextual Meaning(s) : Adjective; represented accurately or precisely
Synonyms : represented, outlined

Embedded
Contextual Meaning(s) : Adjective; inserted as an integral part of a surrounding whole; enclosed firmly in a surrounding mass
Synonyms : implanted

Enduring
Contextual Meaning(s) : Adjective; patiently withstanding continual wrongs or trouble; unceasing
Synonyms : abiding, imperishable

Enigma
Contextual Meaning(s) : Noun; something that baffles beyond understanding and cannot be explained; a difficult problem
Synonyms : mystery, conundrum

Epitome
Contextual Meaning(s) : Noun; a standard or typical example
Other Meaning(s) : noun a brief abstract (as of an article or book);
Synonyms : prototype, paradigm

Fallout
Contextual Meaning(s) : Noun; any adverse and unwanted secondary effect
Other Meaning(s) : noun the radioactive particles that settle to the ground after a nuclear explosion;
Synonyms : side- effect

- **Fastidious**
  Contextual Meaning(s) : Adjective; giving careful attention to detail; hard to please; excessively concerned with cleanliness.
  Other Meaning(s) : Adjective; (microbiology) having complicated nutritional requirements
  Synonyms : squeamish

- **Fostered**
  Contextual Meaning(s) : Adjective; encouraged or promoted in growth or development
  Other Meaning(s) : provided with parental care and nurture especially by a surrogate or surrogates;
  Synonyms : nourished

- **Intangibles**
  Contextual Meaning(s) : Noun; factors which are abstract
  Synonyms : uncountable

- **Intrinsic**
  Contextual Meaning(s) : Adjective; situated within or belonging solely to the organ or body part on which it acts; belonging to a thing by its very nature
  Synonyms : intrinsical

- **Inveterate**
  Contextual Meaning(s) : Adjective; having a habit of long standing
  Synonyms : confirmed, habitual

- **Intrinsic**
  Contextual Meaning(s) : adjective; basic and essential, belonging to something as one of the basic and essential features that make it what it is.
  Synonyms : essential, fundamental

- **Leapfrogged**
  Contextual Meaning(s) : Verb; jumping
  Synonyms : jumped

- **Motif**
  Contextual Meaning(s) : Adjective; a unifying idea a recurrent element in a literary or artistic or branding work
  Synonyms : motive, theme

- **Pervasive**
  Contextual Meaning(s) : Adjective; spreading or spread throughout
  Synonyms : permanent, permeating, permeative

- **Pivotal**
  Contextual Meaning(s) : Adjective; being of crucial importance
  Synonyms : polar

- **Poised**
  Contextual Meaning(s) : Adjective; marked by balance or equilibrium and readiness for action; in full control of your faculties
  Synonyms : collected, equinumerous,

- **Proverbial**
  Contextual Meaning(s) : adjective; widely known and recognized, and often viewed as stereotypical, e.g. their proverbial hospitality
  Other Meaning(s) : noun; used to refer to something in an expression or saying that is not being explicitly stated
  Synonyms : well-known, common

- **Robust**
  Contextual Meaning(s) : Adjective; physically strong; strong enough to withstand or overcome intellectual challenges or adversity; marked by richness and fullness of flavor
  Synonyms : full-bodied, racy, rich

- **Recession**
  Contextual Meaning(s) : noun; a period, shorter than a depression, during which there is a decline in economic trade and prosperity, slump, downturn,
  Synonyms : collapse, decline

- **Strident**
  Contextual Meaning(s) : Adjective; being sharply insistent on being heard;
  Other Meaning(s) : unpleasantly loud and harsh; of speech sounds produced by forcing air through a constricted passage (as `f', `s', `z', or `th' in both `thin' and `then'); conspicuously and offensively loud; given to vehement outcry
  Synonyms : shrill, raucous,

- **Ubiquitous**
  Contextual Meaning(s) : Adjective; present every where
  Synonyms : omnipresent

> **Unpalpable**
> *Contextual Meaning(s)* : Noun; a thing which can not be physically felt.
> *Synonyms* : intangible

> **Vanguard**
> *Contextual Meaning(s)* : Noun; the position of greatest importance or advancement; the leading position in any movement or field;
> *Other Meaning(s)* : the leading units moving at the head of an army; any creative group active in the innovation and application of new concepts and techniques in a given field (especially in the arts)
> *Synonyms* : forefront,

> **Vanquished**
> *Contextual Meaning(s)* : Verb; defeated, lost or beaten
> *Synonyms* : defeated

> **Vernacular**
> *Contextual Meaning(s)* : Adjective; being or characteristic of or appropriate to everyday language; noun the everyday speech of the people (as distinguished from literary language); a characteristic language of a particular group (as among thieves)
> *Synonyms* : common, local

> **Zenith**
> *Contextual Meaning(s)* : Noun; the top most point, apex
> *Other Meaning(s)* : noun the point above the observer that is directly opposite the nadir on the imaginary sphere against which celestial bodies appear to be projected
> *Synonyms* : vertex

Few other industries generate the attention as do the airlines, because flying is an essential need for many individuals, institutions and governments alike. Societies would become **dysfunctional** if airlines were grounded; it won't be an **exaggeration** to say that the earth would stop turning if this happened !

Considering the vital nature of the service the airlines provide and their invaluable contribution to making the world a smaller place, why is the airline industry synonymous with ongoing losses and **insolvency**? Why has the term *airline industry* become an **oxymoron** in that it provides value but is itself bleeding, and that there's no silver lining in sight ?

Perhaps, most ironic fact is that in the industry's value chain; airline catering, aircraft lessors, ground handlers, manufacturers, airports, distribution systems, fueling companies, travel agents, maintenance organizations and freight operations- each of these are quite profitable. All except the airline itself !

So much so that Warren E. Buffett once **quipped** that the best thing that could have happened to the American airline industry was for somebody to shoot down the 'Wright brothers' plane at Kitty Hawk in 1903 itself.

The only ones that are managing to extract a reasonable profit are the *Low cost airlines* or *Budget* airlines.

So why did the historic big airlines (also called **legacy** carriers) started losing out business to these *no frills* carriers ?

Aircraft are very expensive pieces of equipment, and airlines have to continue making large lease or loan repayments against them, regardless of business conditions. The hub-and-spoke networks of the large airlines require them to maintain a fleet of different types of aircraft. This increases their maintenance and staff training costs considerably.

The sooner an aircraft flies back after a landing, the more it can be put to use, and considering the plane is an airline's most expensive asset, it needs to use it as much as possible. However the large network airlines are forced to keep their planes at an airport for long durations, waiting for a connecting flight, decreasing their actual usage time. The airports charge them for using the airport space while lying idle there, thus doubling the expenses. Additionally the crew has to be put up at expensive hotels during this idle time.

All this amounts to a lower revenue per seat of the aeroplane. Now add some more damages.

The traditional ticket selling systems of legacy carriers ,called *global distribution systems* (GDS) and *computerised reservation systems* (CRS) such as Galileo and Amadeus – don't come cheap unlike the internet based ticket selling. The **complimentary** meals, water , snacks and beverages for the traveler actually cost a lot. The trade union agreements and employment contracts often trouble the bigger carriers translating in higher financial **onus**. With fuel prices **spiralling** up **unremmitingly** over the past decade, costs **escalate**. Add in security costs that have **skyrocketed** after 9/11, and it is apparent that few airlines can **surmount** the **formidable handicap** due to their high-cost structure.

Exogenous events like terror attacks, wars, natural disasters like the volcano ash eruptions and earthquakes also cause considerable losses in passenger demand as well as aircraft usage time.

And last but not the least, the business class demand in these times of recession has hit **turbulence**, too and every customer wants to fly **parsimoniously**. Business air travel has been further affected by the increased "security hassle factor". More and more business travelers now look for alternatives to paying premium air fares – teleconferencing and other travel substitutes, alternative travel modes and smaller **contingents**.

Enter the *low-fare no frills airlines* .Starting out in 1971 as a small carrier in Texas with only three jets, *Southwest Airlines* is credited with having given **parturition** to the low-cost-carrier phenomenon. Its founding mission was to fly passengers to short-haul destinations, on time and for the lowest fare possible. Nearly 36 years later, countless carriers have copied this philosophy in flying international , domestic or both sectors.

These carriers tend to keep their prices down by flying out of **nondescript** airports, relying on online booking and providing just the necessary level of onboard services. Food and beverages are on sale and with minimum level of variety. Many carriers stock their fleets with one type of aircraft to minimize the amount of training for crews. As part of the discount category, the airlines also can operate without union agreements and employment contracts that often trouble the bigger carriers. They fly from point to point; they don't sell networked connections. Their aircraft usage is almost upto 15 hours per day compared to barely 8 hours of big airlines. Crew flies back within 20 minutes so no costly hotel bills at the airlines' door.

Reeling under the recession, the ultra price sensitive customers shop the internet and find a discounted sale on an LCC. They may even find the price of a ticket today equal to, or less, in nominal dollars than a fare charged two decades ago. That sounds the death **knell** for the big airlines.

Voted by over 18.8 million airline passengers from 100 different nationalities, the World best LCC for the last three years has been *Air Asia*, operating out of Kulalampur. It operates almost 400 international and domestic destinations. The second spot went to *Jet star* operating out of Melbourne, Australia, and the third place went to *Virgin America*, operating domestically in the USA. Interestingly *Ryan air* a low-cost heavyweight based in Ireland, was carrying more passengers per month than the British Airways.

With so many of the world's airlines in a **perilous** state governments are being forced to step in with financial aid.

In January 2010 Japan Airlines became the latest carrier to declare bankruptcy, joining the swelling ranks of bankrupt airlines in recent years. American Airlines, too, joined a long list of airlines that have filed for bankruptcy protection, including Delta and Northwest airlines. There have been 189 total cases since 1990 including big names like Trans World Airlines (TWA) and Pan American World Airways (Pan Am).

Closing down a large unprofitable airline would involve the loss thousands of jobs, inconvenience to hundreds of thousands of travelers, and millions in losses for the airline's creditors. Thus closing down a **floundering** airline is a politically **unpalatable** decision, governments eventually provide it with a financial lifeline to stay in business.

Switzerland's national flag carrier *Swiss air* and *Sabena*, the national airline of Belgium, had to seek bankruptcy protection and a bail-out from their respective governments. New Zealand has gone so far as to re-nationalise its flag carrier. Mexico is giving its carriers a ten percent discount on jet fuel. Even in America, where the airline industry was deregulated two decades ago, the government is having to decide how best to **dole** out emergency funds without obviously trying to pick winners and losers. Troubled Indian national carrier *Air India* reported a net loss of $1.2bn last year; the Indian government agreed to inject more than $1bn into the carrier to help keep it in business. Kingfisher Airlines, a private player in India is cancelling flights due to cash crunch and **entreating** government for easy loans while the media **pillories** its wasteful work style that led to its crash.

Some unusual ways have been mooted to lift the **sagging** bottom line of the players- say, airlines were to offer a membership to customers – where as if they join they can purchase their tickets at a premium but the incentive for them to do this would be to allow them to fly on an empty or less full flight somewhere as standby.

Governments can help vary the ticket rates using differential tax rates according to departure times. Encourage "low price" flights at non-peak times, so cheapest prices are available at an inconvenient time; business travellers willing to pay the price can get a seat on the departure time as they desire. This is already in use in Europe.

LCCs in India are also looking at new ways to increase revenues. This includes advertisements during the in-flight entertainment -- "We will sell ad space on the TV screen inside the aircraft," says Kingfisher's Wilcox. Air Deccan's aircraft have logos of Sun Microsystem and NDTV painted on the exterior. Then there's the in-flight shopping for gifts and **souvenirs**.

In-flight internet access has the potential to be the **salvation** for struggling carriers. Once the equipment is installed, each interested passenger pays, let's say, 10 bucks a flight for the internet; a lot of them will love to carry out business as well as personal communication all the way. Even more important, internet access has the potential to **palliate** impatient customers. It can even stop kids from kicking the back of the seat in front of them!

A lot of thinking has to happen before the business of flying becomes a win-win situation for both the customer as well as the carrier!

🖎 **Calamities**
Contextual Meaning(s) : Noun; natural disasters
Synonyms : disasters

🖎 **Complimentary**
Contextual Meaning(s) : Adjective; costing nothing
Other Meaning(s) : adjective; conveying or resembling a compliment;
Synonyms : free, gratuitous

🖎 **Contingents**
Contextual Meaning(s) : noun; crew or group or degations for a specific purpose
Other Meaning(s) :
Synonyms : delegations, crews

🖎 **Dole**
Contextual Meaning(s) : noun money received from the state; a share of money or food or clothing that has been charitably given
Synonyms : pogy, charity

🖎 **Dysfunctional**
Contextual Meaning(s) : Adjective; (of a trait or condition) failing to serve purpose; impaired in function; especially of a bodily system or organ
Synonyms : nonadaptive

🖎 **Entreating**
Contextual Meaning(s) : Verb; to beg or plead for something.
Synonyms : beseeching

🖎 **Escalate**
Contextual Meaning(s) : verb increase in extent or intensity
Synonyms : intensify

🖎 **Exaggeration**
Contextual Meaning(s) : Noun the act of making something more noticeable than usual; making to seem more important than it really is;
Synonyms : overstatement, hyperbole

🖎 **Exogenous**
Contextual Meaning(s) : Adjective; derived or originating externally
Synonyms : exogenic

🖎 **Floundering**
Contextual Meaning(s) : Verb; to have difficulties, to stagger
Other Meaning(s) : None; some type of flatfish.
Synonyms : falter, waver

🖎 **Formidable**
Contextual Meaning(s) : adjective; difficult to deal with or overcome, e.g. a formidable task
Synonyms : frightening, dreadful

🖎 **Handicap**
Contextual Meaning(s) : Noun; the condition of being unable to perform as a consequence of financial, physical, mental unfitness;
Other Meaning(s) : noun advantage given to a competitor to equalize chances of winning; something immaterial that interferes with or delays action or progress; put at a disadvantage; attempt to forecast the winner (especially in a horse race) and assign odds for or against a contestant; injure permanently
Synonyms : disable, invalid, incapacitate

🖎 **Ingenious**
Contextual Meaning(s) : Adjective; showing inventiveness and skill; skillful (or showing skill) in adapting means to ends; (used of persons or artifacts) marked by independence and creativity in thought or action
Synonyms : adroit, imaginative, inventive

🖎 **Insolvency**
Contextual Meaning(s) : Noun; the lack of financial resources
Synonyms : bankruptcy

Knell

Contextual Meaning(s) : noun the sound of a bell rung slowly to announce a death or a funeral or the end of something;

Other Meaning(s) : verb ring as in announcing death; make (bells) ring, often for the purposes of musical edification

Synonyms : ring

Legacy

Contextual Meaning(s) : noun (law) a gift of personal or institutional property or attributes by will or by nature.

Synonyms : bequest

Nondescript

Contextual Meaning(s) : Adjective; lacking distinct or individual characteristics; dull and uninteresting;

Other Meaning(s) : noun a person is not easily classified and not very interesting

Synonyms : characterless

Onus

Contextual Meaning(s) : Noun a difficult task

Synonyms : load, encumbrance

Oxymoron

Contextual Meaning(s) : noun conjoining contradictory terms (as in `deafening silence')

Synonyms : trope

Palliate

Contextual Meaning(s) : Verb provide physical relief, as from pain; lessen or to try to lessen the seriousness or extent of

Synonyms : relieve, extenuate

Parsimoniously

Contextual Meaning(s) : Adverb; in a stingy manner

Synonyms : cheaply, miserly

Parturition

Contextual Meaning(s) : Noun; the process of giving birth

Synonyms : birthing

Perilous

Contextual Meaning(s) : Adjective; fraught with danger

Synonyms : precarious

Pillories

Contextual Meaning(s) : verb; to rebuke or criticize harshly

Synonyms : crucifies, harangues

Quipped

Contextual Meaning(s) : Verb; say jokingly

Synonyms : gagged

Reeling

Contextual Meaning(s) : verb; revolve quickly and repeatedly around one's own axis

Synonyms : whirling, spinning

Sagging

Contextual Meaning(s) : Adjective; hanging down (as from exhaustion or weakness)

Synonyms : drooping, droopy

Salvation

Contextual Meaning(s) : Noun saving someone or something from harm of from an unpleasant situation; a means of preserving from harm or unpleasantness; the state of being saved or preserved from harm;

Other Meaning(s) : *the act of deliverance from sin.*

Synonyms : redemption

Souvenirs

Contextual Meaning(s) : Noun; or memorabilia

Synonyms : memorabilia, mementos

Spiralling

Contextual Meaning(s) : noun; continuously accelerating increase or decrease in prices, wages, or interest rates

Synonyms : increase, growth

Skyrocketed

Contextual Meaning(s) : verb; to cause a rise or increase rapidly

Synonyms : shoot up, rise

✒ *Surmount*

Contextual Meaning(s) : verb; to deal with a difficulty successfully
Synonyms : overcome, get through

✒ *Turbulence*

Contextual Meaning(s) : *Noun;* instability in the atmosphere
Other Meaning(s) : noun unstable flow of a liquid or gas; a state of violent disturbance and disorder (as in politics or social conditions generally);
Synonyms : upheaval

✒ *Unpalatable*

Contextual Meaning(s) : Adjective; not pleasant or acceptable to the taste or mind
Synonyms : inedible, distasteful

✒ *Unremmitingly*

Contextual Meaning(s) : adverb; *without interruption*
Other Meaning(s) : with *unflagging resolve.*
Synonyms : ceaselessly, incessantly

HOME SMART HOME

Don't be shocked if someday you run into your neighbor's **poodle** being walked by a robot instead of him, because he has caught a fever. Also don't be shocked if you see another neighbour walking a robot Labrador! All this could be part of scenes from around 20 years from now.

In the near future, Smart home technology will make life easier , more entertaining, eco friendly, and leave us much more time and energy to perform higher level functions. Automation will make machines perform most of our tasks, and as futurist Alwyn Toffler wrote in his **seminal** "Future Shock", humans will become **asynchronous** while machines will be **synchronous** .

The housewife can manage the entire future home; the kitchen will become her command post ! A **tactile** monitor in the kitchen allows the housewife to control every facility . She can dim or brighten lights, open or close any window to a desired size and transparency, choose music, open or lock doors, all of this for any floor, any room. She can put on the shower, which will self adjust to her profile by the time she finishes breakfast.

All sorts of electronics and appliances will be able to communicate with each other and perform a variety of tasks in this futuristic home. Whenever someone wants to have a snack, but does not feel like making something, the refrigerator will suggest something based on what it has inside of it. Samsung, whirlpool and LG Electronics already have developed the Internet Refrigerator, perhaps a predecessor to the networked appliances of future. It allows for users to communicate with it via the Internet, cell phone or PDA. The refrigerator is able to download recipes and then display them on its LCD screen. The refrigerator also takes an automatic **inventory** of items inside of it, alerting the consumer accordingly. Some models already have the ability to order new groceries when they are needed . All that would need to happen is for someone to pick up the groceries, of course only till slave robots are not available.

The next generation microwaves are also smart. Microwaves can communicate with smart refrigerators and suggest recipes based on what items are in the refrigerator. The microwave can even be set to start at certain times while away from home, so when one arrives home, a hot **repast** is waiting for one. Cooking will become more precise with no room for human error as the device automatically sets itself to the right temperature and time. Coffee makers already have smart technology, and can make coffee as per the individual's preferences.

Showers will be able to store individual profiles for each user and will adjust water temperature and pressure settings based on that individuals' preference. No longer will people have to **fidget** with the temperature setting trying to get it right for a comfortable shower. Toilets will have self-clean capabilities and will be able to adjust flush settings depending on the need. Toilets may even be able to notify users when the toilet paper stock is low and order some more for them. An important feature that is available on virtually all smart home technology products is a **self-diagnostic** system. All these devices will be able to notify consumers when there is a malfunction or when some type of service is needed. Many of these devices will also be able to put in a work order automatically. Servicemen will be able to then come and repair the device without a hassle to the consumer.

The living room is another part of the home that can greatly benefit from smart home technologies. The giant TV will also function as a computer and a phone. The ability to buy products on the television with just a push of the button on the remote control is a big opportunity for customers as well as businesses to take advantage of. The ability of companies to give the user the option to buy a particular product immediately after viewing the commercial is a way to increase sales tremendously. The **flip** side of technology for the channels and the corporates is the possibility of a " commercial skipping function". Some of us have an **antipathy** toward TV commercial breaks (I do !). So I can just prioritize the programmes I wish to view at any time, through voice command. The moment the programme I am watching goes into a break, the channels are switched to the next available programme (from my list) that is not in a commercial break. The view **reverts** to the original programme once the commercials are over! Isn't customer the king after all !

The ability to watch sports at any angle the consumer wants is something that will be seen in the future. Another possibility of interactive television is the ability to actually play with contestants on a game show.

The air conditioner can even self adjust to keep the future house cool depending on the amount of people in the home.

The windows will allow a desired intensity of sunlight to come in, in fact they can turn from **opaque** to transparent as day fades into night. Smart glass technologies including **electro chromic** and liquid crystal devices will be **deployed** for this. The use of smart glass can save costs for heating, air-conditioning and lighting and avoid the cost of installing and maintaining blinds or curtains.

Computers will recognize footsteps, tracks movements or other bio signs for personalization and will detect occupants of every room and their movements **vigilantly**. Say in the midst of watching the TV in the living room, you get up and go to the kitchen to get coffee, the kitchen TV starts playing the same channel, while the living room TV shuts down, so no break in your viewing, while the energy is not wasted. And when you finally retire to your bedroom, it lights up, while all unwanted lights close down. Wherever you move in the house, the relevant part lights up and the unrequired lights go off.

Central computer will accept voice commands, distinguishes between occupants for personalized responses and actions. A visitor's presence at the door is immediately **intimated** along with his live video, and in case of a forced entry, alarms will go off at the nearest Police Centre .

Housekeeping is a walk in the park .All surfaces are self-cleaning, table tops cleanse themselves, house makes beds, **raiment** are intelligent , can self wash, dry, and self-fold. So no more those boring repetitive tasks. Even the **attire** suiting your day's schedule as well as the outside weather is suggested by the computer.

The home décor is maintained tastefuly by furniture that shapes itself, can **conceal** itself when not in use, and assumes color as suits the occasion.

The house generates its own energy, owner's cars can be refueled before leaving home and all mobile devices are charged up wirelessly the moment they need it. There is an artificial chlorophyll based green roof , which **replenishes** oxygen.

There is a robot chef, nurse, driver, cleaner and any other assistants we might need. There is virtual medical care available 24/7, remote doctors can examine and treat you while home computers monitor your health.

The challenge that lies would be for human beings not to become lazy and **corpulent**, because all the work they do will be **brainy**. Of course the home will have a state of art gym for burning away all the surplus calories. It will diagnose your physical state the moment you enter and suggest an exercise plan for the session. As you check out, it will display a diet plan for the next 24 hours, and can even order the kitchen accordingly.

🖎 **Aesthetically**
Contextual Meaning(s) : Adverb; in a tasteful way
Synonyms : esthetically

🖎 **Antipathy**
Contextual Meaning(s) : Noun; the object of a feeling of intense aversion; something to be avoided; a feeling of intense dislike
Synonyms : aversion, distaste

🖎 **Asynchronous**
Contextual Meaning(s) : Adjective; not synchronous; not occurring or existing at the same time or having the same period or phase;
Other Meaning(s) : (digital communication) pertaining to a transmission technique that does not require a common clock between the communicating devices; timing signals are derived from special characters in the data stream itself
Synonyms : anachronistic

🖎 **Attire**
Contextual Meaning(s) : Noun; clothing of a distinctive style or for a particular occasion;
Synonyms : apparel

🖎 **Brainy**
Contextual Meaning(s) : Adjective; involving intelligence rather than emotions or instinct; of or relating to the cerebrum or brain
Synonyms : intellectual

🖎 **Conceal**
Contextual Meaning(s) : Verb; hold back; keep from being perceived by others; prevent from being seen or discovered
Synonyms : hold back, hold in, hide

🖎 **Corpulent**
Contextual Meaning(s) : Adjective; excessively fat
Synonyms : fat, rotund

🖎 **Deployed**
Contextual Meaning(s) : Verb; put into use
Synonyms : positioned

🖎 **Electro Chromic**
Contextual Meaning(s) : adjective; of or relating to a substance that changes colour or transparency when subjected to charged electrodes, as in the liquid crystal display in many calculators
Synonyms : electro chromic display

🖎 **Fidget**
Contextual Meaning(s) : Verb; move restlessly
Other Meaning(s) : noun a feeling of agitation expressed in continual motion;
Synonyms : fidgetiness, restlessness

🖎 **Flip**
Contextual Meaning(s) : Adjective; reverse (a direction, attitude, or course of action);
Other Meaning(s) : marked by casual disrespect; noun a dive in which the diver somersaults before entering the water; the act of flipping a coin; hot or cold alcoholic mixed drink containing a beaten egg; (sports) the act of throwing the ball to another member of your team; an acrobatic feat in which the feet roll over the head (either forward or backward) and return; verb go mad, go crazy; turn upside down, or throw so as to reverse; move with a flick or light motion; throw or toss with a light motion; lightly throw to see which side comes up; cause to move with a flick; toss with a sharp movement so as to cause to turn over in the air; cause to go on or to be engaged or set in operation; look through a book or other written material
Synonyms : reverse, back

🖎 **Indolent**
Contextual Meaning(s) : Adjective; disinclined to work or exertion, lazy
Other Meaning(s) : (of tumors e.g) slow to heal or develop and usually painless;
Synonyms : slothful, work-shy

🖎 **Intimated**
Contextual Meaning(s) : Verb; informed or communicated
Synonyms : informed

✉ *Inventory*
Contextual Meaning(s) : Noun; a complete list of items such as property or goods in stock.
Synonyms : list, catalogue

✉ *Opaque*
Contextual Meaning(s) : Adjective; not clear; not transmitting or reflecting light or radiant energy;
Other Meaning(s) : not clearly understood or expressed
Synonyms : obscuring, hiding

✉ *Poodle*
Contextual Meaning(s) : Noun; an intelligent dog with a heavy curly solid-colored coat that is usually clipped; an old breed sometimes trained as sporting dogs or as performing dogs
Synonyms : dog-breed

✉ *Precursor*
Contextual Meaning(s) : Noun; an indication of the approach of something or someone
Other Meaning(s) : noun a person who goes before or announces the coming of another; a substance from which another substance is formed (especially by a metabolic reaction);
Synonyms : forerunner, harbinger,

✉ *Proximity*
Contextual Meaning(s) : Noun; the region close around a person or thing
Other Meaning(s) : noun the property of being close together; a Gestalt principle of organization holding that (other things being equal) objects or events that are near to one another (in space or time) are perceived as belonging together as a unit;
Synonyms : propinquity

✉ *Raiment*
Contextual Meaning(s) : Noun; especially fine or decorative clothing
Other Meaning(s) : verb provide with clothes or put clothes on
Synonyms : regalia, apparel

✉ *Reverts*
Contextual Meaning(s) : Verb; undergoes a reversion, as in a mutation; goes back to a previous state
Synonyms : regresses, returns

✉ *Repast*
Contextual Meaning(s) : Noun; the food served and eaten at one time
Synonyms : meal

✉ *Replenishes*
Contextual Meaning(s) : Verb; fills something that had previously been emptied
Synonyms : refills

✉ *Seminal*
Contextual Meaning(s) : Adjective; containing seeds of later development
Other Meaning(s) : pertaining to or containing or consisting of semen
Synonyms : germinal, originative

✉ *Subservient*
Contextual Meaning(s) : Adjective; compliant and obedient to authority; abjectly submissive; characteristic of a slave or servant; serving or acting as a means or aid
Synonyms : obsequious, servile

✉ *Synchronous*
Contextual Meaning(s) : adjective; happening at the same time, working or moving at the same rate
Synonyms : simultaneously

✉ *Self- Diagnostic*
Contextual Meaning(s) : noun; somebody 's own individual interests and welfare, especially when placed before those of other people
Synonyms : self-interest

✉ *Tactile*
Contextual Meaning(s) : Adjective; producing a sensation of touch; of or relating to or proceeding from the sense of touch
Synonyms : tactual, haptic

✉ *Vapid*
Contextual Meaning(s) : Adjective; lacking significance or liveliness or spirit or zest; lacking taste or flavor or tang
Synonyms : bland, insipid

✉ *Vigilantly*
Contextual Meaning(s) : Adverb; in a watchful manner
Synonyms : watchfully

The William Shakespeare of Stratford-upon-Avon , is widely considered as the " William Shakespeare ", the **bard**, unquestionably the tallest writer of English language. However, a host of theories **surge** now and then suggesting that the legendary works were done under the pseudonym of Shakespeare by someone else, or even a group of writers.

The earliest essays on this authorship question started coming in the late eighteenth century, 150 years after the bard's death. Most of these hinted that Sir Francis Bacon was the factual author of these works.

It must be noted that none of these early **exponents** of the Bacon/Shakespeare theory was a trained Shakespearean scholar. There was passion but little research. They **gainsaid** Shakespeare's authorship on the **presumption** that it was impossible for a "Stratford **rustic**" to write the great plays attributed to him.

Since then, at least 58 different persons have been proposed as the true authors of Shakespeare's works.

The most prominent is Edward de Vere, seventeenth Earl of Oxford, proposed by a group known as "the Oxfordians." There is much evidence to suggest that the Earl was a playwright and a poet, although **curiously** none of his literary output survives. As the Earl of one of England's most affluent and academic cities, the Earl would have been **moneyed** enough to travel to every country Shakespeare ever set a play in, and attend a University in each one. Because the political content in the material could have **ruined** his social standing – did he perhaps need to write under a pseudonym? He was thought to have owned a home in Stratford from 1589 to 1616, which corresponds roughly with the time Shakespeare's literature was written.

Following the earl in popularity is Sir Francis Bacon, favorite of the "Baconians". The theory that Bacon was the only man intelligent enough to write these plays has become known as Baconianism. Although it is unclear why he would have needed to write under a pseudonym, those who **acquiesce** to this theory believe that he left behind **cryptic ciphers** in the texts to reveal his true identity.

Adding to the **bewilderment** are the "Marlovians", who insist that Christopher Marlowe wrote the plays. Marlowe was England's best playwright, before Shakespeare came along. He actually demonstrated genius-level play writing ability, and even died under mysterious circumstances; something that tends to go hand in hand with the **conspiracy** theories. Marlovians believe that Marlowe faked his own death in order to escape the pressures of being a famous writer, and assumed the **moniker** William Shakespeare from then on.

It is a well known fact that Shakespeare was born to a working-class Warwickshire family. A key argument of the authorship question indicates that a poor, lower class man in the 17th century would not have had access to any of the resources such as university education, libraries or capacity for abstract thought that an author would require to complete such an extraordinary body of work.

Even if he got a basic working class education – at Stratford-upon-Avon school, which typically might have lasted until the age of 11; it would not have been enough to furnish Shakespeare with the expert knowledge of foreign languages, politics, law, science and **raunchy** courtly **gossip** that is evident in his plays!

It has also been pointed out that Shakespeare's plays demonstrate a keen knowledge of foreign countries and their landscapes, and therefore they must have been written by a well-travelled Gentleman. The Merchant of Venice for example contains vast amounts of topographical information on the Italian city, including the detailed and accurate descriptions of the canals, castles and Jewish **ghettoes.**

It has also been put forward that Shakespeare could well have been a pseudonym, because of the **hyphenation** between "shake" and "speares" on the cover of his **sonnets**. Critics cite, hyphens were a common convention of Elizabethan pseudonyms, thus trying to give **credence** to their argument.

Many of the scholars who question this are unable to understand why the Bard never **eulogized** any of the monarchs who passed away during his supposed lifespan, despite the fact that he lived to see Queen Elizabeth's demise; a woman he was allegedly quite close to.

Some prominent writers and artistes, including Mark Twain, Helen Keller, Henry James, Sigmund Freud, Charlie Chaplin and Orson Welles, have found the arguments against Shakespeare's authorship **persuasive.**

Many believe that one man simply couldn't have written so many **incisive**, witty and beautiful plays, and that it must have been a group effort, involving some or all of the other candidates for authorship.

Many feminists have been quick to suggest that Shakespeare's works were actually written by a woman. Countess of Pembroke and wealthy upper-class patron of Shakespeare's publishers Mary Sidney is considered the most likely female candidate, although many also speculate that Queen Elizabeth I herself could also have been the secret author !

However, all but a few Shakespeare scholars and literary historians consider the conspiracy theories a **peripheral** belief and for the most part disregard the negative description of his abilities.

William Shakespeare was born in April, 1564, the oldest son of John Shakespeare. His father, a glover, trader, and landowner, married the daughter of an affluent landowner of Wilmcote. John Shakespeare was ambitious, and he filled many municipal offices in Stratford , eventually he was elected Bailiff (equivalent to mayor). Young William got an education at Stratford Grammar school, and was certainly not illiterate !

Nearly all academic Shakespeareans believe that the author referred to as "Shakespeare" was the same William Shakespeare who was born in Stratford-upon-Avon in 1564 and who died there in 1616. He became an actor and shareholder in the Globe Theatre, which had the exclusive rights to produce Shakespeare's plays then. Shakespeare was also allowed the use of the **honorific** "gentleman" after 1596 when his father was granted a "coat of arms".

Shakespeare scholars see no reason to suspect that Shakespeare was the writer of his body of work; other playwrights such as Ben Jonson and Christopher Marlowe came from similar backgrounds, and no peer is known to have expressed doubts about Shakespeare's authorship. While information about some aspects of Shakespeare's life is **sketchy**, this is true of many other playwrights of the time !

Opinions continue to be **volatile** and its a controversy which may not drop dead any time soon!

🖎 **Acquiesce**
Contextual Meaning(s) : Verb; to agree or express agreement
Synonyms : assent, accede

🖎 **Bard**
Contextual Meaning(s) : Noun; a lyric poet;
Synonyms : lyric-poet

🖎 **Bewilderment**
Contextual Meaning(s) : Noun; confusion resulting from failure to understand
Synonyms : obfuscation, bafflement

🖎 **Conspiracy**
Contextual Meaning(s) : Noun; a plot to carry out some harmful or illegal act (especially a political plot); a secret agreement between two or more people to perform an unlawful act; a group of conspirators banded together to achieve some harmful or illegal purpose
Synonyms : cabal, confederacy

🖎 **Contemporary**
Contextual Meaning(s) : Adjective; belonging to the present time; characteristic of the present; occurring in the same period of time; noun a person of nearly the same age as another
Synonyms : coeval, present-day,

🖎 **Credence**
Contextual Meaning(s) : Noun; the mental attitude that something is believable and should be accepted as true;
Other Meaning(s) : Noun; a kind of sideboard or buffet
Synonyms : acceptance, credenza

🖎 **Curiously**
Contextual Meaning(s) : Adverb; in a manner differing from the usual or expected; with curiosity
Synonyms : oddly, peculiarly

🖎 **Cryptic Ciphers**
Contextual Meaning(s) : adjective; deliberately mysterious and seeming to have a hidden meaning, secret or hidden in some way
Synonyms : mysterious, enigmatic

🖎 **Eulogised**
Contextual Meaning(s) : Verb; accorded very high praise
Synonyms : extolled, panegyrized

🖎 **Exponents**
Contextual Meaning(s) : Noun; promoters of a cause or idea
Other Meaning(s) : Noun; a mathematical function
Synonyms : advocates, proponents

🖎 **Gainsaid**
Contextual Meaning(s) : Verb; strongly denied or refuted.
Synonyms : disputed, challenged

🖎 **Ghettoes**
Contextual Meaning(s) : Noun; a neighborhood for economically or socially constrained people
Synonyms : slum

🖎 **Gossip**
Contextual Meaning(s) : Noun; a report (often malicious) about the behavior of other people; light informal conversation for social occasions;
Other Meaning(s) : a person given to gossiping and divulging personal information about others; verb talk socially without exchanging too much information; wag one's tongue; speak about others and reveal secrets or intimacies
Synonyms : scuttlebutt, gab

🖎 **Honorific**
Contextual Meaning(s) : Noun; an expression of respect
Other Meaning(s) : adjective conferring or showing honor or respect;
Synonyms : title

🖎 **Hyphenation**
Contextual Meaning(s) : noun; separating or joining words or parts of words using a hyphen

Incisive

Contextual Meaning(s) : Adjective; suitable for cutting or piercing; having or demonstrating ability to recognize or draw fine distinctions
Synonyms : discriminating, penetrating,

Moneyed

Contextual Meaning(s) : Adjective; based on or arising from the possession of money or wealth; having an abundant supply of money or possessions of value
Synonyms : affluent, , wealthy

Moniker

Contextual Meaning(s) : Noun; a familiar name for a person (often a shortened version of a person's given name)
Synonyms : nickname, cognomen, sobriquet,

Pejorative

Contextual Meaning(s) : Adjective; expressing disapproval
Synonyms : dyslogistic, expletive

Peripheral

Contextual Meaning(s) : Adjective; on or near an edge or constituting an outer boundary; the outer area; related to the key issue but not of central importance;
Other Meaning(s) : noun (computer science) electronic equipment connected by cable to the CPU of a computer
Synonyms : superficial, marginal

Persuasive

Contextual Meaning(s) : Adjective; capable of convincing; tending or intended or having the power to induce action or belief
Synonyms : cogent, compelling

Presumption

Contextual Meaning(s) : noun; a belief based on the fact that something is considered to be reasonable or likely, e.g. I acted on the presumption that their IDs were genuine.
Synonyms : assumption, supposition

Raunchy

Contextual Meaning(s) : Adjective; earthy and sexually explicit; thickly covered with ingrained dirt or soot; suggestive of or tending to moral looseness
Synonyms : obscene, salacious

Ruined

Contextual Meaning(s) : Adjective; brought to destruction; destroyed physically or morally; doomed to extinction
Synonyms : finished, undone

Rustic

Contextual Meaning(s) : Adjective; noun an unsophisticated country person
Other Meaning(s) : Adjective; awkwardly simple and provincial; characteristic of the fields or country; used of idealized country life; characteristic of
Synonyms : bucolic, pastoral

Sketchy

Contextual Meaning(s) : Adjective; giving only major points; lacking completeness
Other Meaning(s) :
Synonyms : unelaborated, vague

Surge

Contextual Meaning(s) : Noun; a sudden or abrupt strong increase;
Other Meaning(s) : a large sea wave; a sudden forceful flow; verb see one's performance improve; rise or heave upward under the influence of a natural force such as a wave; rise or move forward; rise rapidly; rise and move, as in waves or billows
Synonyms : billow, zoom

Sonnets

Contextual Meaning(s) : noun; a short poem with 14 lines, usually ten-syllable rhyming lines
Synonyms : ballad, rhyme

Volatile

Contextual Meaning(s) : Adjective; tending to vary often or widely; marked by erratic changeableness in affections or attachments;
Other Meaning(s) : evaporating readily at normal temperatures and pressures; liable to lead to sudden change or violence; noun a volatile substance; a substance that changes readily from solid or liquid to a vapor
Synonyms : fickle, explosive

ARE 3D MOVIES WORTH IT?

Silent movies were **bettered** by the introduction of sound. Black and white movies were **adorned** by the introduction of colour. Technicolor first came in the mid-1930s; it was first used in 1935 with "Becky Sharp" and again famously in "The Wizard of Oz" made in 1939. For next 10-15 years, technicolor was **demoted** to musicals, comedies and westerns. It wasn't intended for the serious genres, but today everything is in color. **Transition** from 2D to 3D is also equally **tumultuous**.

3-D films have existed in some form since the 1950s, but were largely limited to a limited segment of the motion picture industry because of costly hardware and processes required to produce and display a 3-D film. Nonetheless, 3-D films were prominently featured in the 1950s in American cinema. **Pertinently**, the first 3D film ever made was in 1953, a horror film *The house of wax*.

Back then the industry felt the **menace** of growing popularity of television and decided to launch an experimental format of film to give audiences something they couldn't get from the TV. However, this 3D format proved to be a short lived flash in the pan – primarily due to the motion sickness the **fuzzy** images induced. Moreover, 3D induced headaches, **repelling** the audience instead of attracting them. 3D made its next **incarnation** in the eighties, when there was another trend that prompted wide-spread panic across the movie industry: Home-video. Home-video though, is now confined to the history books , its younger sibling DVD is the new **nemesis** of moviemakers. Yet another **scourge**, so the third wave of 3D rolled in, bringing its idiotic glasses with it. Driven by IMAX high-end theaters and Disney themed venues, 3-D films became more successful throughout the 2000s, **culminating** in the **unprecedented** success of 3-D presentations of *Avatar* in December 2009 .

Critics feel, this latest version of 3D , in the entire landscape from Hollywood to Bollywood, sums up as an attempt to reduce cinema to an entirely visual experience. But this is at the expense of other attributes that make a film watchable, such as the script, dialogue, and characters. It's these things that make a film an **engulfing** experience, perhaps more than the **shallow** visual thrills. Say 3D is the future of cinema – then this would be the final nail in the coffin of intelligent, **narrative** cinema. Technically, a monkey **hurling** ground nuts out at an audience for two hours could pass as a new visual experience - a 3D movie! Cinema would need little creativity at all if visual **illusions suffice**. Likewise, if a film did have a strong narrative, then you might be distracted from following the story if you were ducking every five minutes from say, flying bullets. It's hard to engage the brain when you are having your senses **battered.** Maybe, 3D should be limited to fantasy or sci-fi films only. Some even say wasn't cinema 3D already? One never sat there looking at the screen feeling that one were watching something, like a Mickey Mouse cartoon movie. Truth is, 2D cinema has depth behind the screen. 3D cinema has depth in front of the screen. These are quite different from each other. **Proponents** of 3D are quite vocal, too. **Raconteurs** like Steven Spielberg, Peter Jackson and of course, James Cameron have all agreed to make films in the 3D format.

After all, six of the top 10 highest **grossing** movies of all time are 3D films that were released since Avatar in 2009. That represents 63% of the total gross from the top 10 films of all time.

Currently, there are more than 30,000 3D screens internationally, which is twice as many as those available to audiences just one year ago. This growth represents the **waxing** consumer demand for the third wave of 3D.

The Oscar-winning film-maker, Martin Scorsese, has said he would prefer to shoot all his future films in 3D following his experiences with his new movie Hugo, which has received impressive critical notices and is being **tipped** for awards season success as I write this piece.

Scorsese also suggested that his previous films Taxi Driver and The Aviator might have benefited from being shot in **stereoscope**. Once the technology advances maybe you can eliminate glasses that are **hindrances** to some moviegoers.

After all, if people download movies, its mainly because in these tough times, people can't afford going to theatres. Now consider the fact that 3D film tickets have to be priced up to £2 more than a regular film .This just creates another obstruction for the theatre **buffs**. And with the advent of DVD and HD TV, people are likely to download the 3D versions of movies on their DVDs and watch it on their home DVD tv !

Movie makers are now reportedly **contemplating** adding further dimensions of **aroma** and climate to lure back the audience. I bet the television would follow suit.

Some things can be never **prophesied** ! As long as the price of a ticket is within budgets, people won't complain !

Adorned
Contextual Meaning(s) : Adjective; provided with something intended to increase its beauty or distinction
Other Meaning(s) : Adjective; clothed or adorned with finery
Synonyms : decorated, bedecked

Aroma
Contextual Meaning(s) : Noun; a distinctive odor that is pleasant; any property detected by the olfactory system
Synonyms : fragrance, perfume

Battered
Contextual Meaning(s) : Adjective; damaged by blows or hard usage; damaged especially by hard usage
Other Meaning(s) : Adjective; exhibiting symptoms resulting from repeated physical and emotional injury
Synonyms : beaten-up

Bettered
Contextual Meaning(s) : Verb; to have improved the quality of something
Synonyms : ameliorated

Buffs
Contextual Meaning(s) : Adjective; an ardent follower and admirer
Other Meaning(s) : Adjective; of the yellowish-beige color of buff leather; noun an implement consisting of soft material mounted on a block; used for polishing (as in manicuring); bare skin; naked; a soft thick undyed leather from the skins of e.g. buffalo or oxen; a medium to dark tan color;; verb polish and make shiny; strike, beat repeatedly
Synonyms : enthusiast

Celebrated
Contextual Meaning(s) : Adjective; having an illustrious past; widely known and esteemed
Synonyms : storied, noted, renowned

Contemplating
Contextual Meaning(s) : Verb; Considering as a possibility.
Other Meaning(s) : Verb; meditating, looking at something thoughtfully.
Synonyms : considering

Culminating
Contextual Meaning(s) : Verb; to reach final or climatic stage
Other Meaning(s) : Verb; to reach the highest altitude or meridian.
Synonyms : Resulting

Decimated
Contextual Meaning(s) : Verb; to be destroyed totally.
Synonyms : destroyed

Demoted
Contextual Meaning(s) : Verb; to move someone to a lower rank or position.
Synonyms : downgrade, relegate

Engulfing
Contextual Meaning(s) : Adjective; absorbing or occupying the mind
Synonyms : consuming, absorbing

Fuzzy
Contextual Meaning(s) : Adjective; confused and not coherent; not clearly thought out; covering with fine light hairs; indistinct or hazy in outline
Synonyms : bleary, foggy

Grossing
Contextual Meaning(s) : Verb; earning (before tax) or collections
Synonyms : collecting

Hindrances
Contextual Meaning(s) : Noun; (plural) a blockade or instruction
Synonyms : encumbrances, handicaps

*   *Hurling*
    Contextual Meaning(s) : Verb; throwing something at someone
    Other Meaning(s) : rushing and whirling; noun a traditional Irish game resembling hockey; played by two teams of 15 players each
    Synonyms : throwing

*   *Illusions* (Noun)
    Synonyms : conjurations, legerdemains

*   *Incarnation*
    Contextual Meaning(s) : Noun; a new personification of a familiar idea
    Other Meaning(s) : noun (Christianity) the Christian doctrine of the union of God and man in the person of Jesus Christ; time passed in a particular bodily form; the act of attributing human characteristics to abstract ideas etc.
    Synonyms : personification, embodiment, avatar

*   *Inducing*
    Contextual Meaning(s) : Noun act of bringing about a desired result
    Synonyms : inducement

*   *Menace*
    Contextual Meaning(s) : Noun a threat or the act of threatening; something that is a source of danger
    Other Meaning(s) : Verb; act in a threatening manner; express a threat either by an utterance or a gesture; pose a threat to; present a danger to
    Synonyms : peril

*   *Narrative*
    Contextual Meaning(s) : Adjective; consisting of or characterized by the telling of a story
    Other Meaning(s) : noun a message that tells the particulars of an act or occurrence or course of events; presented in writing or drama or cinema or as a radio or television program
    Synonyms : narration, story, tale

*   *Nemesis*
    Contextual Meaning(s) : Noun; something causes misery or death
    Other Meaning(s) : noun (Greek mythology) the goddess of divine retribution and vengeance
    Synonyms : bane, curse, scourge

*   *Niche*
    Contextual Meaning(s) : Noun; (ecology) a position particularly well suited to the person who occupies it
    Other Meaning(s) : noun (ecology) the status of an organism within its environment and community (affecting its survival as a species); an enclosure that is set back or indented; a small concavity
    Synonyms : recess, corner

*   *Pertinently*
    Contextual Meaning(s) : Adverb in a pertinent way
    Synonyms : fittingly, appropriately

*   *Prophesied*
    Contextual Meaning(s) : Verb; predict the to here
    Synonyms : presaged

*   *Proponents* (Noun)
    Contextual Meaning(s) : Noun; someone who pleads for or addiction a cause
    Synonyms : champion, protagonist

*   *Raconteurs*
    Contextual Meaning(s) : Noun; (plural) story tellers
    Synonyms : anecdotists

*   *Relegated*
    Contextual Meaning(s) : Verb; pushed to a lower state or position
    Synonyms : demoted

*   *Repelling*
    Contextual Meaning(s) : verb; to ward something off, or keep something away, e.g. a cram that is effective in repelling mosquitoes
    Synonyms : aversion, revulsion

*   *Scourge*
    Contextual Meaning(s) : Noun; something causes misery or death
    Synonyms : terror, bane, curse

Shallow

Contextual Meaning(s) : Adjective; not deep or strong; not affecting one deeply; lacking depth of intellect or knowledge; concerned only with what is obvious;
Other Meaning(s) : Adjective; lacking physical depth; having little spatial extension downward or inward from an outer surface or backward or outward from a center; noun a stretch of shallow water; verb become shallow; make shallow
Synonyms : shoal

Suffice

Contextual Meaning(s) : Verb; be sufficient; be adequate, either in quality or quantity
Synonyms : do, serve

Stereoscope

Contextual Meaning(s) : noun; a device resembling a pair of binoculars in which two-dimensional pictures of a scene taken at slightly different angles are viewed concurrently, one with each eye, creating the illusion of three dimensions.

Transition

Contextual Meaning(s) : Noun; a change from one place or state or subject or stage to another; the act of passing from one state or place to the next; an event that results in a transformation

Other Meaning(s) : Noun; a passage that connects a topic to one that follows; a musical passage moving from one key to another; verb make or undergo a transition (from one state or system to another); cause to convert or undergo a transition
Synonyms : passage, conversion, changeover

Tumultuous

Contextual Meaning(s) : Adjective; characterized by unrest or disorder or insubordination
Synonyms : riotous, troubled

Tipped

Contextual Meaning(s) : verb; to push or knock over
Synonyms : bend, inclined

Unprecedented

Contextual Meaning(s) : adjective; having no earlier parallel or equivalent
Synonyms : extraordinary, unique

Waxing

Contextual Meaning(s) : Adjective; a gradual increase in magnitude or extent
Other Meaning(s) : adjective (of the moon) pertaining to the period during which the visible surface of the moon increases; noun the application of wax to a surface
Synonyms : enlarging

Recently my hometown was struck with a mild earthquake. A good friend of mine immediately started to update his twitter account with this event rather than **scramble** outside the residence to safer outdoors!

An about-to-be mom recently broadcasted her entire child delivery experience through a mobile social media account !

Why talk of others ? Facebook is now virtually *my* family tree with 8 year to 80 year old **perched** on various branches, updating their latest adventures with photographs and comments.

Social networking sites have become an **indispensable** way to find old friends, schedule events , play games and even send virtual gifts. You wake up early in the morning and first thing you do is log onto your Facebook account to check what **transpired** when you were fast asleep at night. Maybe your last online prank just **boomeranged**. And that spoils your mood for the day!

If you're doing more living online than off, it might be time to **excogitate**. There is no way the virtual life can **supplant** your real life. Especially if you are socially shy, you try to find **succor** in the digital society, but this tendency to **circumvent** real life encounters can be bad in the long run. This electronic **gregariousness** is ,well electronic after all!

Notifications, messages ,invites and comments on your remarks reward you with a temporary high, much like gambling. That **blitheness** of spirit can get dangerously addictive.

 Many folks are now pronouncing social networking sites more as an addiction than a networking tool, and psychologists **countenance** this view.

Are personal relationships taking a backseat to internet friendships ? Do you think about Facebook even when you're offline? Do you use Facebook to escape problems or homework? Do you stay on Facebook **incessantly** ? Have you ever concealed Facebook use?

If you answered yes to any, you might be a borderline addict - no joke.

Relentlessly updating your Facebook status, Twittering your every move and spying on your friends, relatives and coworkers can increase stress levels, damage sleep patterns and even **debase** meaningful personal relationships.

Rob Bedi, a registered psychologist and assistant professor at the University of Victoria, said that Internet addictions are common on university campuses, often helped by unlimited free Internet access, web-based assignments and unstructured blocks of time.

Some students are so addicted to social networking sites that they **squander** upwards of 21 hours a day connected to the site in some way, whether through their computers or through their mobile phones, leaving only a couple hours for uninterrupted sleep. Many have no time whatsoever for quality, face-to-face interaction with their friends and family members as a result.

Many students have now come to the abrupt **trepidation** that social network addiction is destroying their health both physically and emotionally. Some admit that they need to make some **radical** changes in their daily habits and **truncate** their online presence.

Bedi suggests make a Facebook schedule. Limit time spent on social media to whatever is required to meet your original goals behind joining such networks. Update your e-mail addresses to avoid relying on Facebook messages.

For some people, talking with someone might be the answer. Many universities offer addiction counselling through student services.

If you're not quite ready for that, you could join one of the 155 Facebook Addicts Anonymous groups on Facebook itself - but that might defeat the purpose !

Ample
Contextual Meaning(s) : Adjective; affording an abundant supply; more than enough in size or scope or capacity; fairly large
Synonyms : plenteous ,sizeable

Blitheness
Contextual Meaning(s) : Noun a feeling of spontaneous good spirits
Synonyms : cheerfulness, mirth

Boomeranged
Contextual Meaning(s) : Verb; backfired on the originating source.
Synonyms : backfired

Boomeranged
Contextual Meaning(s) : Verb; something that does inadvertently harm to its initiator, to backfire on the initiator of an action, causing that person harm, return to the initial position from where it came
Other Meaning(s) : Noun; a flat curved, usually wooden missile configured so that when hurled it returns to the thrower.
Synonyms : to come back or return

Circumvent
Contextual Meaning(s) : Verb; avoid or try to avoid fulfilling, answering, or performing (duties, questions, or issues);
Other Meaning(s) : Verb; beat through cleverness and wit; surround so as to force to give up
Synonyms : skirt, dodge, duck,

Countenance
Contextual Meaning(s) : Noun; the appearance conveyed by a person's face; the human face (`kisser' and `similar' and `mug' are informal terms for `face' and `phiz' is British); formal and explicit approval;
Other Meaning(s) : Verb; consent to, give permission
Synonyms : visages

Debase
Contextual Meaning(s) : Verb; lower in value by increasing the base-metal content; corrupt, debase, or make impure by adding a foreign or inferior substance; often by replacing valuable ingredients with inferior ones; corrupt morally or by intemperance or sensuality
Synonyms : demoralise, profane, vitiate, deprave,

Excogitate
Contextual Meaning(s) : Verb; reflect deeply on a subject;
Other Meaning(s) : Verb; come up with (an idea, plan, explanation, theory, or principle) after a mental effort
Synonyms : ruminate

Fickle
Contextual Meaning(s) : Adjective; marked by erratic changeableness in affections or attachments; liable to sudden unpredictable change
Synonyms : quicksilver

Gregariousness
Contextual Meaning(s) : Noun; the quality of being gregarious having a dislike of being alone
Synonyms : sociability

Incessantly
Contextual Meaning(s) : Adverb; with unflagging resolve
Synonyms : ceaselessly

Indispensable
Contextual Meaning(s) : Adjective; unavoidable; not to be dispensed with; essential; absolutely necessary; vitally necessary
Synonyms : essential

- *Perched*
  Contextual Meaning(s) : Verb; sit, as on the branch; to come to rest
  Synonyms : roosted

- *Radical*
  Contextual Meaning(s) : Adjective; Revolutionary
  Other Meaning(s) : Adjective; especially of leaves; located at the base of a plant or stem;
  Synonyms : extreme, revolutionary

- *Relentlessly*
  Contextual Meaning(s) : Adverb; in a relentless manner
  Synonyms : unrelentingly

- *Ruin*
  Contextual Meaning(s) : Noun; failure that results in a loss of position or reputation; the process of becoming dilapidated;
  Other Meaning(s) : Noun; a ruined building; an event that results in destruction; an irrecoverable state of devastation and destruction; destruction achieved by causing something to be wrecked or ruined;
  Synonyms : dilapidation

- *Scramble*
  Contextual Meaning(s) : Noun; an unceremonious and disorganized struggle; rushing about hastily in an undignified way;
  Other Meaning(s) : Verb; make unintelligible; bring into random order; to move hurriedly; stir vigorously; climb awkwardly, as if by scrambling
  Synonyms : scamper, scurry,

- *Supplant*
  Contextual Meaning(s) : Verb; take the place or move into the position of
  Synonyms : replace

- *Succor*
  Contextual Meaning(s) : Noun; assistance in time of difficulty;
  Other Meaning(s) : Verb; help in a difficult situation
  Synonyms : ministration

- *Squander*
  Contextual Meaning(s) : Verb; spend extravagantly; spend thoughtlessly; throw away
  Synonyms : waste, ware, blow

- *Transpired*
  Contextual Meaning(s) : Verb. Occurred or took place or was discussed
  Synonyms : happened

- *Trepidation*
  Contextual Meaning(s) : Noun; a feeling of alarm or dread
  Synonyms : dread

- *Truncate*
  Contextual Meaning(s) : Verb; terminating abruptly by having or as if having an end or point cut off; verb make shorter as if by cutting off; approximate by ignoring all terms beyond a chosen one;
  Other Meaning(s) : Verb; replace a corner by a plane
  Synonyms : prune

Undoubtedly a war is **abominable** and leaves behind misery, pain , loss and bad memories. **Ironically**, wars in general and the second world war in particular **sired** a number of inventions, developments and discoveries.

One does not go to the extent of **opining** that wars are good but they do provide a motivating atmosphere as well as **wherewithal** for ground breaking research.

Whether in science, technology, medicine or communications, the original objective behind the research was certainly to feed the war machinery and make it more efficient and deadly. Nevertheless the new inventions kept being used after the war, and underwent **improvisations** and developments which made the life of mankind happier and healthier.

Most of the Research and Development in wartime had to be done **covertly,** the enemy spies were always a threat.

Penicillin invented by Howard Florey & Ernst Chain as a "practical" antibiotic, might be rated as the number one invention as it saved lives not only during the war but continues to **ameliorate** lives of people globally.

Several pioneers developed early versions of dialysis machines during World War II when many injured soldiers and civilians were **inflicted** kidney damage and died. In 1937, a young Dutch physician, *Willem Kolff*, working in Groningen, Holland, had already put together a **rudimentary** dialyzing machine and worked to refine it. After the Germans occupied the Netherlands in 1941, Kolff moved to Kampen where, in spite of wartime shortages, he constructed a dialysis machine using cellophane tubing and beer cans

During the pressures of world war I, Germany developed synthetic rubber of industrial variety, this became a spring board for further developments of **elastomers** all over the world. During second world war when Japan occupied Malaysia and **impeded** the sourcing of natural rubber to the allies, more **finesse** got added to synthetic rubber in America.

The biggest problem with war is that it tends to put holes in people, thus encouraging blood to take a scenic flow through places it's not supposed to visit. During World War I, a cotton shortage made the bandaging of bleeding soldiers a pain in the neck. At that time, Kimberly-Clark was a paper mill company that realized you could do more with wood pulp besides just make it into paper. In fact, if you prepared the right combination of pulp, you could get a material that was five times more absorbent than cotton, yet significantly cheaper to produce. Kimberly-Clark named their newly discovered material **cellucotton** and the Allied Forces were on it like white on rice. It turned out those super absorbent bandages worked really well as disposable sanitary napkins, something that was not readily available to women at that point. So once the war ended, Kimberly-Clark packaged cellucotton as feminine hygiene products and was hailed as the **savior** of women everywhere.

And, there's Walter "Fred" Morrison. Fred, like most other college kids in the 1930s, spent a great deal of time throwing around pie pans from the Frisbie Baking Company. But it wasn't until he joined the Air Force that he learned about aerodynamics and he realized he was doing science during those pan-flinging sessions. So, Fred took what he learned about basic aerodynamics from the Air Force and made a prototype of a better flying disc, that didn't have bits of pie crust stuck to it. And instead of tin, he went with plastic. He dubbed his creation the "Pluto Platter," which was ultimately renamed the "Frisbee" and went on to provide hard core leaping motivation for extreme college kids everywhere.

During WWI, When Japan cut off the West from their silk, life became a **hazard** for American women. Dupont, put the best chemists of the day to work on synthetic polymers to replace the silk and what they came up with was Nylon. Nylon was stronger than silk, but the war effort really needed all of America's nylon for Parachutes, Tires and Flak Vests. Once the war was over, the women got an improved variety of Nylon to wear.

Its natural for wars to invent and improvise on weapons of destruction, like Ballistic Missiles, Atomic Weapons, Norden bomb sights, Owen sub machine guns, but these would hardly qualify as "gifts"! An exception could be the Jet Aircraft engine which makes travel so easy.

The famous Mark I, was the world's first electro mechanical computer and was used during World War 2 by the U.S. Navy. In comparison to 20th-century systems, it could be likened to a battleship in size!

The need for communication between the homelands and many far-flung theatres of war gave rise to the need for improved long-range overseas communication systems.

High-powered mobile radio sets and Radio relay **telephony** became common at division and regimental level during the WWII.

Television - had its start in the war as a screen with a camera. Transistors, Hundreds of medical equipment, tools and medicines, Nuclear Energy, Nuclear Medicine, Heart transplants and many other transplants, mechanical hearts, hydrogen peroxide, tools that run on battery power, portable gasoline container, small disposable batteries and radar all are gifted to mankind by the second World-War.

No wonder the phrase "war footing" is in common **parlance** whenever some work is being done on a mission critical priority, on a large scale , with big budgets and above all with a "killer" instinct ! The **saturnine** clouds of war do have a silver lining.

✎ Abominable

Contextual Meaning(s) : Adjective; unequivocally detestable; exceptionally bad or displeasing
Synonyms : detestable, execrable

✎ Ameliorate

Contextual Meaning(s) : Verb; to improve the condition or allay the damage of something or someone
Synonyms : amend

✎ Cellucotton

Contextual Meaning(s) : noun; used for a soft absorbent creped cellulose used in surgical dressings
Synonyms : nitrocotton, pyrocotton

✎ Covert

Contextual Meaning(s) : Adjective; not openly acknowledged or displayed
Synonyms : secret, stealthy

✎ Elastomers

Contextual Meaning(s) : noun; a natural material such as rubber or synthetic material such as polyvinyl that has elastic properties
Synonyms : ulsters

✎ Espionage

Contextual Meaning(s) : Noun; the systematic use of spies to get military or political secrets
Synonyms : spying

✎ Fecund

Contextual Meaning(s) : Adjective; capable of producing offspring or vegetation; intellectually productive
Synonyms : fertile

✎ Finesse

Contextual Meaning(s) : Noun; subtly skillful handling of a situation
Synonyms : finish

✎ Hazard

Contextual Meaning(s) : Noun; an obstacle on a golf course; a source of danger; a possibility of incurring loss or misfortune; an unknown and unpredictable phenomenon that causes an event to result one way rather than another;
Other Meaning(s) : Verb; put forward, of a guess, in spite of possible refutation; take a risk in the hope of a favorable outcome; put at risk
Synonyms : jeopardy, peril

✎ Ironically

Contextual Meaning(s) : Adverb; not according to what is logically expected
Synonyms : wryly

✎ Improvisations

Contextual Meaning(s) : Noun; unplanned expedients; creations spoken or written or composed extemporaneously (without prior preparation
Other Meaning(s) : performances given extempore without planning or preparation
Synonyms : extemporizations

✎ Inflicted

Contextual Meaning(s) : Verb; caused pain or suffering or misery to
Synonyms : wreaked

✎ Impeded

Contextual Meaning(s) : Adjective; made difficult or slow
Synonyms : occlude, block

✎ Lethal

Contextual Meaning(s) : Adjective; of an instrument of certain death
Synonyms : baleful

✎ Opining

Contextual Meaning(s) : Verb; expressing one's opinion or views
Synonyms : animadverting

- *Parlance*
  Contextual Meaning(s) : Noun; a manner of speaking that is natural to native speakers of a language
  Synonyms : idiom

- *Rudimentary*
  Contextual Meaning(s) : Adjective; being in the earliest stages of development;
  Other Meaning(s) : Adjective; not fully developed in mature animals; being or involving basic facts or principles
  Synonyms : elementary

- *Sired*
  Contextual Meaning(s) : Verb; produces, gave birth to, became parent of
  Synonyms : begot

- *Stroll*
  Contextual Meaning(s) : Noun; a leisurely walk (usually in some public place); (other) verb walk leisurely and with no apparent aim
  Synonyms : amble, perambulation

- *Savior*
  Contextual Meaning(s) : Noun; a person who rescues you from harm or danger; (other) a teacher and prophet born in Bethlehem and active in Nazareth; his life and sermons form the basis for Christianity (circa 4 BC - AD 29)
  Synonyms : Redeemer, Deliverer

- *Saturnine*
  Contextual Meaning(s) : Adjective; something which is dark or sullen or gloomy
  Synonyms : morose, doleful

- *Telephony*
  Contextual Meaning(s) : noun; the science, technology, or system of communication by telephone
  Synonyms : telephone system

- *Wherewithal*
  Contextual Meaning(s) : Noun; the necessary means (especially financial means)
  Synonyms : means

CELEBRATING THEIR WAY TO THE BANKS

Ever since Lux launched its advertisements in 1930s, screen Divas Marilyn Monroe, Sophia Loren, Natalie Wood, Brigitte Bardot, Demi Moore, Catherine Zeta-Jones, Sarah Jessica Parker and Aishwarya Rai ,to **enumerate** a few, have featured in them, **extolling** the benefits of its soap.

Top celebrities, and even the **trivial** ones, receive truckloads of cash for this. Justin Timberlake got £3.4m for his 'I'm Lovin' It' one liner for McDonalds.

Venus Williams, Wimbledon champion , at a stage signed a five-year $40 million contract with sportswear manufacturer Reebok International Inc.

In 2000, Tiger Woods renegotiated a five-year contract estimated at $125 million with Nike for their Golf balls.

Celebrity endorsements have been the **bedrock** of Pepsi as well as arch rival coke's advertising.

Indian cricket God Sachin Tendulkar is **ebullient** after getting his Pepsi, **perked** up by Boost, **exudes** pride for his Fiat Palio car, **groovy** about his TVS victor scooter, finds Colgate Total toothpaste **prophylactic**, regularly **ingests** Britannia Biscuits, **swears** on Visa credit cards, **coaxes** us to use Airtel mobile , and we are still counting.

Bollywood superstar Shahrukh khan's product promotion deals run parallel to Sachin's, they have even appeared for Pepsi commercials together. Not to be outdone, Coke has been using Shahrukh's **puckish** rival Aamir Khan for its ads.

Super **sleuth** James bond played by actor Pierce Brosnan is **enamored** by Omega watches, BMW, and Noreico.

All the money and publicity for a comparatively **minuscule** amount of **toil** !

Approximately 20% of all television commercials feature famous people. The basic idea behind celebrity endorsement of a brand remains to cash on the **hero-worship, credibility** and mass appeal of the celebrities which is expected to help **hoist** awareness of the brand, reinforce the image of the brand , and ultimately **inveigle** the buyers to choose the brand over others.

Celebrities can bring a much needed human angle, especially to fairly 'cold' products like razors or '**chore**' jobs like shopping. A brand that got it right here would be Gillette and its partnership with David Beckham. A **mundane** daily task for millions of men was transformed into an important **grooming** process associated with the self control, success and **precision** of a top footballer.

On a more charitable side, Live Aid, a mega rock and pop concert was held simultaneously in US and UK in 1984 ,which first **harnessed** the power of celebrity on a mass scale to highlight the need to help the Ethopian famine cause. Most celebrities have nowadays adopted their own pet cause and support some NGO or aid agency.

Sometimes things go wrong, too.

Sainsbury's encountered a problem with Hollywood **diva** Catherina Zeta Jones. She was endorsing their **recipe** , while actually she was found **slyly** shopping at their rival super-store Tesco. A similar case happened with Britney Spears who endorsed one cola brand and was repeatedly **snitched** drinking another brand of cola .

Pepsi Cola's suffered when its endorsers - Mike Tyson, Madonna, Michael Jackson and Shane Warne, all were **tarnished** for something or other. Warne **doping** controversy occurred bang in the middle of the Cricket World Cup 2003 and Pepsico found itself on an uneasy wicket. And Naomi Campbell was blamed of **turpitude** doing an anti-fur ad, and later wearing fur in a product ad.

Rocker Bruce Springsteen famously **objurgated** the requests to use his song "Born in the U.S.A." in commercials for Chrysler cars, turning down an offer worth several million dollars during the 80s. He felt he owed to his song writing and music a sacred **fidelity**, much above monetary considerations. Sadly that breed of **luminaries** is rare in today's world of **fickle** and **fragile** stardom!

🔖 **Allegiance**

Contextual Meaning(s) : Noun; the act of binding yourself (intellectually or emotionally) to a course of action

Other Meaning(s) : noun the loyalty that citizens owe to their country (or subjects to their sovereign);

Synonyms : fealty, commitment, loyalty, dedication

🔖 **Bedrock**

Contextual Meaning(s) : Noun; a foundation for any strategy

Other Meaning(s) : noun solid unweathered rock lying beneath surface deposits of soil; principles from which other truths can be derived

Synonyms : foundation

🔖 **Buttress**

Contextual Meaning(s) : Verb make stronger or defensible;

Other Meaning(s) : noun a support usually of stone or brick; supports the wall of a building; reinforce with a buttress

Synonyms : buttressing

🔖 **Chore**

Contextual Meaning(s) : Noun a specific piece of work required to be done as a duty or for a specific fee

Synonyms : job, task

🔖 **Coaxes**

Contextual Meaning(s) : Verb; to persuade diligently

Synonyms : palavers

🔖 **Credibility**

Contextual Meaning(s) : Noun the quality of being believable or trustworthy

Synonyms : credibleness, believability

🔖 **Diva**

Contextual Meaning(s) : Noun a distinguished female operatic singer; a female operatic movie or popstar

Synonyms : prima donna

🔖 **Doping**

Contextual Meaning(s) : noun; an act or instance of giving a narcotic, usually a steroid, to an athlete to unfairly boost performance in a competition

Synonyms : addictive drugs

🔖 **Ebullient**

Contextual Meaning(s) : Adjective; joyously unrestrained

Synonyms : exuberant

🔖 **Enamored**

Contextual Meaning(s) : Adjective; marked by foolish or unreasoning fondness

Synonyms : crazy, dotty, gaga, infatuated, in love, smitten, soft on, taken with

🔖 **Enumerate**

Contextual Meaning(s) : Verb specify individually; determine the number or amount of

Synonyms : count

🔖 **Extolling**

Contextual Meaning(s) : Verb; praising the nature of something or someone

Synonyms : exalt

🔖 **Exudes**

Contextual Meaning(s) : Verb; make apparent by one's mood or behaviour

Synonyms : transmits

🔖 **Fickle**

Contextual Meaning(s) : Adjective; changing frequently, especially as regards of one's loyalties or affections.

Synonyms : volatile, variable

🐦 **Fidelity**

Contextual Meaning(s) : Noun; the quality of being faithful
Other Meaning(s) : accuracy with which an electronic system reproduces the sound or image of its input signal
Synonyms : dedication

🐦 **Fragile**

Contextual Meaning(s) : Adjective; vulnerably delicate; easily broken or damaged or destroyed; lacking solidity or strength and liable to break
Synonyms : delicate, frail, flimsy

🐦 **Grooming**

Contextual Meaning(s) : Noun; the activity of getting dressed; putting on clothes;
Synonyms : dressing, training, preparation

🐦 **Groovy**

Contextual Meaning(s) : Adjective; (British informal) very chic; very good
Synonyms : swagger, bang-up, bully, corking, cracking, dandy, great, keen, neat, nifty, not bad, peachy, slap-up, swell, smashing

🐦 **Harnessed**

Contextual Meaning(s) : Adjective; brought under control and put to use
Synonyms : exploit, convert

🐦 **Hoist**

Other Meaning(s) : noun lifting device for raising heavy or cumbersome objects; verb raise or haul up with or as if with mechanical help; verb; move from one place to another by lifting
Synonyms : lift, wind

🐦 **Hero-worship**

Contextual Meaning(s) : noun; great admiration for somebody, especially if it borders on the excessive*
Synonyms : admiration, idealization

🐦 **Ingests**

Contextual Meaning(s) : Verb; to eat or devour something*
Synonyms : consume

🐦 **Inveigle**

Contextual Meaning(s) : Verb influence or urge by gentle urging, caressing, or flattering
Synonyms : wheedle, cajole, palaver, blarney, coax, sweet-talk

🐦 **Luminaries**

Contextual Meaning(s) : Noun, people of eminence or fame
Synonyms : celebrities

🐦 **Minuscule**

Contextual Meaning(s) : Adjective; very small
Other Meaning(s) : adjective of or relating to a small cursive script during 7th to 9th centuries; used in medieval manuscripts; the characters that were once kept in bottom half of a compositor's type case
Synonyms : miniscule, minuscular, small letter, lowercase, lower-case letter, little, small

🐦 **Mundane**

Contextual Meaning(s) : Adjective; lacking interest or excitement.
Synonyms : dull, boring

🐦 **Objurgated**

Contextual Meaning(s) : Verb; to express strong disapproval of
Synonyms : chastened, excoriated

🐦 **Perked**

Contextual Meaning(s) : Verb; to get energised, motivated.
Synonyms : energised

🐦 **Precision**

Contextual Meaning(s) : noun the state of being accurate or consistent
Synonyms : preciseness

🐦 **Prophylactic**

Contextual Meaning(s) : Adjective; preventing or contributing to the prevention of disease; tending to ward off; noun remedy that prevents or slows the course of an illness or disease

Other Meaning(s) : adjective; capable of preventing conception or impregnation; *Synonyms* : salubrious, preventive.

☙ **Puckish**
Contextual Meaning(s) : Adjective; naughtily or annoyingly playful
Synonyms : impish, mischievous,

☙ **Recipe**
Contextual Meaning(s) : Noun; directions for making something manually, a dish
Synonyms : formula

☙ **Sleuth**
Contextual Meaning(s) : Noun; a detective who follows a trail;
Synonyms : stag, snoop

☙ **Slyly**
Contextual Meaning(s) : Adverb; in an artful manner using deception
Synonyms : craftily, cunningly, foxily, knavishly, trickily, artfully

☙ **Snitched**
Contextual Meaning(s) : Verb; reported a misdeed to authorities
Synonyms : informed

☙ **Swears**
Contextual Meaning(s) : Verb; to have faith or confidence in (succeeded with 'by')
Synonyms : vows

☙ **Tarnished**
Contextual Meaning(s) : Adjective; tainting, especially of reputation
Synonyms : besmirched, sullied

☙ **Toil**
Contextual Meaning(s) : Noun productive work (especially physical work done for wages);
Synonyms : travail, grind, drudge

☙ **Trivial**
Contextual Meaning(s) : Adjective; obvious and dull; concerned with trivialities; not large enough to consider or notice; (informal) small and of little importance; of little substance or significance
Synonyms : picayune

☙ **Turpitude**
Contextual Meaning(s) : Noun; a corrupt or depraved or degenerate act or practice
Synonyms : depravity

THE GLASS CEILING

Women's rise in corporate leadership is said to be **trampled** by a discriminatory "glass ceiling. Infact almost all disciplines of work are **fraught** with issues that **throttle** a female's **ascendency** to the **apex** .

The term *glass ceiling* refers to "the unseen, yet unreachable **impediment** that keeps minorities and women from rising to the upper **echelons** of the corporate ladder, regardless of their qualifications or achievements." Initially, the metaphor applied to barriers in the careers of women but was quickly extended to refer to **ramparts** hindering the advancement of minority men, as well. Moreover besides corporates, other careers like bureaucracy, police, army and politics - almost all hierarchical structures have a **pejorative** view of women at top. The **dogma** continues to be the cause of **disillusionment** of capable women .

It is a **ceaseless** theme in work that women worry **fervently** about being **constrained** in their career progress because they are females. These women **hypothesize** about how they might be perceived, whether they are being taken seriously or **frivolously**, rather than spend the energy doing a great job. The **irony** is that usually they are very **uptight** about this even before anything negative has happened. This can **manifest** itself in **acrimony** and suspicion that grows if unchecked, until eventually they become less **efficacious** in their professional roles and find themselves dropping behind their peer group on the career ladder. A painful example of the self-fulfilling **prophecy** at work!

As a **rookie** 20-year old **recounts** : " Myself stepping foot onto a trading floor for the first time many years ago, I remember **bracing** myself for a bombardment of comments about blonde hair correlating with intellect and a daily **critique** on my wardrobe. Did it happen? Of course, but equally the **alpha** males who stepped onto that same trading floor with me were **sneered** at as being too fat, too thin, too posh, too geeky or too **garish**. In short, we were identified by our most obvious **delineating** factor, which in my case was that I was a blonde girl, and that formed the basis for comments intended to engage the floor. The important point is that the comments were not made because I was a girl, but because I had chosen to work in an environment where **banter** is as certain as lots of computer screens and anyone looking for a **cosseted** working environment simply shouldn't choose that one".

Women should celebrate their natural ability to multi task, their high EQ and their **plethora** of choices and stop being **queasy** about a glass ceiling until they hit it. One can't imagine that Margaret Thatcher spent a lot of time **cogitating** how far she could go, she simply got on with the job in hand. Likewise, the Body Shop's Anita Roddick, Lastminute.com's Martha Lane Fox and Ultimo's chief executive Michelle Mone have all believed that they could do it rather than hesitating that a glass ceiling might **impede** them. Indra Nooyi, CEO of PepsiCo, **erstwhile** U.S. Secretary of State Condoleeza Rice and first female 4-star general, Ann E. Dunwoody of U.S. Army also rose to the top , probably an **anomaly.**

It is a **lamentable** fact that often it is women themselves who **bridle** their female peers. I know of high-powered female professionals who would remove expensive jewellery or 'dress down' before a **pitch** with female clients for fear of being too threatening. Some of the worst workplace bullying starts in ladies toilets and continues with a round of **noxious** chinese whispers aimed at an unlucky colleague. Even worse, the media still enjoy to stereotype women according to their looks.

The women who succeed are those who choose to focus on the opportunities not the obstacles. They put their **vigor** into what they can achieve and not into considering what they cannot. They earn **laudation** and are taken seriously because they perform well.

Bollywood's *Vidya Balan* should make a great role model for women at work, especially the way she is earning **encomiums** for making superb movies around a female **protagonist** who doesn't need any **underpinning** from male stars. These movies have won over the classes as well as the masses !

👁 ***Acrimony***

Contextual Meaning(s) : Noun; a rough and bitter relationship
Synonyms : bitterness, acerbity, jaundice, tartness, thorniness

👁 ***Anomaly***

Contextual Meaning(s) : Something that deviates from what is normal or standard
Synonyms : exception, oddity

👁 ***Apex***

Contextual Meaning(s) : Noun; the highest point (of something)
Other Meaning(s) : noun the point on the celestial sphere toward which the sun and solar system appear to be moving relative to the fixed tars;
Synonyms : solar apex, apex of the sun's way, vertex, peak, acme

👁 ***Ascendency***

Contextual Meaning(s) : Noun the state that exists when one person or group has power over another
Synonyms : dominance, ascendance, ascendence, ascendancy, control

👁 ***Alpha***

Contextual Meaning(s) : adjective; first in order of importance; e.g. the alpha male in the group of chimpanzees
Other Meaning(s) : noun; the first letter of Greek alphabet, the brightest star or main star in a constellation; e.g. Alpha Centauri

👁 ***Banter***

Contextual Meaning(s) : Noun; light teasing repartee;
Other Meaning(s) : Verb; be silly or tease one another
Synonyms : gossip, chaff

👁 ***Bridle***

Contextual Meaning(s) : Verb; to restrain or limit somebody's progress or powers
Other Meaning(s) : Noun; headgear for a horse to give the rider control.
Synonyms : check, curb

👁 ***Bracing***

Contextual Meaning(s) : verb; making you feel refreshed or invigorated, e.g. a bracing cold shower
Other Meaning(s) : Noun; braces supporting something, a system of braces that are used to support or strengthen a structure
Synonyms : invigorating, refreshing

👁 ***Cogitating***

Contextual Meaning(s) : Verb; consider carefully and deeply, reflect upon.
Synonyms : cerebrating, thinking

👁 ***Constrained***

Contextual Meaning(s) : under a restraint
Other Meaning(s) : Adjective; lacking spontaneity; not natural
Synonyms : encumbered

👁 ***Cosseted***

Contextual Meaning(s) : Verb; treat with excessive indulgence
Synonyms : mollycoddled, pampered

👁 ***Critique***

Contextual Meaning(s) : noun; a serious examination and judgment of something
Other Meaning(s) : Noun; a written or broadcast assessment of something, usually a creative work, with comments on its good and bad qualities
Synonyms : review

👁 ***Ceaseless***

Contextual Meaning(s) : adjective; repeated in action, full of or involving repetition; e.g. a boring repetitive task
Synonyms : recurring, cyclical

👁 ***Disillusionment***

Contextual Meaning(s) : Noun: freeing from false belief or illusions, a state of disaperintment
Synonyms : disenchantment, disillusion

👁 ***Dogma***

Contextual Meaning(s) : Noun: a doctrine or code of beliefs accepted as authoritative; a religious doctrine that is proclaimed as true without proof
Synonyms : tenet

- **Delineating**
  Contextual Meaning(s) : Noun; defining
  Other Meaning(s) : Verb; to describe or explain something in detail, to sketch or draw something in outline
  Synonyms : describe with precision

- **Echelons**
  Contextual Meaning(s) : Noun; bodies of troops arranged in a line.
  Other Meaning(s) : Noun; a diffraction grating consisting of a pile of plates of equal thickness arranged stepwise with a constant offset
  Synonyms : garrisons, regiments

- **Efficacious**
  Contextual Meaning(s) : Adjective: marked by qualities giving the power to produce an intended effect; producing or capable of producing an intended result or having a striking effect
  Synonyms : effective, effectual

- **Encomiums**
  Contextual Meaning(s) : Noun; a formal expression of praise
  Synonyms : paeans, panegyrics

- **Erstwhile**
  Contextual Meaning(s) : adjective; formerly holding a particular position or relationship; e.g. Since leaving the bank, she has been ostracized by her erstwhile colleagues.
  Synonyms : previous, former

- **Fervently**
  Contextual Meaning(s) : Adverb; with passionate fervor
  Synonyms : fierily, fervidly

- **Fraught**
  Contextual Meaning(s) : Adjective; filled with or attended with; marked by distress
  Synonyms : pregnant

- **Frivolously**
  Contextual Meaning(s) : Adverb; in a casual manner
  Synonyms : farivolous

- **Garish**
  Contextual Meaning(s) : Adjective; tastelessly showy
  Synonyms : ostentatious, gaudy

- **Hypothesize**
  Contextual Meaning(s) : Verb; to believe especially on uncertain or tentative grounds
  Synonyms : speculate, theorize, theorise, conjecture, hypothesise, hypothecate, suppose

- **Irony**
  Contextual Meaning(s) : Noun: incongruity between what might be expected and what actually occurs;
  Other Meaning(s) : a trope that involves incongruity between what is expected and what occurs; witty language used to convey insults or scorn
  Synonyms : sarcasm, satire, caustic remark

- **Impede**
  Contextual Meaning(s) : Verb; to interfere with the movement, progress, or development of something or somebody
  Synonyms : obstruct, hinder

- **Impediment**
  Contextual Meaning(s) : noun; something that hinders progress, an impairment, especially one affecting speech
  Synonyms : obstruction, obstacle

- **Lamentable**
  Contextual Meaning(s) : Adjective; bad; unfortunate
  Synonyms : distressing, pitiful

- **Laudation**
  Contextual Meaning(s) : Noun; applause or admiration for somebody
  Synonyms : appreciation

- **Manifest**
  Contextual Meaning(s) : Verb: reveal its presence or make an appearance;
  Other Meaning(s) : Noun; clearly revealed to the mind or the senses or judgment; noun a customs document listing the contents put on a hip or plane; record in a ship's manifest; provide evidence for; stand as proof of; show by one's behavior, attitude, or external attributes
  Synonyms : attest, certify, demonstrate, evidence, apparent, evident, patent, plain, unmistakable

🕭 **Noxious**
Contextual Meaning(s) : Adjective; injurious to physical or mental health
Synonyms : baneful, pernicious

🕭 **Pejorative**
Contextual Meaning(s) : Adjective; expressing disapproval
Synonyms : dyslogistic, dislogistic

🕭 **Pitch**
Contextual Meaning(s) : Verb; sell or offer for sale from place to place
Other Meaning(s) : the action or manner of throwing something; (baseball) the act of throwing a baseball by a pitcher to a batter; promotion by means of an argument and demonstration; verb set to a certain pitch; lead (a card) and establish the trump suit; hit (a golf ball) in a high arc with a backspin; erect and fasten; fall or plunge forward; set the level or character of; throw or hurl from the mound to the batter, as in baseball; throw or toss with a light motion; move abruptly; heel over; be at an angle
Synonyms : promote

🕭 **Plethora**
Contextual Meaning(s) : Noun; a large or excessive amount of something
Synonyms : abundance, plenty

🕭 **Prophecy**
Contextual Meaning(s) : Noun: knowledge of the future (usually said to be obtained from a divine source); a prediction uttered under divine inspiration
Synonyms : prognostication, vaticination, divination

🕭 **Protagonist**
Contextual Meaning(s) : Noun; the most important character in a novel, play, story, or other literary work
Synonyms : main character, hero, leading role

🕭 **Queasy**
Contextual Meaning(s) : Adjective; causing or fraught with or showing anxiety
Synonyms : anxious, uneasy

🕭 **Ramparts**
Contextual Meaning(s) : Noun; walls meant for blocking
Synonyms : fortifications

🕭 **Recounts**
Contextual Meaning(s) : Verb; narrate or give a detailed account of
Synonyms : recites

🕭 **Rookie**
Contextual Meaning(s) : Noun; an awkward and inexperienced youth
Synonyms : beginner, greenhorn

🕭 **Vigour**
Contextual Meaning(s) : Noun; great physical or mental strength and energy, intensity or forcefulness in the way something is done
Synonyms : energy, dynamism, vitality, force

🕭 **Sneered**
Contextual Meaning(s) : Verb; smile contemptuously; express through a scornful smile
Other Meaning(s) : Noun; a facial expression of contempt or scorn; the upper lip curls; a contemptuous or scornful remark
Synonyms : leers

🕭 **Throttle**
Contextual Meaning(s) : Noun; place limits on (extent or access);
Other Meaning(s) : Verb; kill by squeezing the throat of so as to cut off the air noun a valve that regulates the supply of fuel to the engine; a pedal that controls the throttle valve; verb reduce the air supply;
Synonyms : choke, restrict, restrain, trammel

🕭 **Trampled**
Contextual Meaning(s) : Adjective; crushed or broken by being stepped upon heavily
Synonyms : trodden

🕭 **Underpining**
Contextual Meaning(s) : Verb; supporting from beneath; supporting with evidence or authority or making more certain or confirm
Synonyms : buttressing, bolstering

🕭 **Uptight**
Contextual Meaning(s) : Adjective; being in a tense state
Synonyms : jittery, jumpy, nervy, overstrung, restive

Leapfrogging involves adopting a new technology directly, and skipping over the earlier, **middling** versions that **predated** it. This is **epitomized** by the sudden **proliferation** of mobile phones in the developing world. Fixed-line networks were poor or non-existent in many developing countries because these required a **titanic** infrastructure, so the telecom companies there have leapfrogged straight to mobile phones, instead. The number of mobile phones now far outnumbers the number of fixed-line telephones in China, India and sub-Saharan Africa. By their very nature, mobile networks are far easier, faster and cheaper to **deploy** than fixed-line networks.

Incandescent light bulbs, introduced in the late 1870s, are slowly being displaced in the developed world by more energy-efficient light-emitting **diodes** (LEDs), in applications from traffic lights to domestic lighting. LEDs could, however, have an even greater **efficacy** in parts of the developing world that lack mains power and electric lighting altogether. LEDs' greater energy efficiency makes it possible to run them **nocturnally** from batteries charged by solar panels **diurnally.** So there is the prospect of another leapfrog, as the rural poor skip over centralised electric grids and straight to a world of energy-efficient appliances run using local "micropower" energy sources. Other leapfrogs include the embrace by China and Brazil of open-source software, and China's plan to build a series of "eco-cities" from scratch based on new green technologies.

Being behind the *bleeding edge* of technological development can nowadays, actually be a good thing! It means that early versions of a technology, which have been **erratic**, unreliable or otherwise inferior, can be avoided. America, for example, was the first country to adopt colour television, which explains why American Television Sets look **stagnated** : consumers won't keep on buying newer models every now and then. Other countries that came to the technology later, had to **adapt** to an advanced **paradigm** in TVs, and **ensuant** to this one could see more sophisticated TVs in these countries .

It's believed that people all over the world that have never owned a PC might get their first computer in the form of a handheld. Why not? A consumer priced smartphone today has as much computing power as any PC did five years ago. But instead of a huge desktop box you have a smartphone you can slip into your pocket.

Leapfrog technologies can also spread faster, because within the designing company they do not face **pugnacity** from the managers of the **entrenched** systems. And leapfrogging straight to a green technology means there is no need to dispose of the **obsolete**, **sullied** one. By the time Chinese consumers started buying fridges in large numbers, for example, refrigeration technology no longer depended on ozone-destroying CFCs.

The lesson to be drawn from all of this is that it is wrong to assume that developing countries will follow the same technological course as developed nations. Some parts of the world may skip the desktop computers in favour of portable devices, just like an entire generation never saw a typewriter. Entire economies may even spring from **agrarian** straight to high-tech industries. That is what happened in Israel, which went from citrus farming to microchips; India, similarly, is doing its best to jump straight to a high-tech service economy. Its **behemoth** English speaking middle class has become the envy of outsourcing industry. Rwanda even hopes to turn itself into an African tech hub.

Those who anticipate and **advocate** leapfrogging can **thrive** as a result. Those who fail to see it coming, risk becoming **antiquated**. Kodak, for example, hit by the sudden rise of digital cameras in the developed world, wrongly assumed that it would still be able to sell old-fashioned film and film cameras in China instead. But the emerging Chinese middle classes leapfrogged straight to digital cameras—and even those are now outnumbered by camera-phones.

The very infrastructure that enabled American merchants to accept credit cards before any other place in the world, has now become an **albatross**; other countries that never developed one have now leapfrogged directly to cell phones as the payment device. Its like the need to run new trains on the old tracks. If one starts with a clean slate, it is beautiful. That's why Toyota and other carmakers are killing American and European cars , they don't have the legacy cost.

Mobile Operators who haven't made the jump from 2G to 3G could benefit from early 4G adoption as a leap-frog strategy, thus providing significant performance enhancements for data services. Thus they can **obviate** entire time, energy and resources of commissioning 3G services and **reap** a **harvest** from the state of the art 4G services.

✉ **Adapt**

Contextual Meaning(s) : Verb; make fit for, or change to suit a new purpose; adapt or conform oneself to new or different conditions

Synonyms : adjust

✉ **Advocate**

Contextual Meaning(s) : Verb; speak, plead, or argue in favour of; push for something

Other Meaning(s) : noun a person who pleads for a cause or propounds an idea; a lawyer who pleads cases in court;

Synonyms : exponent, counsel, counselor, counsellor, counselor-at-law, pleader, preach, recommend, urge

✉ **Agrarian**

Contextual Meaning(s) : Adjective; relating to rural matters

Synonyms : agricultural, farming

✉ **Albatross**

Contextual Meaning(s) : Noun; something that hinders or handicaps

Other Meaning(s) : noun large web-footed birds of the southern hemisphere having long narrow wings; noted for powerful gliding flight; (figurative)

Synonyms : mollymawk, millstone

✉ **Antiquted**

Contextual Meaning(s) : Adjective; something that has become out of fashion or usage

Synonyms : obsolete

✉ **Behemoth**

Contextual Meaning(s) : Noun; a person of exceptional importance and reputation; someone or something that is abnormally large and powerful

Synonyms : colossus, giant, heavyweight, titan, goliath, monster

✉ **Conform**

Contextual Meaning(s) : Verb; be similar, be in line with; adapt or conform oneself to new or different conditions

Synonyms : adjust, adapt

✉ **Deploy**

Contextual Meaning(s) : Verb; to distribute systematically or strategically

Synonyms : marshal

✉ **Descry**

Contextual Meaning(s) : Verb; catch sight of

Synonyms : spot, espy, spy

✉ **Diurnally**

Contextual Meaning(s) : Adverb; during the day time

Synonyms : day time-active

✉ **Diodes**

Contextual Meaning(s) : Noun; an electronic device that has two electrodes and is used to convert alternating current to direct current

Synonyms : electronic current converter

✉ **Efficacy**

Contextual Meaning(s) : Noun; capacity or power to produce a desired effect

Synonyms : effectiveness, potency

✉ **Ensuant**

Contextual Meaning(s) : Adverb; happening as a consequence

Synonyms : consequent

✉ **Entrenched**

Contextual Meaning(s) : Adjective; established firmly and securely;

Synonyms : implanted

✉ **Erratic**

Contextual Meaning(s) : Adjective; liable to sudden unpredictable change; likely to perform unpredictably; having no fixed course

Synonyms : mercurial, temperamental

Epitomized

Contextual Meaning(s) : Verb; to be a highly representative example of a type, class or characteristic, e.g. This incident epitomizes all that is wrong with modern society

Synonyms : exemplify

Harvest

Contextual Meaning(s) : Verb; to gain as a result of special effort.

Other Meaning(s) : Noun; the season for gathering crops; the gathering of a ripened crop; the consequence of an effort or activity; the yield from plants in a single growing season; verb remove from a culture or a living or dead body, as for the purposes of transplantation; gather, as of natural products

Synonyms : crop, reap

Leapfrogging

Contextual Meaning(s) : Verb; jumping over something

Synonyms : jumping

Middling

Contextual Meaning(s) : Adjective; lacking exceptional quality or ability

Other Meaning(s) : adverb to a moderately sufficient extent or degree; noun any commodity of intermediate quality or size (especially when coarse particles of ground wheat are mixed with bran)

Synonyms : mediocre

Nocturnally

Contextual Meaning(s) : Adverb; done during the night

Synonyms : nightly

Obsolete

Contextual Meaning(s) : Adjective; old; no longer in use or valid or fashionable; no longer in use

Synonyms : superannuated, disused

Obviate

Contextual Meaning(s) : Verb; make something unnecessary.

Synonyms : deflect, avert

Paradigm

Contextual Meaning(s) : Noun; the generally accepted perspective of a particular discipline at a given time; a standard or typical example;

Other Meaning(s) : systematic arrangement of all the inflected forms of a word; the class of all items that can be substituted into the same position (or slot) in a grammatical sentence (are in paradigmatic relation with one another)

Synonyms : prototype, image

Paradoxically

Contextual Meaning(s) : Adverb; in an illogical manner

Synonyms : contradictorily

Predated

Contextual Meaning(s) : Verb; happened before something else

Synonyms : preceded

Proliferation

Contextual Meaning(s) : Noun; production in massive quantities

Synonyms : escalation

Pugnacity

Contextual Meaning(s) : Adjective; noun a natural disposition to be hostile

Synonyms : aggressiveness, belligerence

Reap

Contextual Meaning(s) : Verb; gather, as of natural products; get or derive

Synonyms : harvest, glean, draw

Stagnated

Contextual Meaning(s) : Verb; stand still; be idle; exist in a changeless situation

Other Meaning(s) : cease to flow; stand without moving; cause to stagnate

Synonyms : idle, laze

❰ *Sullied*

Contextual Meaning(s) : Adjective; dirty or stained
Synonyms : besmirched, stained, tainted

❰ *Thrive*

Contextual Meaning(s) : Adjective; verb gain in wealth; grow stronger
Synonyms : prosper, fly high, flourish, boom, get ahead, expand

❰ *Titanic*

Contextual Meaning(s) : Adjective; of great force or power or size
Other Meaning(s) : consisting of or forming human or animal figures
Synonyms :

❰ *Unwieldy*

Contextual Meaning(s) : Adjective; difficult to work or manipulate; difficult to use or handle or manage because of size or weight or shape; lacking grace in movement or posture
Other Meaning(s) : consisting of or forming human or animal figures
Synonyms : unmanageable, gawky, clumsy, clunky, ungainly

SHOPAHOLISM

Omniomania, or compulsive shopping is perhaps the most socially acceptable and an apparently **serene** behavior but can still be **blustery** and can secretly **impair** one's personal and family life.

Social acceptance happens because, for all we know the shopper might be shopping for a wedding, festival or any other special occasion; it's only the shopper or her nearest friends and family members know that this is a behavioral **anomaly** and requires attention.

We are surrounded by **piquant** advertising, telling us that buying will make us happy. We are **prodded** by politicians to spend as a way of giving economy a **fillip**. And we all long for what those around us have – consumerism has become the **motif** of our social life.

Although widespread **consumerism** has **escalated** in recent years, the shopping addiction is not a new **malaise**. It was recognized as far back as the early nineteenth century, and was **cited** as a psychiatric disorder in the early twentieth century.

Almost everyone shops to some degree, but only about 6% of the general population is thought to have a shopping addiction. **Incipient** in the late teens and early adulthood, shopping addiction often co-occurs with other disorders, including mood and anxiety disorders, substance use disorders, eating disorders, other **impulse** control disorders, and personality disorders.

So what makes the difference between normal shopping, occasional **splurges**, and **shopaholism** ? As with all addictions, shopping becomes the person's main way of **grappling** with stress, to the point where she continues to shop excessively even when it is **vitiating** many areas of her life. Even as finances and relationships are damaged, the shopping addict feels unable to stop her **binges**.

Like other behavioral addictions, shopping addiction is a **disputatious** idea. Many experts find the idea that excessive spending can be an addiction, rather **incredulous**. They believe that addiction has to be to a chemical substance which produces " feel good " symptoms such as a mood change and personality transformation. Likewise, a with-drawl of the substance from the addict's system would lead to reduction of these enzymes and the **upshot** would be a depression and anxiety in him.

There are several characteristics that shopping addiction shares with other addictions. As with other addictions, shopping addicts become preoccupied with , and devote significant time and riches to the activity. Actual spending is important to the process of shopping addiction; window shopping does not constitute an addiction, just like an alcoholic will not get **inebriated** just by looking at wine bottles. But he will certainly crave a drink.

Growing number of online shopping sites add another reason for excessive shopping. They influence them to shop more and more as it is easy sitting at home, economical, accessible from anywhere and incurs less expenses as well. Online shopping sites provide them an insight into a world where everything is just one click away and available under one roof.

As with other addictions, shopaholism is highly **ritualized** and follows a typical pattern of thoughts about shopping, planning shopping trips, and the shopping act itself, often described as pleasurable even, **ecstatic.** It **elevates** the mood of the shopper and provides relief from negative feelings. However ,often after reaching home the shopper crashes with feelings of disappointment, particularly with the herself, and **bemoans** the damage to her bank balance. Other symptoms that occur are almost parallel to any addict. She will **wallow** in **compunction,** may have to face the **wrath** of her spouse, and would definitely make promises never to **relapse.**

The **profligate** shopper uses shopping as a way of escaping negative feelings, such as depression, anxiety, boredom, self-critical thoughts, and anger. Unfortunately, the escape is **momentary**. The purchases are often simply **hoarded**, unused, and **compulsive** shoppers will then begin to plan the next spending **spree**. Most shop alone, although some shop with others who enjoy it. Generally, it will lead to embarrassment to shop with people who don't share this type of enthusiasm for shopping. Which is a waste of time money and energy.

Research indicates that around three-quarters of compulsive shoppers are willing to admit their shopping is problematic, particularly in areas of finances and relationships. Of course, this may reflect the zeal of those who participate in research to admit to having problems. Fortunately, although not yet well-researched, compulsive shopping does appear to respond well to a range of treatments, including medication, self help books, self help groups, financial counseling, etc. It should be noted, however, that although some medication shows promise, results are mixed. Hence it should not be considered a sole or reliable treatment. Like coming out from other addictions, shopaholics too go through a cycle of recovery and **recidivism** and **perseverance** is required for curbing this disorder on a long term basis.

If you believe you are a **prodigal** shopper, discuss possible treatments with your doctor. You may also find it helpful to get financial counseling, particularly if you have run up debts by spending. It is recommended that you **abstain** from use of checkbooks and credit cards, as the easy access to funding tends to fuel the addiction.

Shopping only with friends or relatives who do not compulsively spend is also a good idea, as they can help you to **curb** your spending. Finding alternative ways of enjoying your leisure time is essential to breaking the cycle of using shopping as way of trying to feel better about yourself. Engaging in activities like cooking, reading, outing eq. going for a movie or picnic may some movement prove helpful. Remember, you are a worthwhile person, no matter how much or how little you buy.

Word – Watch

☙ Anomaly

Contextual Meaning(s) : Noun; something that deviates from what is standard or normal
Synonyms : peculiar, odd

☙ Abstain

Contextual Meaning(s) : verb; to choose not to something, refrain from something
Synonyms : desist, refrain

☙ Bemoans

Contextual Meaning(s) : Verb; means over something waits
Synonyms : rafter, resist, jib

☙ Binges

Contextual Meaning(s) : Noun; unrestrained acts (later often regretted)
Synonyms : indulgences

☙ Blustery

Contextual Meaning(s) : Adjective; noisily domineering; tending to browbeat others; blowing in violent and abrupt bursts
Synonyms : stormy

☙ Cited

Contextual Meaning(s) : Verb; mentioned
Synonyms : quoted

☙ Compunction

Contextual Meaning(s) : Noun; a feeling of deep regret (usually for some misdeed)
Synonyms : remorse, self-reproach

☙ Consumerism

Contextual Meaning(s) : Noun; an attitude that values the acquisition of material goods
Other Meanings(s) : Noun; the protection of the rights and interests of consumers, especially with regard to price, quality and safety
Synonyms : materialistic attitude

☙ Compulsive

Contextual Meaning(s) : adjective; driven to something, driven by an irresistible inner force to do something; e.g. a compulsive liar
Other Meaning(s) : noun; somebody under psychological compulsion, somebody whose actions are driven by a usually irrational psychological force
Synonyms : obsessive, neurotic

☙ Curb

Contextual Meaning(s) : verb; impose limitation,
Other Meaning(s) : hold something back, to restrain, control, or limit something; e.g. hope to curb inflation
Synonyms : limit, check

☙ Disputatious

Contextual Meaning(s) : Adjective; inclined or showing an inclination to dispute or disagree, even to engage in law suits
Synonyms : contentious, litigious

☙ Ecstatic

Contextual Meaning(s) : Adjective; feeling great rapture or delight
Synonyms : enraptured, rapturous, rapt

☙ Elevates

Contextual Meaning(s) : Verb; raises up
Synonyms : raise

☙ Escalated

Contextual Meaning(s) : Verb; increased, grown higher
Synonyms : increment

☙ Fillip

Contextual Meaning(s) : Noun; anything that tends to arouse or boost
Synonyms : boost

✎ *Grappling*

Contextual Meaning(s) : Verb; fighting or trying to beat

Other Meaning(s) : noun the sport of hand-to-hand struggle between unarmed contestants who try to throw each other down; the act of engaging in close hand-to-hand combat

Synonyms : wrestling, rassling

✎ *Hoarded*

Contextual Meaning(s) : Verb; gathered in large quantity

Synonyms : accumulated

✎ *Impairs*

Contextual Meaning(s) : Verb; damages or reduces effectiveness

Synonyms : vitiates

✎ *Incipient*

Contextual Meaning(s) : Adjective; only partly in existence; imperfectly formed

Synonyms : inchoate

✎ *Incredulous*

Contextual Meaning(s) : Adjective; not disposed or willing to believe

Synonyms : skeptical

✎ *Inebriated*

Contextual Meaning(s) : Adjective; stupefied or excited by a chemical substance (especially alcohol)

Synonyms : intoxicated, drunk

✎ *Impulse*

Contextual Meaning(s) : noun; an instinctive drive or natural tendency; e.g. She couldn't resist the impulse to ask him.

Synonyms : desire, inclination

✎ *Incredulous*

Contextual Meaning(s) : adjective; unable or unwilling to believe something or completely unconvinced by it, showing or characterized by disbelief

Synonyms : doubtful, skeptical, dubious

✎ *Malaise*

Contextual Meaning(s) : Noun; physical discomfort (as mild sickness or depression)

Synonyms : unease, uneasiness

✎ *Motif*

Contextual Meaning(s) : Noun; a design that consists of recurring shapes or colors; a theme that is elaborated on in a piece of music; a unifying idea that is a recurrent element in a literary or artistic work

Synonyms : motive, theme

✎ *Momentary*

Contextual Meaning(s) : adjective; lasting for a very short time, living or continuing for only a relatively short time

Synonyms : brief, temporary

✎ *Perseverance*

Contextual Meaning(s) : Noun; the act of persisting or persevering; continuing or repeating behavior; persistent determination

Synonyms : tenacity, pertinacity

✎ *Piquant*

Contextual Meaning(s) : Adjective; engagingly stimulating or provocative; having an agreeably pungent taste; attracting or delighting

Synonyms : spicy, engaging

✎ *Prodded*

Contextual Meaning(s) : Verb; pushed into doing something

Synonyms : pushed

✎ *Prodigal*

Contextual Meaning(s) : Adjective; marked by rash extravagance; very generous; recklessly wasteful; noun a recklessly extravagant consumer

Synonyms : profligate, spendthrift

✎ *Profligate*

Contextual Meaning(s) : Adjective; unrestrained by convention or morality; recklessly wasteful;

Other Meaning(s) : noun a recklessly extravagant consumer; a dissolute man in fashionable society
Synonyms : prodigal, squanderer, rake, spendthrift

🖎 **Recidivism**
Contextual Meaning(s) : Noun; habitual relapse into crime or psychological any disorder
Synonyms : retrogression

🖎 **Relapse**
Contextual Meaning(s) : Verb; go back to bad behavior; deteriorate in health
Other Meaning(s) : noun a failure to maintain a higher state;
Synonyms : recidivate, regress

🖎 **Ritualized**
Contextual Meaning(s) : Verb; made or evolved into a ritual
Synonyms : traditionalized

🖎 **Serene**
Contextual Meaning(s) : Adjective; completely clear and fine; not agitated; without losing self-possession
Synonyms : unagitated, tranquil

🖎 **Splurges**
Contextual Meaning(s) : Noun; spending money in an unrestrained manner.
Synonyms : wastes

🖎 **Spree**
Contextual Meaning(s) : Noun; a brief indulgence of one's impulses;
Other Meaning(s) : verb engage without restraint in an activity and indulge, as when shopping
Synonyms : fling

🖎 **Shopaholism**
Contextual Meaning(s) : Noun; Shopping or spending money as a result of feeling disappointed, angry or scared
Synonyms : Compulsive buying disorder, omniomania, shopping addiction

🖎 **Upshot**
Contextual Meaning(s) : Noun; a phenomenon that follows and is caused by some previous phenomenon
Synonyms : consequence, , outcome

🖎 **Vitiating**
Contextual Meaning(s) : Verb; harming or causing decrease in quality or value
Synonyms : harms, hurts, damages

🖎 **Wallow**
Contextual Meaning(s) : Verb; devote oneself entirely to something;
Other Meaning(s) : noun an indolent or clumsy rolling about; a puddle where animals go to wallow; delight greatly in; indulge in to an immoderate degree, usually with pleasure; be ecstatic with joy; roll around, "pigs were wallowing in the mud"; rise up as if in waves
Synonyms : rejoice, triumph, welter, billow

🖎 **Wrath**
Contextual Meaning(s) : Noun; belligerence aroused by a real or supposed wrong (personified as one of the deadly sins); intense anger (usually on an epic scale)
Synonyms : anger, ire

🖎 **Zeal**
Contextual Meaning(s) : noun; energetic and unflagging enthusiasm, especially for a cause or idea
Synonyms : enthusiasm, keenness

You could say the safest sports in the world are table tennis, badminton, golf and wrestling; we all know by now that the last one is fake, so in these sports you can never even think of a serious injury.

The world's most dangerous sports are too many. It will take a lot of time to classify them. Driving a road car on public roads can also be dangerous, so just think how dangerous can motorsports be. Any form of motorsports can be dangerous, whether it's Formula racing, NASCAR, Touring Car, Motogp, Motor cross, or rallying. In formula 1 in the last 14 years no driver has been killed, the last casualty being Ayrton Senna but that does not mean that motorsports is not dangerous. Infact, 25 drivers have died since its **inception** in 1950.but the number of **dire** injuries would be **substantial**.

Dangerous sports are often activities that people take part in exactly because there is an element of danger involved. The fact that these dangerous sports have killed a number or people does not prevent some people from trying them out.

Fatality figures are hard to determine, as event organizers understandably do not wish bad publicity for the event. Nevertheless, there are a few sports that can claim to be the world's most dangerous sports. Although there is no official ranking, there are a few sports that pop up on the list time and time again.

High up on the list of dangerous sports, literally, is base jumping. In this activity, the participant jumps from high buildings, bridges, or the sides of cliffs. The purpose of base jumping is to wait as long as possible before eventually pulling the parachute chord. There is no safety net and no alternative means of stopping before you hit the ground. Figures estimate that around 15 people are killed each year due to base jumping. BASE jumpers have leapt from the Golden Gate Bridge, the Eiffel Tower and the Empire State Building. People who try this sport almost always end up getting arrested because its **illicit** and some don't even live long enough to get **incarcerated**.

In Free Diving - divers will **plunge** up to 400 feet underwater in a single breath. At the 2001 Free Diving World Cup, 15 people had to be rescued because of blackouts caused by their brains not getting enough oxygen.

Imagine being more than 100 feet underwater in a deep, cold and dark cave. Those who do Cave diving are well trained but there are so many things that can go wrong which is why this is one of the world's most dangerous sports. You can lose your way, run out of air, your equipment can fail or you can be eaten alive by a cave creature.

Speed Skiing is the world's fastest non-motorized sport and one of the world's most dangerous sports. Skiers wear special skis and **aerodynamic** suits to fly down a hill at speeds up to 250 kms. per hour! That's almost as fast as a race car ! One crash often means death.

Unless you're a fish, how can fishing be one of the world's most dangerous sports? Rock Fishing involves casting a line into the ocean from the shoreline. People often forget about the tides and are swept away or are dragged underwater by massive waves. In 2001, 15 people in Australia died while rock fishing.

Not risky enough for you? How about getting on top of a **bucking** bull and trying to hang on as the bull tries its best to throw you off. Some of these bulls can weigh up to 900 kg and are understandably **infuriated** at having someone jumping about on their backs. A rider who is thrown off can be **brutally stomped** on by the bull. Broken bones, **ruptured** organs, and of course death may await the fearless bull rider.

Heli-skiing involves being taken to untouched snow via helicopter. Extreme weather conditions and **avalanches** do nothing to **deter** the determined heli-skier; they only add to the **adrenalin** kick. There are so many budding heli-skiers that waiting lists for the activity must be booked up to a year in advance.

Lately, a new surprising contender has gained **infamy** as one of the world's most dangerous sports. Kite flyers in the Punjab Province of Pakistan can now face murder charges and the death penalty. Kite flying in Pakistan and India is a popular pastime that reaches its climax at the Basant Festival each spring. Kite flyers have been taking part in dog fights, trying to cut their opponents kite strings. Some kites have been found to have metallic strings or to have been coated with glass **shards**. The kites pose a threat to observers and bike riders. Many people have **incurred** injuries due to the kite strings, and some have been killed by falling from high buildings while flying their kites. What was once an innocent pastime now ranks as one of the world's most dangerous sports.

Cheer leading takes countless hours of practice, conditioning and skill. It takes **endurance**. They don't get pads or a ball to play with. Other mates throw cheerleaders who sometimes weigh more than the bases do into the air and mates are expected to catch them, not hurt them and safely put them back on the ground.

Cheer is a very **dodgy** sport. If all goes well, they get caught after doing a pretty flip in the air. If not, one could die, or kill a base. You're being tossed 5-10 feet in the air and have no padding, no helmet, no safety-nets, and you're expecting girls or guys of your age to catch you.

Some would argue that naming cheer in this list is **vacuous**. Gymnastics is twice as dangerous as cheer leading. Gymnasts swing on the bars and land on their hands, the level of **pliability** and accuracy required is nothing if not **exacting**.

Horse riding is also very dangerous. One must remember that horse racing is a legally permissible variety of gambling, hence a number of riders are groomed every year for this risky sport. A rider ,only 13 years old , has fallen off the horse about 10 times. He claims riding horses is definitely more difficult and dangerous than cheer. In cheer there is a 100 pound human falling on you, compared with a 1,000 pound and more animal, trampling you at top speed! When you **tumble** off a horse , if you aren't too badly hurt, you're expected to catch the horse and get back on. You will most likely be **squelched** by 10-plus horses who can't stop in time.

Also very deadly sports are **lacrosse** and rugby. In rugby gigantic men try to kill you and when you have no pads and crap, it hurts to be tackled by a 145 pound man. Players break arms and legs in every game.

Don't be **astounded** but even golf can be dangerous. Many people don't notice that. If someone on a hole parallel to yours hooks or slices the ball and it hits you it will break a bone or kill you. Golf balls go a hell of a lot faster than people think; they go anywhere between 80 and 140 mph.

Another viewpoint claims most dangerous sport in the world is obviously air racing! Accidents in this sport are almost always fatal.

Apparently, **jousting** is also a dangerous pastime, with 636 killed for every 106 who die skiing or divin g. The combination of charging horses, **armour** and pointed **lance** is naturally a risky enterprise.

Your mom will certainly **proscribe** Supercross. Athletes fly in the air on a motorcycle while doing back flips, taking their hands off the handlebars and other death-defying stunts.

In a Solo Yacht race around the world, sailors encounter waves, sharks, hurricanes and even pirates. The nearest help can be hundreds of miles away and racers have no control over the conditions they run into. With no one nearby to help them out, racers can lose the race and their lives, too.

One would not advice Street Lugging as a safe pastime. Highly modified skateboards are used to race down a hill at speeds up to 128 kms per hour. The **pioneers** of this sport originally raced down hills in the middle of traffic which made it even more risky. There are now special **luges** and equipment for the sport which make it much safer. But , you're still hitting pavement when you crash.

And this will certainly take the cake. A guy says, the most dangerous sport in existence is baby sitting ! Those kids can be terrible. One time he almost got killed by a 2 year old! The toddler pulled out a knife and threatened to stab this guy because he was bad and was intending to put him in the corner!

🐦 **Armour**
Contextual Meaning(s) : Noun; tough more-or-less rigid protective covering of an animal or plant; protective covering made of metal and used in combat;
Synonyms : kevlar

🐦 **Astounded**
Contextual Meaning(s) : Adjective; filled with the emotional impact of overwhelming surprise or shock
Synonyms : amazed, astonished, stunned

🐦 **Avalanches**
Contextual Meaning(s) : Noun; sudden appearances of an overwhelming number of things;
Other Meaning(s) : Noun; slide of large masses of snow and ice and mud down a mountain; verb gather into a huge mass and roll down a mountain, of snow
Synonyms : bombardments, barrages

🐦 **Aerodynamic**
Contextual Meaning(s) : Adjective; designed to reduce air resistance, especially to increase fuel efficiency or maximum speed
Synonyms : sleek, smooth, slick

🐦 **Adrenalin**
Contextual Meaning(s) : A catecholamine secreted by the adrenal medulla in response to stress (trade name Adrenalin); stimulates autonomic nerve action
Synonyms : adrenaline

🐦 **Brutally**
Contextual Meaning(s) : Adverb; in a vicious manner
Synonyms : viciously, savagely

🐦 **Bucking**
Contextual Meaning(s) : verb; Jump vertically, with legs stiff and back arched
Synonyms : charging

🐦 **Deter** *(Adverb)*
Contextual Meaning(s) : try to prevent; show opposition to
Other Meaning(s) : turn away from by persuasion
Synonyms : discourage, dissuade

🐦 **Dire**
Contextual Meaning(s) : Adjective; causing fear or dread or terror; fraught with extreme danger; nearly hopeless
Synonyms : awful, horrific, desperate

🐦 **Dodgy**
Contextual Meaning(s) : Adjective; marked by skill in deception; of uncertain outcome; especially fraught with risk
Synonyms : crafty, cunning, foxy, dicey

🐦 **Endurance**
Contextual Meaning(s) : Noun; the power to withstand hardship or stress; a state of surviving; remaining alive
Synonyms : survival

🐦 **Exacting**
Contextual Meaning(s) : Adjective; requiring precise accuracy; severe and unremitting in making demands;
Synonyms : exigent, stern, strict, fastidious

🐦 **Illicit**
Contextual Meaning(s) : Adj.; contrary to accepted morality (especially sexual morality) or convention; contrary to or forbidden by law
Synonyms : illegitimate, outlaw, outlawed, unlawful

🐦 **Incarcerated**
Contextual Meaning(s) : Verb; locked up or confined, in or as in a jail
Synonyms : interned, immured

- *Inception*

  Contextual Meaning(s) : Noun; an event that is a beginning; a first part or stage of subsequent events
  Synonyms : origin, origination

- *Incurred*

  Contextual Meaning(s) : Verb; make oneself subject to; bring upon oneself; become liable to; receive a specified treatment (abstract)
  Synonyms : undergone

- *Infamy*

  Contextual Meaning(s) : Noun; evil fame or public reputation; a state of extreme dishonor
  Synonyms : opprobrium

- *Infuriated*

  Contextual Meaning(s) : Adjective; marked by extreme anger
  Synonyms : angered, enraged, furious, maddened

- *Jousting*

  Contextual Meaning(s) : noun; a form of combat in medieval times held between two mounted knights in full armour who charged at and tried to unseat each other with a lance
  Other Meaning(s) : verb; to take part in a contest against others; e.g. candidates jousting for ninety minutes in a televised debate
  Synonyms : banter, repartee

- *Lance*

  Contextual Meaning(s) : Noun; a surgical knife with a pointed double-edged blade; used for punctures and small incisions; a long pointed rod used as a weapon; an implement with a shaft and barbed point used for catching fish; verb open by piercing with a lancet; pierce with a lance, as in a knights' fight
  Synonyms : spear

- *Lacrosse*

  Contextual Meaning(s) : Noun; a sport in which two teams of ten players use sticks with a net pouch crosse at one end to throw and catch a small hard rubber ball. The objective is to score a goal by throwing the ball into the opposing team's goal net. Lacrosse was originated by Native North Americans, e.g. a lacrosse stick

- *Luges*

  Contextual Meaning(s) : Noun; a sporting event in which competitors race down a snow track in a luge, trying to complete the descent in the shortest time.

- *Pioneer*

  Contextual Meaning(s) : Noun; a person who is one of the first people to do something
  Synonyms : developer, innovator

- *Pliability*

  Contextual Meaning(s) : Noun; adaptability of mind or character; the property of being easily bent without breaking
  Synonyms : ductility

- *Proscribe*

  Contextual Meaning(s) : Verb; command against
  Synonyms : forbid, disallow

- *Plunge*

  Contextual Meaning(s) : verb; to move suddenly downward or forward, or move something in this way; e.g. plunged into the undergrowth and disappeared
  Synonyms : dive, plummet

- *Ruptured*

  Contextual Meaning(s) : Verb; to break, burst or tear something, or become broken, burst or torn
  Other Meaning(s) : Noun; a break in something, or breaking apart of something, e.g. a rupture in a water main, a breakdown in a friendly or peaceful relationship
  Synonyms : broken tissue, break, burst, or tear something

- *Shards*

  Contextual Meaning(s) : Noun; small pieces

  Synonyms : fragments, pieces

- *Squelched*

  Contextual Meaning(s) : Adjective; subdued or overcome

  Synonyms : quelled, quenched

- *Substantial*

  Contextual Meaning(s) : Adjective; having substance or capable of being treated as fact; not imaginary; having a firm basis in reality and being therefore important, considerable;

  Synonyms : significant, solid, hearty

- *Stomped*

  Contextual Meaning(s) : Verb; to bring a foot down heavily on something or somebody with the intention f causing damage or injury, to tread heavily and noisily

  Synonyms : walk with heavy steps

- *Tumble*

  Contextual Meaning(s) : fall suddenly and sharply

  Synonyms : collapse

- *Vacuous*

  Contextual Meaning(s) : Adjective; devoid of matter; void of expression; devoid of significance or point; devoid of intelligence

  Synonyms : inane, asinine, mindless

STEREOTYPES

The happiest man on earth lives in a British house, gets an American salary, has a Chinese wife, and eats Japanese food.

The saddest man on earth lives in a Japanese house, gets a Chinese salary, has an American wife, and eats British food.

These are of course, traditional jokes. People often take their own mental picture of a type of person, and generalize it to all people in that group. This image then becomes a stereotype for that group.

Stereotypes also exist about cultures and countries as a whole. Some stereotypes suggest that most Germans are industrious, Italians are passionate and the English are **phlegmatic.** Homer Simpson of the TV series *The Simpsons* is the personification of the American stereotype. Often take their own mental picture of a type of person and generalize it to all that group

Germans are also considered mechanical, organized, boring, without sense of humor and **conscientious.** They are supposedly born with a monkey **wrench** in their hands, eating vast quantities of sausage and **sauerkraut.** They loathe inefficiency, love the Fatherland, have never been late for anything in their lives, and are **fastidious** about rules and regulations They would secretly like to invade Europe, even if they have to do it via the EU. They probably eat about five huge meals a day besides drinking beer in gallons.

Ethiopian seem to suffer an **eternal** famine and possess big Foreheads. They also make the best long distance runners.

Australians are considered party animals, nature lovers, sports lovers and **extroverted.** They are also honest, **unbiased** and **bohemians.** People think they surf all day and drink all night !

Americans are difficult to stereotype because they are such an **eclectic** bunch, but extreme patriotism seems to be a **trait** many possess. They are over consuming, **ethnocentric**, obese and dim witted but also optimistic, caring, and **intrepid.** Americans are considered independent and very entrepreneurial.

Arabs are visualized as living in one big massive desert **devoid** of any technology whatsoever, getting around by riding camels which is also their main and only source of nutrition. They keep their women in veils and are **polygamous.**

Brazilians are body-centric, party animals, impulsive; They are carnival addicts, mad about soccer and coffee , and can't stop doing *samba* all day. They are also active, and **ingenious** people though they are always trying to outwit government and have no **qualms** about bending regulations. There has to be a reason why most outlaws are hidden away in Brazil ! They tend to be family- and community-oriented.

British can be stiff upper-lips, ultra-traditional, bulldog spirit, have bad teeth and hygiene. Can be rude, thin, smoke cigar or pipe, swear all day long. Because they are artistic, deep thinkers, intelligent and articulate, they have produced ground breaking literature, theater and rock music.

Chinese stereotype is **stingy** and business-oriented. They think money rules the world and are preparing for world domination. They are credited with being fast-learners, open-minded, ambitious and progressive. They also are materialistic, do kung fu and other martial arts, are great at mathematics. However, they can't hold their liquor, drive terribly. They wear glasses, pirate and copy everything, don't value contracts and provide cheap labour. They drink green tea, eat everything that lives – rats, bear, gall bladder, rhino horns and sea cucumber.

Dutch are considered polite, open-minded, well-traveled, and harmless in general. Netherlands is "a nation of rosy-cheeked farmers who live in windmills, wear clogs, have a house **redolent** of tulips and sit on piles of yellow cheese".

French make good lovers and own the best **cuisine** in the world. However are **chaotic, remiss**, introverted and selfish. They are cultured but do not like to work – prefer to strike. They always surrender in war, won't speak English, are rude to tourists and are anti-American. They avoid using soap, are **supercilious**, distant and difficult to meet. They don't respect religious freedom.

Greek can be big, overweight and lazy. They eat **souvlaki** and olives and drink Ouzo or red wine all day. They always break their plates after meals, can't drive especially when its dark. They can be disorganized, live the easy life and are **corruptible**. They own all the oil-tankers in the world.

Indians are adaptive, open-minded, agreeable, cerebral and hardworking . On the negative side they can be manipulative and politically inactive. They are also studious, intelligent, **prolific;** inoffensive and generally poor. They maintain poor personal hygiene, have huge families , are obsessed with movies and cricket. They are spiritual, meditators, snake charmers, and legendary bureaucrats. Great at computer programming and will soon outsource the whole world.

Jamaicans are **indolent** grass-smokers. They are Reggae and Rasta maniacs, loud, **boisterous** and aggressive. They make innovative musicians who influence many genres. They believe God is Bob Marley!

Swiss are rich, competent, private, modest; they are also , serious, multi-lingual, hard bargainers and the best watch makers. They sit in the mountains, **'yodel'** and milk their cows; they play 12m long Alpine horns, are **ruddy** cheeked; they tend to be pretty **smug** because of the fresh mountain air. Their trains always run on time; their diet is chocolate and holey-cheese; the women are mostly blond, never grow old, and are usually named *Heidi*; But the swiss living in Zurich are different: those are sharp-suited secretive bankers hoarding Nazi gold and dirty money from all over the world; they are obsessed with the environment, cleanliness and punctuality; tight on the rules.

Japanese are disciplined, organized, very techy, fearful, neurotic but competent. Always short but wealthy due to being workaholics. Their women are subordinate to men and make perfect devoted wives. They eat raw-fish , can be suicidal and always travel in packs!

For Koreans **'kimchi'** is the only food. They are open-minded, ambitious, progressive, efficient, materialistic and assertive. They are tech-savy, love gossip, and may soon become a superpower next only to china .

Italians live with their Mamas all their life. They are even more chaotic than the French and very possessive, passionate and pizza or pasta freaks. They are creative and smooth-talking but manipulative and dishonest. They are soccer-addicted and either **Casanovas, felons** or mafioso .They make by far the best sports cars in the world, and they rule the world of fashion and styling.

Nigerians are internet scam artists & drug dealers besides being violent and **neurotic**. They are can also be, open-minded, modest , and creative. They practice bizarre cults like sacrificing their first-born children.

Mexicans are heavy tequila drinkers, always come into America illegally. They wear huge **sombreros**, are religious, family-oriented, modest. Their men are **corpulent**, have golden teeth and a 3-day-beard, all women are as attractive as Salma Hayek !

Romanians make you **flinch**, aren't they directly related to Dracula ? Everyone in Romania owns a mystic castle and is primitive or communist.

Stereotyping is not only hurtful, it is also unfair. Even if the stereotyping is happening **involunatarily**, constantly repudiating someone based on your **prejudices** will lead to a fragmented society.

Stereotyping can lead to bullying from a young age. Stereotyping encourages **hectoring** behavior that children carry into adulthood.

Stereotyping can also lead people to live lives driven by hate, and can cause the victims of those stereotypes to be driven by fear.

But we use the subconscious stereotypes all the time. Assume that you are walking down the street and you have only two choices — either walk on the left side of the street or the right side of the street. Before you choose, you notice that on the left side there are ten tattooed, muscular men with shaved heads walking and talking together, while on the right side you see ten "clean-cut" men wearing dress shirts and ties carrying Bibles. Now, which side would you choose to walk ?

☞ **Bohemians**

Contextual Meaning(s) : Adjective; noisy and lacking in restraint or discipline; full of rough and exuberant animal spirits

Other Meaning(s) : violently agitated and turbulent;

Synonyms : gypsies

☞ **Boisterous**

Contextual Meaning(s) : noisy and lacking in restraint or discipline; full of rough and exuberant animal spirits

Other Meaning(s) : Adjective; adj. violently agitated and turbulent

Synonyms : obstreperous, defiant

☞ **Casanovas**

Contextual Meaning(s) : Noun; men who are chronic flirts

Synonyms : playboys

☞ **Chaotic**

Contextual Meaning(s) : Adjective; lacking a visible order or organization; completely unordered and unpredictable and confusing;

Other Meaning(s) : of or relating to a sensitive dependence on initial conditions

Synonyms : helter-skelter, disorderly

☞ **Conscientious**

Contextual Meaning(s) : Adjective; guided by or in accordance with conscience or sense of right and wrong

Other Meaning(s) : characterized by extreme care and great effort;

Synonyms : painstaking, scrupulous

☞ **Corpulent**

Contextual Meaning(s) : Adjective; excessively fat

Synonyms : obese, weighty, rotund

☞ **Cuisine**

Contextual Meaning(s) : Adjective; noun the practice or manner of preparing food or the food so prepared

Synonyms : culinary art

☞ **Corruptible**

Contextual Meaning(s) : adjective; immoral or dishonest, especially as shown by the exploitation of a position of power or trust for personal gain

Synonyms : cowardly, weak-willed

☞ **Devoid**

Contextual Meaning(s) : Adjective; completely lacking; completely wanting or lacking

Synonyms : barren, destitute, innocent

☞ **Eclectic**

Contextual Meaning(s) : Adjective; selecting what seems best of various styles or ideas;

Other Meaning(s) : noun someone who selects according to the eclectic method

Synonyms : eclecticist

☞ **Eternal**

Contextual Meaning(s) : Adjective; tiresomely long; seemingly without end; continuing forever or indefinitely

Synonyms : ageless, perpetual

☞ **Extroverted**

Contextual Meaning(s) : Adjective; at ease in talking to others; not introspective; examining what is outside yourself; being concerned with the social and physical environment

Synonyms : outgoing

☞ **Ethnocentric**

Contextual Meaning(s) : adjective; centered on a specific ethnic group, usually one's own

Synonyms : nationalism, fanatical patriotism

- *Felons*

  Contextual Meaning(s) : Noun; someone who has committed a crime or has been legally convicted

  Synonyms : criminals, crooks

- *Flinch*

  Contextual Meaning(s) : verb; to make an involuntary small backward movement in response to pain or something frightening or shocking

  Synonyms : recoil, balk

- *Fastidious*

  Contextual Meaning(s) : adjective; concerned that even the smallest details should be just right, e.g. fastidious about his appearance

  Synonyms : particular, precise

- *Hectoring*

  Contextual Meaning(s) : Adjective; a behaviour marked by bullying other

  Synonyms : bullying

- *Indolent*

  Contextual Meaning(s) : Adjective; disinclined to work or exertion

  Other Meaning(s) : (of tumors e.g.) slow to heal or develop and usually painless;

  Synonyms : slothful, work-shy

- *Ingenious*

  Contextual Meaning(s) : Adjective; showing inventiveness and skill; skillful (or showing skill) in adapting means to ends; (used of persons or artifacts) marked by independence and creativity in thought or action

  Synonyms : inventive

- *Intrepid*

  Contextual Meaning(s) : Adjective; invulnerable to fear or intimidation, brave

  Synonyms : valiant

- *Involunatarily*

  Contextual Meaning(s) : Adjective; not done willfully, not of one's non volition

  Synonyms : forced

- *Jingoism*

  Contextual Meaning(s) : Adjective; noun fanatical patriotism; an appeal intended to arouse patriotic emotions

  Synonyms : chauvinism

- *Kimchi*

  Contextual Meaning(s) : noun; a pickle made with vegetables such as cabbage and white radish seasoned with chili, garlic, and ginger, regarded as the national dish of Korea

- *Neurotic*

  Contextual Meaning(s) : adjective; obsessive about everyday things

  Synonyms : overanxious, obsessed

- *Phlegmatic*

  Contextual Meaning(s) : Adjective; showing little emotion

  Synonyms : apathetic, stoic

- *Polygamous*

  Contextual Meaning(s) : Adjective; having more than one mate at a time; used of relationships and individuals;

  Other Meaning(s) : having several forms of gametoecia on the same plant

  Synonyms : heteroicous, polyoicous

- *Prejudices*

  Contextual Meaning(s) : Noun; partialities in choice

  Synonyms : biases

- *Prolific*

  Contextual Meaning(s) : adjective; producing ideas or works frequently and in large quantities

  Synonyms : productive, creative

- *Qualms*

  Contextual Meaning(s) : Noun; uneasiness about fitness of one's actions

  Synonyms : scruples

- *Reclusive*

  Contextual Meaning(s) : Adjective; providing privacy or seclusion; withdrawn from society; seeking solitude

  Synonyms : cloistered, sequestered

- **Redolent**

  Contextual Meaning(s) : Adjective; (used with `of' or `with') noticeably odorous; having a strong pleasant odor; serving to bring to mind

  Synonyms : aromatic, evocative,

- **Remiss**

  Contextual Meaning(s) : Adjective; failing in what duty requires

  Synonyms : delinquent, neglectful

- **Ruddy**

  Contextual Meaning(s) : adjective; with a healthy reddish glow

  Synonyms : reddish, rosy

- **Stingy**

  Contextual Meaning(s) : Adjective; unwilling to spend; deficient in amount or quality or extent

  Synonyms : scrimpy

- **Subservient**

  Contextual Meaning(s) : Adjective; compliant and obedient to authority; abjectly submissive; characteristic of a slave or servant; serving or acting as a means or aid

  Other Meaning(s) : consisting of or forming human or animal figures

  Synonyms : slavish, submissive

- **Supercilious**

  Contextual Meaning(s) : Adjective; expressive of contempt; having or showing arrogant superiority to and disdain of those one views as unworthy

  Synonyms : snide, haughty

- **Sauerkraut**

  Contextual Meaning (s) : noun; a German dish of shredded cabbage fermented in its own juice with salt

  Synonyms : broccoli

- **Souvlaki**

  Contextual Meaning(s) : noun; a Greek dish consisting of pieces of seasoned meat roasted on skewers

  Synonyms : kebab, shish kebab

- **Smug**

  Contextual Meanings(s) : adjective; conceited and self-satisfied

  Synonyms : self-satisfied, self- righteous

- **Sombreros**

  Contextual Meaning(s) : noun; a straw or felt hat with a very wide upturned brim, originally worn by men in Mexico and some other Spanish-speaking countries

- **Trait**

  Contextual Meaning(s) : Adjective; noun a distinguishing feature of one's personal nature

  Synonyms : characteristic

- **Unbiased**

  Contextual Meaning(s) : Adjective; without bias; characterized by a lack of partiality or prejudices

  Other Meaning(s) : consisting of or forming human or animal figures

  Synonyms : fair

- **Wrench**

  Contextual Meaning (s) : verb; to move with a forceful twisting movement

  Other Meaning(s) : noun; a difficult parting from a person or place, or the feelings of sadness and loss that accompany such as parting, e.g. Leaving New York was a terrible wrench after having lived there for 30 years.

  Synonyms : pull, jerk

- **Yodel**

  Contextual Meaning(s) : verb; to sing, changing rapidly between a normal and falsetto voice

  Synonyms : sing high

LEAN AND MEAN I'M POLYTHENE

Almost every product we buy, most of the food we eat and many of the liquids we drink come encased in polythene. Some say our life seems to be wrapped in polythene !

Every once in a while the authorities pass out an order **interdicting** shop keepers from providing plastic bags to customers for carrying their purchases, its effect is ,however **fugacious**. Plastic bags are very popular with both retailers as well as consumers because they are cheap, **impregnable, impervious**, lightweight and **utilitarian.** They are certainly a *convenient* means of carrying food as well as other goods ; but we forget their long term **ramifications**.

However seemingly **innocuous,** they secretly destroy our ecology. They are responsible for causing pollution, killing wildlife, and using up the **treasured** resources of the earth.

The decomposition of polythene bags takes about 1000 years. For all practical purposes, they can be called non-biodegradable. The reason traditional plastics are not biodegradable is because their long polymer molecules are too large and too tightly bonded together to be broken apart and **assimilated** by living organisms.

Traditional plastics are manufactured from non-renewable resources – oil, coal and natural gas. That means another large misuse of the precious resource the earth has.

Even though they are one of the modern conveniences that seem to be a necessity , their usage is simply **deleterious** in the long run for our planet from either angle. Too costly to produce and impossible to **extirpate** !

About a hundred billion plastic bags are used each year in the US alone. And then, when one considers the massive economies and **flummoxing** populations of India, China, Europe, and other parts of the world, the numbers can be **staggering**. The problem is further worsened by the developed countries which often ship off their plastic waste to developing countries.

Harmful effects of plastic bags are numerous. Once they are used, most plastic bags go into landfill, or rubbish tips. Each year more and more plastic bags end up **littering** the environment. Once they become litter, plastic bags find their way into our waterways, parks, beaches, and streets. And, if they are burned, they infuse the air with toxic fumes.

About 100,000 animals such as dolphins, turtles whales, penguins are killed every year due to plastic bags. Many animals **ingest** plastic bags, mistaking them for food, and therefore die. And worse, the **ingested** plastic bag remains intact even after the death and decomposition of the animal. Thus, it lies around in the landscape till another **ravenous** animal consumes it.

With the banning of plastic bags appearing to be such a sensible idea, what possible problems could there be?

People who are against the banning of plastic bags often cite the fact that plastic bags are very low priority when all the environmental issues of concern are taken into account. Even some green supporters are against the banning of bags, preferring instead to educate people and change habits rather than forcing the issue. Other people refer to the fact that the banning of plastic bags simply moves the problem elsewhere. Cities that have banned plastic bags often report an increase in the sale of plastic bin bags. Instead of plastic, paper bags are often used. These raise other issues, for instance the use of virgin paper pulp.

Some environmentalists who are opposed to the banning of bags fear that it breeds **complacency**. They are concerned that people may feel that they are making their contribution towards green living by not using plastic bags and overlooking the bigger issues. They argue that the big picture needs to be considered rather than focusing on smaller issues.

While it is undeniable that **disposable** plastic bags are a relatively small problem in the overall scheme of things, reducing their use is something we can all do. Governments and world organizations need to make decisions on some of the bigger environmental issues, however the reduction of the use of plastic bags is our individual **obligation** regardless of whether or not there is an official **proscription**.

Single-use bags, both paper and plastic, represent a huge threat to the environment. This threat is not only related to the sheer volume of them ending up in landfill, but also to the resources needed to produce, transport and (occasionally) recycle them, and the emissions resulting from these processes. Single-use plastic bags are also well known for their interference in ecosystems and the part they play in flood events, where they clog pipes and drains. Other animals or birds become entangled in plastic bags and drown or can't fly as a result.

How about taking previously used bags with you next time you go to the shops? Or even better - turn back time and do as grandma did. Take a sturdy bag with you every time you go shopping. We do have an obligation towards the nature, lets restore it and make it as **pristine** as Grandma's love !

🔖 **Assimilated**

Contextual Meaning(s) : verb; to consume and incorporate nutrients into the body after digestion

Synonyms : absorb, take in

🔖 **Complacency**

Contextual Meaning(s) : noun the feeling you have when you are satisfied with yourself

Synonyms : smugness

🔖 **Deleterious**

Contextual Meaning(s) : Adjective; harmful to living things

Synonyms : hazardous

🔖 **Disposable**

Contextual Meaning(s) : Adjective; designed to be disposed of after use; free or available for use or disposition;

Other Meaning(s) : noun an item that can be disposed of after it has been used

Synonyms : dispensable

🔖 **Exacerbated**

Contextual Meaning(s) : Adjective; diminished to be reduced to (a worse condition)

Synonyms : worsened

🔖 **Extirpate**

Contextual Meaning(s) : Verb; destroy completely, as if down to the roots

Other Meaning(s) : verb surgically remove (an organ); pull up by or as if by the roots;

Synonyms : uproot

🔖 **Flummoxing**

Contextual Meaning(s) : Adjective; totally confusing or puzzling.

Synonyms : confounding

🔖 **Fugacious**

Contextual Meaning(s) : Adjective; lasting a very short time

Synonyms : ephemeral, transient, transitory

🔖 **Impervious**

Contextual Meaning(s) : Adjective; not admitting passage or capable of being affected

Synonyms : imperviable

🔖 **Impregnable**

Contextual Meaning(s) : Adverb; able to withstand attack;

Other Meaning(s) : adjective; incapable of being overcome, challenged or refuted; capable of conceiving

Synonyms : inviolable

🔖 **Indispensable**

Contextual Meaning(s) : Adjective; unavoidable; not to be dispensed with; essential; absolutely necessary; vitally necessary

Synonyms : obligatory

🔖 **Ingest**

Contextual Meaning(s) : Verb; serve oneself to, or consume regularly

Synonyms : devour

🔖 **Innocuous**

Contextual Meaning(s) : Adjective; not injurious to physical or mental health; not causing disapproval; lacking intent or capacity to injure; unlikely to harm or disturb anyone

Synonyms : harmless

🔖 **Insidiously**

Contextual Meaning(s) : Adverb; in a hidden harmful manner

Synonyms : perniciously

🔖 **Interdict**

Contextual Meaning(s) : Verb; ordering to refrain from doing something

Synonyms : prohibition , edict

Interdicting

Contextual Meaning(s) : Noun; showing inventiveness and skill; skillful (or showing skill) in adapting means to ends; (used of persons or artifacts) marked by independence and creativity in thought or action
Synonyms : resourceful, clever

Ingested

Contextual Meaning(s) : verb; to take food, liquid, or some other substance into the body by swallowing or absorbing
Synonyms : absorb, consume

Littering

Contextual Meaning(s) : act of dirtying or spoiling place
Synonyms : strewing

Obligation

Contextual Meaning(s) : Noun; the social force that binds you to the courses of action demanded by that force
Other Meaning(s) : noun a legal agreement specifying a payment or action and the penalty for failure to comply; a personal relation in which one is indebted for a service or favor; the state of being obligated to do or pay something;
Synonyms : indebtedness

Pristine

Contextual Meaning(s) : Adjective; immaculately clean and unused; completely free from dirt or contamination
Synonyms : pure

Proscription

Contextual Meaning(s) : Noun; rejection by means of an act of banishing or prohibiting; a decree that prohibits something
Synonyms : banishment

Ramifications

Contextual Meaning(s) : Noun; a development that complicates a situation
Other Meaning(s) : Noun; an arrangement of branching parts; the act of branching out or dividing into branches; a part of a forked or branching shape
Synonyms : complications

Ravenous

Contextual Meaning(s) : Adjective; devouring or craving food in great quantities; extremely hungry
Synonyms : edacious

Staggering

Contextual Meaning(s) : Adjective; so surprisingly impressive as to stun or overwhelm
Synonyms : astounding

Titanic

Contextual Meaning(s) : Adjective; of great force or power or size
Synonyms : gargantuan

Treasured

Contextual Meaning(s) : Adjective; characterized by feeling or showing fond affection for
Synonyms : cherished

Utilitarian

Contextual Meaning(s) : Adjective; having a useful function; having utility often to the exclusion of values;
Other Meaning(s) : noun someone who believes that the value of a thing depends on its utility
Synonyms : useful

THE STATISTICAL LIAR

Statistically an average man lives till 60. The truth is most men die before 50 or after 70, and few die at 60. People have said statistics is common sense seen upside down. I agree !

We live in a world of statistics: you can find numbers **buttressing** just about any idea. The problem arises when you find statistics that support every possible way of **deconstructing** an idea. You can find statistics that verify that cigarettes are killers and also that they have no effect on anyone's health. You can find statistics that say the consumption of dairy products should be reduced and also that dairy products are **salubrious**. You can find statistics that **vilify** the soft drinks because they will give you cancer and that they have no effect on anything but your thirst. Every one of these sets of statistics is absolutely **veracious**.

However, what you need to **probe** is who is publishing the numbers, and what are they trying to **attest** with them. Are the statistics provided by the Cancer Society or the Tobacco association ? Are they provided by the Medical Association or the Dairy Association?

Every point of view uses statistics to support their ideas. It's your job to examine all statistics supporting all points of view, to arrive at your own conclusions based on your **sapience.**

Once you have determined whether or not there is **prejudice** involved in the statistics only then take it on **face-value**. It is possible some **knavish** person is using the figures to either **repudiate** or **espouse** a certain point of view convenient to him.

Numbers can be a **camouflage** for stories, events and emotions that they deliberate **obscure**.

Numbers, statistics – are **incompetent** of telling anything in absence of context, stories, people and their motivations.

Lets say, I want to statistically prove that computers in Nigeria are now very high in usage. So I **corroborate** it with the statistic that every third person you see on Nigerian roads is carrying a laptop. The same data can be **fudged** by stating that about 67 % of Nigerians haven't even "seen" a computer. Thus using exactly the same data, I am presenting it in a language that suits my mission. Just a game of **semantics**, that's what statistical proof is all about!

Consider these driving accident statistics - 45% of crashes are caused by **intoxicated** drivers, but that means *55%* were caused by *sober* drivers. The latter fact ,if stressed ,would seem to **trivialize** the need for sober driving! Consider these crime statistics - 5000 murders were committed in one city but only 500 were committed in another; a person might assume the second city is safer, but if the **former** city had 100 times the population then it is actually only one-tenth, not ten times as dangerous as the **latter**.

People have always **construed** the numbers at the backdrop some stories that they would like to believe or sell.

So it is not about what those numbers are but it is about "how do people feel" about them.

One must first, try to determine whether the statistics are hard or soft science based. The simplest way to do this is simply find out whether human behavior/ opinion or factual incidents are being studied.

The former is soft science, the latter is hard.

Second, if the statistics are hard science, check to see what results other researchers who have repeated the study obtained. If the second study has results that are very **divergent** from the first, find a third and/or fourth and use the results that are consistent overall.

Of course, hard science statistics often require that you examine the sample that was considered. If the statistics say that 30% of the US population has AIDS, what was the sample? The entire population of the US? The population of New York or San Francisco? The population of Otumwa, Iowa? Or a selection of towns and cities, rural, urban and suburban, in all parts of the country? Statistics on the incidence of rape in the US vary wildly depending on whether the study asks law enforcement or rape counseling centers (one set is based on the number of reported rapes, the other on the number of women needing counseling whether or not they reported the rape to law enforcement). No doubt the first statistic will prove the incidence to be much less than that proposed by the Counselors. Both examples above appear to be hard science, since they are based on "hard" facts, but nonetheless must be examined for who was asked.

Soft science statistics are even more **guileful** than hard science statistics. If you wish to show how people react to violence, how do you define violence? And how do the people in your study define violence. A victim of a **mugging** may define violence as the mugger getting within five feet of him, while a mugger may define it as some action that has caused serious physical damage.

Also bear in mind that any study that uses human subjects is **defenseless** because of numerous reasons.

First is the fact that all people have different mental makeup. Second, individuals are inconsistent; what they feel today may change totally tomorrow. Lastly, if the question involves self image, they may not tell the truth. Ask men whether they watch tv soaps and they are likely to say no, even if they do watch them as much as two hours a day.

The way that the questions are framed can also **slant** the results. For example, one study asked people who were homeless ,if they have felt "down", "depressed" or "anxious" in the past four weeks. Is it surprising that many people who were homeless answered "yes"? The question was meant to statistically confirm that homelessness is correlated to mental illness, and no wonder it did ! Leading questions like these literally **coerce** the **respondent** into a desired answer.

Don't be surprised if tomorrow you read a news that "a correlation was found between a person's shoe size and math ability" !

Attest

Contextual Meaning(s) : Verb; authenticate, affirm to be true, genuine, or correct, as in an official capacity; establish or verify the usage of; provide evidence for; stand as proof of; show by one's behavior, attitude, or external attributes;

Other Meaning(s) : give testimony in a court of law

Synonyms : certify, testify

Buttressing

Contextual Meaning(s) : Verb; supporting or bolstering

Other Meaning(s) : noun a support usually of stone or brick; supports the wall of a building

Synonyms : bolstering

Camouflage

Contextual Meaning(s) : Noun; device or stratagem for concealment or deceit;

Other Meaning(s) : fabric dyed with splotches of green and brown and black and tan; intended to make the wearer of a garment made of this fabric hard to distinguish from the background; the act of concealing the identity of something by modifying its appearance; an outward semblance that misrepresents the true nature of something; verb disguise by camouflaging; exploit the natural surroundings to disguise something

Synonyms : disguise

Coerce

Contextual Meaning(s) : Verb; to cause to do through pressure or necessity, by physical, moral or intellectual means.

Synonyms : hale, squeeze, pressure, force

Construed

Contextual Meaning(s) : Verb; interpreted or understood as

Synonyms : deconstructed

Corroborate

Contextual Meaning(s) : Verb; support with evidence or authority or make more certain or confirm; establish or strengthen as with new evidence or facts; give evidence for

Synonyms : substantiate, validate

Deconstructing

Contextual Meaning(s) : Adjective; understanding the Meaning(s) of

Synonyms : perceiving

Divergent

Contextual Meaning(s) : Adjective; tending to move apart in different directions; diverging from another or from a standard

Synonyms : diverging

Defenseless (US)

Contextual Meaning(s) : adjective; lacking any form of protection and therefore vulnerable

Synonyms : weak, powerless

Endorse

Contextual Meaning(s) : Verb; sign as evidence of legal transfer; guarantee as meeting a certain standard; be behind; approve of; give support or one's approval to

Synonyms : indorse, certify

Espouse

Contextual Meaning(s) : Verb; take up the cause, ideology, practice, method, of someone and use it as one's own; choose and follow; as of theories, ideas, policies, strategies or plans;

Other Meaning(s) : take in marriage

Synonyms : embrace, adopt

Face-value

Contextual Meaning(s) : Noun; the apparent worth as opposed to the real worth;

Other Meaning(s) : the value of a security that is set by the company issuing it; unrelated to market value
Synonyms : par value, nominal value

✍ *Former*

Contextual Meaning(s) : Adjective; referring to the first of two things or persons mentioned (or the earlier one or ones of several); (used especially for persons) of the immediate past; belonging to the distant past; belonging to some prior time; noun the first of two or the first mentioned of two
Synonyms : previous

✍ *Fudged*

Contextual Meaning(s) : Adjective; manipulated for cheating
Synonyms : tweaked

✍ *Guileful*

Contextual Meaning(s) : Verb; marked by skill in deception
Synonyms : crafty, cunning, dodgy, foxy, wily

✍ *Incompetent*

Contextual Meaning(s) : Adjective; not qualified or suited for a purpose; not doing a good job; not meeting requirements; showing lack of skill or aptitude;
Other Meaning(s) : noun someone who is not competent to take effective action
Synonyms : incapable, bungling, clumsy, fumbling

✍ *Intoxicated*

Contextual Meaning(s) : Adjective; stupefied or excited by a chemical substance (especially alcohol); as if under the influence of alcohol
Synonyms : drunk, inebriated,

✍ *Knavish*

Contextual Meaning(s) : Adjective; marked by skill in deception
Synonyms : sly, tricksy, tricky, wily

✍ *Latter*

Contextual Meaning(s) : Adjective; referring to the second of two things or persons mentioned (or the last one or ones of several); noun the second of two or the second mentioned of two
Synonyms : second

✍ *Mugging*

Contextual Meaning(s) : noun; the crime of attacking and robbing somebody in a public image, crime of robbery
Synonyms : attack, robbery

✍ *Obscure*

Contextual Meaning(s) : Verb; make unclear; make difficult to perceive or sight; make undecipherable or imperceptible by obscuring or concealing; make less visible or unclear; make unclear, indistinct, or blurred
Other Meaning(s) : adjective not clearly understood or expressed; not drawing attention; not famous or acclaimed; marked by difficulty of style or expression; remote and separate physically or socially; difficult to find;
Synonyms : bedim, veil, befog, becloud,

✍ *Prejudice*

Contextual Meaning(s) : Verb; influence (somebody's) opinion in advance; disadvantage by prejudice
Other Meaning(s) : noun a partiality that prevents objective consideration of an issue or situation;
Synonyms : prepossess, bias, preconception

✍ *Probe*

Contextual Meaning(s) : Verb; question or examine thoroughly and closely; examine physically with or as if with a probe
Other Meaning(s) : noun an investigation conducted using a flexible surgical instrument to explore an injury or a body cavity; an exploratory action or expedition; a flexible slender surgical instrument used to explore wounds or body cavities; an inquiry into unfamiliar or questionable activities
Synonyms : investigation, examine

Repudiate

Contextual Meaning(s) : Verb; refuse to acknowledge, ratify, or recognize as valid; reject as untrue, unfounded, or unjust; refuse to recognize or pay; cast off or disown
Synonyms : renounce

Respondent

Contextual Meaning(s) : Adjective; someone who responds;
Other Meaning(s) : Noun; the codefendant (especially in a divorce proceeding) who is accused of adultery with the corespondent
Synonyms : answerer

Salubrious

Contextual Meaning(s) : Adjective; favorable to health of mind or body; promoting health; healthful
Synonyms : healthy, good for you

Sapience

Contextual Meaning(s) : Noun; ability to apply knowledge or experience or understanding or common sense and insight
Synonyms : sagacity

Semantics

Contextual Meaning(s) : Noun; the study of language meanings and fineries.
Synonyms : linguistics

Slant

Contextual Meaning(s) : Noun; a biased way of looking at or presenting something;
Other Meaning(s) : degree of deviation from a horizontal plane; verb present with a bias; lie obliquely; heel over; to incline or bend from a vertical position
Synonyms : tilt, lean, tip

Trivialize

Contextual Meaning(s) : Verb; make less serious or insignificant
Synonyms : minimalize

Veracious

Contextual Meaning(s) : Adjective; precisely accurate; habitually speaking the truth
Synonyms : honest

Vilify

Contextual Meaning(s) : Verb; spread negative information about
Synonyms : revile, vituperate, rail

Vulnerable

Contextual Meaning(s) : Adjective; capable of being wounded or hurt; susceptible to criticism or persuasion or temptation; susceptible to attack
Synonyms : exposed

The United States and the Soviet Union have had deep-rooted ideological, economic and political differences since much before the second world war. The USSR and the United States were allies during *World War II* if only because both countries did not **endorse** Hitler's Nazi ideologies. They ,however did maintain the required **modicum** of alignment required in fighting the **megalomaniac** Adolf Hitler.

Once the WW II left Germany in **tatters**, the Allies split it into two ; western part was **apportioned** to the allies and became known as the Federal Republic of Germany). The eastern part went to USSR and was named the German Democratic Republic .

America, because of its geographic isolation, had avoided permanent alliances with other countries till the second world war. However, President Truman then realized that **providence** lay in breaking this tradition. In 1949 ten European nations entered into a pact with the United States and Canada. This created the North Atlantic Treaty Organization (NATO), a military alliance for defending all members from outside attack. This represented a military coalition of all the major allied forces except USSR.

On the eastern side of Europe, USSR under Stalin took control of most eastern European countries and imposed communist rule there- these came to be named the Eastern bloc. The Warsaw Pact is the name commonly given to the treaty between eastern European countries, and the Soviet Union. In a way this was a response of the communist bloc countries to the democratic countries' NATO alliance.

The following decades witnessed *the cold war* – a conflict between the Soviet Union led nations and the nations led by the United States. It was fought by all means - **propaganda**, economic war, diplomatic **haggling,** spying and occasional military clashes. It was fought by **proxy** in all places - in neutral states, in newly independent nations in Africa, Asia and even in outer space.

The **inveterate** differences between USA and USSR were intensified as a result of their mutual suspicions immediately after the Second World War.

The United States wanted to encourage free trade throughout the world. The Soviet Union wanted to shield off her own sphere from international commerce. Russia feared that trade with the West would involve the risk of Russia being opened to western influences which would have eroded the strength of their **totalitarian** regime. These differences led to much **reciprocal** ill feeling.

The Vietnam War was a **distended** proxy war between the United States and the Soviet Union aided by China, which had become a Communist country. The Soviet Union and China worked together to help North Vietnam fight South Vietnam. The United States directly fought in the war against North Vietnam. The war went on from 1955 to 1973, and symbolized the military equivalent of the cold war.

During the 1950s, there was a "red scare" in the United States. The American establishment was worried about Communists becoming powerful in the United States. Many Americans were accused of being Communists. Accusing someone of being a communists was like being charged with **blasphemy**. Many artists, writers and actors were **blackballed** and were not allowed to act in any movies after they were accused of being Communists. This was called *McCarthyism*; senator Joseph McCarthy was an **emblem** of the communist **paranoia** in USA. He **stigmatized** and wiped out his political opponents in the process. Ultimately the establishment became **leery** of his tactics; he was **censured** after 1953 when the United States came under the presidency of Dwight Eisenhower.

Eisenhower created a policy to reduce military defense spending while rapidly increasing the amount of nuclear weapons it had. It was a policy of nuclear **deterrence** which means that the United States built so many nuclear weapons, it intimidated the Soviet Union from attacking them.

Eisenhower's Vice-President Richard Nixon engaged in several talks with Nikita Khrushchev during the 1950's. One of these was called the "Kitchen Debate" because it happened in a kitchen at the World's Fair. At the end of the decade, a United States plane which spied on the Soviet Union, called U2, crashed. This was very bad for U.S.-Soviet relations, and the **fissure** between the two countries reopened after this relatively peaceful Eisenhower presidency.

In 1959, Fidel Castro took over power in Cuba. He followed anti-american trade policies and built strong links with USSR. This was very threatening to the USA because Cuba was right next to America. This was the highest period of tension during the Cold War .While the Soviet Union tried to supply Cuba with nuclear missiles, the United States sent a large amount of ships and B-52 bombers around Cuba. Thankfully, the United States under Kennedy and Soviet Union under Khrushchev came to a **climactic** agreement and diffused the tension. It was the closest the world was to having a nuclear war.

After this episode, Khrushchev lost prestige while, China broke away from Russia. But American president J .F. Kennedy was **lionized** and acquired **cult** status. He was seen as the man who faced down the Russians. Both sides had a fright; they set up a telep 'hotline' to talk directly in any such crisis situation. In 1963, they agreed on a Nuclear Test Ban Treaty. Cuba was the start of the end of the Cold War.

A phase called " détente" began after the Cuban Missile Crisis in 1962, and ended around 1980. The word "**detente**" meant less tension between the two superpowers. Around this time, the United States built a good relationship with China, giving the Soviet Union a disadvantage during the Cold War. During the 1970's, the United States and the Soviet Union both signed several treaties which reduced the amount of nuclear weapons each country had.

The policy of détente ended in 1981, when president Ronald Reagan ordered a massive military **fortification** to challenge the Soviet Union's influence around the world. The United States began to support (by giving money and weapons to them) anti-communists all over the world who wanted to overthrow their communist governments.

The Soviet Union had a devolving economy during this decade and was trying to keep up with the United States in military spending, but could not. The Soviet Union invaded Afghanistan in 1979, but had a very difficult time winning against the Afghanistan freedom fighters. The Soviet Union's failed invasion of Afghanistan is often compared to the United States' failure during the Vietnam War.

In the late 1980s the new Soviet President Mikhail Gorbachev made an effort to make an ally of the United States and the soviets realized that communism, inspite of an 80 year long trial, is not paying the dividends besides curbing personal freedom.

After the fall of the Berlin Wall in 1989 and without Communist rule holding the countries that compiled the Soviet Union together, the USSR broke into many smaller countries, like Russia, Ukraine, Lithuania and Georgia. The nations of Eastern Europe became democratic governments, and the period of the Cold War was over. The Soviet Union formally folded up in December 1991.

Not all historians agree on when the Cold War ended. Some think it ended when the Berlin Wall fell. Others think it ended when the Soviet Union ended.

Cold war era conflicts were aptly exploited by novelists who wrote classic spy stories, many of these novelists were themselves ex-spies or war veterans.

A noteworthy **fictional** Cold War spy is the heroic, upper-class James Bond, secret agent 007 of the British Secret Service, a mixture of assassin and counter-intelligence officer introduced by Ian Fleming. Despite the commercial success of Fleming's fantastical anti-Communist novels, other former spies, such as John le Carré and Len Deighton, created anti-heroic **protagonists** who were almost your guy-next-door.

Then there was also a **cornucopia** of cold war based politico–military thrillers from Frederick Forsyth, Ken Follett and Robert Ludlum; the last one created the legendary Jason Bourne series.

Hollywood films, too, were busy during the cold war ,exposing life behind the Iron Curtain and **ferreting** out spies and **subversive** at home. *Walk East on Beacon* (1952), based on an article by J. Edgar Hoover, the long time FBI director was a **harbinger** of this genre. Most notable ones dealing with **espionage** and political **intrigue** were Ice Station Zebra, The Package and The Hunt for Red October.

Many science fiction Hollywood movies were made in the 1950's such as Invasion of the Body Snatchers, War of the Worlds and the Day the Earth Stood Still ; a lot of these films reflected the Red Scare that took place at the time. The aliens in these films reflected communists, and the fear of them taking over all earthlings and converting them into aliens mirrored spread of communism !

The end of cold war makes USA the single superpower in the world. But this *post cold war* era is again full of **strife** of a stranger variety. There are religious, regional and racial assaults on world peace, besides the never ending economic and environmental hazards. Mankind keeps living on a prayer !

Apportioned
Contextual Meaning(s) : Adjective; given out in portions to different entities
Synonyms : dealt out

Blackballed
Contextual Meaning(s) : Verb; expelled from a community or group.
Synonyms : banished

Blasphemy
Contextual Meaning(s) : Noun; blasphemous language (expressing disrespect for God or for something sacred); blasphemous behavior; the act of depriving something of its sacred character
Synonyms : profanation, desecration, sacrilege

Censured
Contextual Meaning(s) : Adjective; officially and strongly disapproved; officially rebuked or found blameworthy
Synonyms : condemned

Climactic
Contextual Meaning(s) : Adjective; consisting of or causing the decisive moment
Synonyms : culminating point

Cornucopia
Contextual Meaning(s) : Noun; the property of being extremely abundant;
Other Meaning(s) : a goat's horn filled with grain and flowers and fruit symbolizing prosperity
Synonyms : profuseness, richness

Cult
Contextual Meaning(s) : Noun; an extreme or excessive admiration for a person, philosophy of life, or activity, e.g. the cult of youth, a cult hero
Other Meaning(s) : adjective; trendy, offbeat, alternative, out of the ordinary, religious group
Synonyms : craze, idolization of somebody or some thing

Detente
Contextual Meaning(s) : Noun; the easing of tensions or strained relations (especially between nations)
Synonyms : cease fire

Distended
Contextual Meaning(s) : Adjective; abnormally expanded or increased in size; ('swollen' is sometimes used in combination); abnormally distended especially by fluids or gas
Synonyms : bloated, turgid

Deterrence
Contextual Meaning(s) : Verb; restrain from taking action, to discourage somebody from taking action or prevent something from happening, especially by making somebody feel afraid or anxious
Synonyms : avoidance, prevention, anticipation

Emblem
Contextual Meaning(s) : Noun; special design or visual object representing a quality, type, group, etc.; a visible symbol representing an abstract idea
Synonyms : allegory

Endorse
Contextual Meaning(s) : Noun; be behind; approve of; give support or one's approval to
Synonyms : certify

Espionage
Contextual Meaning(s) : Noun; the systematic use of spies to get military or political secrets
Synonyms : spying

Ferreting
Contextual Meaning(s) : hounding or harrying relentlessly; searching and discovering through persistent investigation
Synonyms : hound

- **Fictional**
  Contextual Meaning(s) : Adjective; related to or involving literary fiction; formed or conceived by the imagination
  Synonyms : fabricated, invented

- **Fissure**
  Contextual Meaning(s) : Verb; break into fissures or fine cracks
  Synonyms : cleft, crevice

- **Fortification**
  Contextual Meaning(s) : Noun; the addition of an ingredient for the purpose of enrichment (as the addition of alcohol to wine or the addition of vitamins to food); defensive structure consisting of walls or mounds built around a stronghold to strengthen it;
  Other Meaning(s) : the art or science of strengthening defenses
  Synonyms : munition

- **Haggling**
  Contextual Meaning(s) : Noun; an instance of intense argument (as in bargaining)
  Synonyms : wrangling

- **Harbinger**
  Contextual Meaning(s) : Noun; an indication of the approach of something or someone; verb foreshadow or presage
  Synonyms : announce

- **Intrigue**
  Contextual Meaning(s) : Noun; a crafty and involved plot to achieve your (usually sinister) ends; a clandestine love affair; verb cause to be interested or curious; form intrigues (for) in an underhand manner
  Synonyms : machination, scheme

- **Inveterate**
  Contextual Meaning(s) : Adjective; having a habit of long standing
  Synonyms : confirmed, habitual

- **Leery**
  Contextual Meaning(s) : Adjective; openly distrustful and unwilling to confide
  Synonyms : mistrustful

- **Lionized**
  Contextual Meaning(s) : Verb; made into a hero
  Synonyms : glorified

- **Megalomaniac**
  Contextual Meaning(s) : Noun; a pathological egotist
  Synonyms : pathological-egotist

- **Modicum**
  Contextual Meaning(s) : Noun a small or moderate or token amount
  Synonyms : iota

- **Paranoia**
  Contextual Meaning(s) : Noun; a psychological disorder characterized by delusions of persecution or grandeur
  Synonyms : psychosis

- **Propaganda**
  Contextual Meaning(s) : Noun; information that is spread for the purpose of promoting some cause
  Synonyms : publicity

- **Providence**
  Contextual Meaning(s) : Noun; the prudence and care exercised by someone in the management of resources;
  Other Meaning(s) : noun the guardianship and control exercised by a deity; the capital and largest city of Rhode Island; located int northeastern Rhode Island on Narragansett Bay; ite of Brown University; a manifestation of God's foresightful care for his creatures
  Synonyms : prudence

- **Protagonist**
  Contextual Meaning(s) : Noun; the leading character or one of the major characters in a play, film or novel.
  Synonyms : lead, star

- **Proxy**
  Contextual Meaning(s) : Noun; a person authorized to act for another

Other Meaning(s) : noun a power of attorney document given by shareholders of a corporation authorizing a specific vote on their behalf at a corporate meeting;
Synonyms : placeholder, procurator

✎ *Reciprocal*

Contextual Meaning(s) : Adjective; especially given or done in return;
Other Meaning(s) : noun something (a term or expression or concept) that has a reciprocal relation to something else; hybridization involving a pair of crosses that reverse the sexes associated with each genotype; (mathematics) one of a pair of numbers whose product is 1: the reciprocal of 2/3 is 3/2; the multiplicative inverse of 7 is 1/7
Synonyms : *mutual,*

✎ *Stigmatized*

Contextual Meaning(s) : Verb; to accuse or condemn or openly or formally or brand as disgraceful
Other Meaning(s) : Verb; mark with a stigma or stigmata
Synonyms : branded, denounced

✎ *Strife*

Contextual Meaning(s) : Noun; bitter conflict; heated often violent dissension; lack of agreement or harmony
Synonyms : discord, unrest

✎ *Subversive*

Contextual Meaning(s) : Adjective; in opposition to a civil authority or government;
Other Meaning(s) : Noun; a radical supporter of political or social revolution
Synonyms : seditious

✎ *Tatters*

Contextual Meaning(s) : Noun; badly damaged or completely spoiled
Synonyms : shreds, ruined

✎ *Totalitarian*

Contextual Meaning(s) : Adjective; characterized by a government in which the political authority exercises absolute and centralized control; of or relating to the principles of totalitarianism according to which the state regulates every realm of life; noun an adherent of totalitarian principles or totalitarian government
Synonyms : autocratic

It's no secret that newspapers are in trouble in the new media age. Circulation is dropping, ad revenue is shrinking, and as a result the industry has experienced an unprecedented wave of layoffs, cutbacks, **bankruptcies** and even the complete shutdown of some papers. The big question now is, can newspapers survive, or are they bound to become web-only operations or disappear entirely? Will the internet hammer the last nail in the coffin of printed papers?

After all, once *The New York Times* admits print's days are numbered, it's a long, slow and **excruciating** downward spiral to the point that the newspaper, like the vinyl record, is a **relic** for collectors and **anachronists.**

No, newspapers still have a role to fill, and even if you're not NASA, you can still appreciate the wisdom of having a **contingency** plan, just in case something goes **haywire** with the main internet engine. One tends to forget, newspapers serve another function ,namely continuity. Any publication here is a public record and is **archived** for **posterity**. Yes, you can access those archives on the web news too, but what happens if the parent company **detracts** something controversial and further the website simply **vaporizes** one fine day!

Newspapers can also assign professional writers to a given subject or issue and maintain coverage over an extended period, whereas freelance 'web'-sters grow restless and tend to move to the Next Big Thing with great rapidity. Most major newspapers have correspondents specializing in covering education, crime, technology, **psephology** and the like. They nurture and develop "sources" and can provide in depth analysis and **prognosis** of various stories on a continuous basis. Newspaper journalists have a reputation and a fan following which they can't let down unlike the **frivolous** internet bloggers or the **dilettante** web correspondent.

Nevertheless these very same Newspaper journalists' articles can also be accessed through the e-newspaper which turns the argument upside down.

You have to make some concessions to the web as a medium. Stories, paragraphs and sentences are shorter because a screen just isn't as readable as a paper page. And you have to make concessions to our ever-shortening attention spans, a phenomenon that **predates** the internet. You can also expect many more of those **abstruse** abbreviations , usually belonging to college campuses or the digital world like *lol, asap* and the works.

The good part for a net journalist is that there are fewer people looking over your shoulder, catching your misspellings, factual **indiscretion** and grammatical **gaffes**, **deprecating** your word choices and imposing their own style. Put **pithily,** there is little editorial **intrusion.**

We're also all learning that some of the most important readers are not human, they're search engines. And, if we want hits, the rough equivalent of newspaper readers, we have to include certain key words, which are often **expletives**. That would mean a compromise with the journalist's story writing **etiquette**!

Looking at the long term future one would agree that for the classic newspapers, the outlook isn't good. They simply do not have the same adaptability that online news does. The staff in newsrooms have shrunk by 25% in three years, and just under 27% since the beginning of the decade. This is **ominous** for the print media **genre**. If this trend were to continue, simple math can show that it would not take long before what was left of standard newspaper businesses all but evaporated.

The internet is superior to classic newspapers in terms of providing content in almost every way. For example, producing online articles does not require ink or paper, so it is more friendly to the environment. Also, server storage and website creation is fairly inexpensive in comparison to the physical components necessary to produce a standard newspaper, such as printing presses. It's also much cheaper to display beautiful, colored pictures on a monitor than it is to print them in a newspaper.

Also, online news can be delivered almost instantly. Newspapers come out once per day; news online is being released by the minute and as stories evolve, they are updated. If there is a change in the story at the last minute, standard newspapers either need to be completely reprinted or the story needs to be saved for another day. Online, a simple edit and re-upload of the article anytime, from anywhere, can bring a story up to speed.

Even the newspaper's one main strength, its mobility, is being challenged. Smartphones and portable computers are becoming ever more popular. Things like the Kindle, iPad, Netbooks, Smartphones, etc. can be taken almost anywhere and with a wireless internet connection, these can update the news as it arrives.

There will probably always be a **niche** market that simply prefers the old fashioned method, but the question is how long will the size of this niche group be large enough for someone to continue **catering** to. Printed type will be popular with people not accustomed to technology, as well as with people who encounter severe eye strain when staring at a screen for extended periods of time.

I think the final factor in the **demise** of printed type will be environmental concerns. As the world tries to become more and more environmentally friendly, habits like mass felling of trees will be reduced and eliminated whenever possible. Mother Nature would prefer we do our reading electronically, and while I do not foresee an immediate collapse of the classic newspaper, it will happen sooner or later.

Unfortunately, the argument for the environmental positives of the abandonment of print media neglects to consider the other side of the table.

Like the costs of staying online are substantial too. The attainment, refinement, transformation and disposal of the rare elements and chemicals found within the computer you are using to read this comment likely outweigh the savings in paper and emissions.

And before putting the old newspaper out on the curb for the weekly pick up, there are **myriad** useful things one could do with them.

On the lighter side, since Newsprint absorbs grease very well, one can use it under a paper towel to **wick** away oil from fried foods. You can insulate hot or cold food with crumpled or layered newsprint. One can use a stack of old newspaper for pressing flowers. The paper absorbs the moisture well. There is nothing like old newspaper to wash and dry windows as well as car windshields for a streak-free shine. Crumpled old newsprint is great for packing material besides absorb odors and will help leather shoes keep their shape. Newspaper can be **composted**. Just shred it and mix it in with fresh lawn clippings for fastest results. My mom uses newspaper to cover plants at night during cold snaps.

Additionally, I can use as newspaper as an umbrella when i get caught in a sudden rain. They are also usable to protect car-seats from muddy or wet clothing .They can be spread over outdoor benches to protect clothing. I see people cover store or home windows when **remodeling**. Families cover furniture with them when away on vacation. Can an ipad or smart phone perform even a **scintilla** of these tasks ?

Every established newspaper has some classic columns, which have substantial readers . Readers who can not imagine beginning their day without the read. God forbid, if the newspaper sinks in the internet tsunami, where will one read its **obituary** ?

- **Abstruse**
  Contextual Meaning(s) : Adjective difficult to penetrate; incomprehensible to one of ordinary understanding or knowledge
  Synonyms : deep, recondite

- **Anachronists**
  Contextual Meaning(s) : Noun; people or thinking living not synchronization with time
  Synonyms : misdated

- **Archived**
  Contextual Meaning(s) : Verb; tiled or stored for future reforms
  Synonyms : stored, filed

- **Bankruptcies**
  Contextual Meaning(s) : noun; the state of having been legally declared bankrupt
  Synonyms : insolvency, indebtedness

- **Catering**
  Contextual Meaning(s) : Noun; providing food and services
  Synonyms : providing, servicing

- **Composted**
  Contextual Meaning(s) : Verb; Converted to manure
  Synonyms : converted

- **Contingency**
  Contextual Meaning(s) : Noun; a possible event or occurrence or result
  Other Meaning(s) : the state of being contingent on something;
  Synonyms : eventuality, contingence

- **Demise**
  Contextual Meaning(s) : Noun; the time when something ends or dies
  Synonyms : death, dying

- **Deprecating**
  Contextual Meaning(s) : Adjective; tending to diminish or disparage
  Synonyms : belittling, slighting

- **Detracts**
  Contextual Meaning(s) : Verb; takes away from a desired direction; diminishes
  Synonyms : misleads

- **Dilettante**
  Contextual Meaning(s) : Adjective; showing frivolous or superficial interest; amateurish;
  Other Meaning(s) : noun an amateur who engages in an activity without serious intentions and who pretends to have knowledge
  Synonyms : dabbler

- **Excruciating**
  Contextual Meaning(s) : Adjective; extremely painful
  Synonyms : agonizing, torture-some

- **Expletives** (Noun)
  Contextual Meaning(s) : Noun; unparliamentary words or terms
  Synonyms : swearword

- **Etiquette**
  Contextual Meaning(s) : noun; the rules and conventions governing correct or polite behaviour in society in general or in a specific social or professional group or situation
  Synonyms : manners, decorum

- **Fickle**
  Contextual Meaning(s) : Adjective; marked by erratic changeableness in affections or attachments; liable to sudden unpredictable change
  Synonyms : volatile, erratic, mercurial, quicksilver

- **Frivolous**
  Contextual Meaning(s) : Adjective; not serious in content or attitude or behavior
  Synonyms : flighty

- **Gaffes**
  Contextual Meaning(s) : Noun; (plural) socially or professionaly awkward acts.
  Synonyms : blunders

- **Genre**
  Contextual Meaning(s) : Noun; a category, style or class of an art form
  Synonyms : category, style

Haywire

Contextual Meaning(s) : Adjective; not functioning properly;
Other Meaning(s) : informal or slang terms for mentally irregular; noun wire for tying up bales of hay
Synonyms : awry, whacky

Indiscretion

Contextual Meaning(s) : Noun a petty misdeed; the trait of being injudicious
Synonyms : peccadillo, injudiciousness

Intrusion

Contextual Meaning(s) : Noun entrance by force or without permission or welcome;
Other Meaning(s) : rock produced by an intrusive process; the forcing of molten rock into fissures or between strata of an earlier rock formation; entry to another's property without right or permission; any entry into an area not previously occupied
Synonyms : trespass, encroachment, usurpation, invasion

Myriad

Contextual Meaning(s) : Adjective; too numerous to be counted; noun a large indefinite number
Synonyms : countless, infinite

Niche

Contextual Meaning(s) : Noun a position particularly well suited to the person who occupies it;
Other Meaning(s) : noun (ecology) the status of an organism within its environment and community (affecting its survival as a species); an enclosure that is set back or indented; a small concavity
Synonyms : ecological niche, recess, recession, corner

Obituary

Contextual Meaning(s) : Noun a notice of someone's death; usually includes a short biography
Synonyms : obit, necrology

Ominous

Contextual Meaning(s) : Adjective presaging ill fortune; threatening or foreshadowing evil or tragic developments
Synonyms : inauspicious, threatening

Pithily

Contextual Meaning(s) : Adverb; in a brief manner
Synonyms : sententiously

Posterity

Contextual Meaning(s) : Noun all future generations; all of the offspring of a given progenitor
Synonyms : descendants

Prognosis

Contextual Meaning(s) : Noun a prediction about how something (as the weather) will develop
Other Meaning(s) : noun a prediction of the course of a disease;
Synonyms : medical projection, forecast

Psephology

Contextual Meaning(s) : Noun the branch of sociology that studies election trends (as by opinion polls)
Synonyms : election-study

Predates

Contextual Meaning(s) : verb; to come before something else in time
Synonyms : preexist

Relic

Contextual Meaning(s) : Noun an antiquity that has survived from the distant past; something of sentimental value
Synonyms : souvenir, token

Remodelling

Contextual Meaning(s) : verb; to renovate or alter the structure or style of something such as building, room, or design
Synonyms : refurnishing, reconstruction

Scintilla

Contextual Meaning(s) : Noun a tiny or scarcely detectable amount
Other Meaning(s) : noun a sparkling glittering particles;
Synonyms : shred iota

Vaporizes

Contextual Meaning(s) : Verb; when something disappearing or vanishing
Other Meaning(s) :
Synonyms : disappears, vanishes

Wick

Contextual Meaning(s) : Noun a loosely woven cord (in a candle or oil lamp) that draws fuel by capillary action up into the flame; any piece of cord that conveys liquid by capillary action
Synonyms : taper

After Walter Mondale was soundly **trounced** by Ronald Reagan who won 49 states in the 1984 election, "loser" was added to the list of **abusive** words ; it became the kiss of death for any politician to be so labeled. This word could no longer be spoken out loud in mixed company.

A school in Seattle renamed its Easter eggs 'spring spheres' to avoid causing offence to people who did not celebrate Easter. Any terms using the word 'man' as a prefix or suffix have been ruled as not being politically correct. 'Manhole' is now referred to as a 'utility' or 'maintenance' hole!

Political correctness first **germinated** in a think tank called The Frankfurt School in Germany in 1923. The purpose was to find a solution to the biggest problem facing the implementers of communism in Russia. Maybe the politically correct phrases would lead to a level playing field and **induce** an **egalitarian** society, they thought. However, it's the eighties when the term really caught on.

But now its just about being "nice to people", and treating them with proper respect. It could be also called good manners. People are sentimental about many things, and all measures must be taken so as to not offend somebody. So those who have died are referred to as "differently alive", and we say "Companion animal" instead of pet !

Somebody with "Ample proportions" is actually obese or fat, "Armed intervention" is a phrase, the **diplomats** use for "war", "Between jobs" is what the **genteel** use instead of "unemployed".

A traditional figure of speech called **Euphemism** has always been used to **cloak** an offending word and replace it with a better sounding and less **explicit** substitution. Political correctness is just a **novel** term for the same literary device.

The **sprouting** of these "morally correct" expressions can be attributed to the spread of media, increased intermingling of cultures, and the **burgeoning** communication technology. As one's communication reaches people of a different background, more and more unacceptable words are discovered and have to be replaced by **benign** words or phrases. Even if these phrases are much longer and at times appear **satirical**, they are now in **vogue**.

Thus **"Disinformation"** replaces "Lie", "Rebels" become "Freedom fighters", **"Indisposed"** means "Sick" and **"Inventory** leakage" is a **subtler** though longer way of saying "Theft"!

A writer or speaker has a responsibility to ensure that his content does not offend or **prejudice** children, even if his sentences don't remain **succinct**. So we substitute **midget** with "vertically challenged", "fat" with " horizontally challenged", "dishonest" with "ethically disoriented" "fired" with "laid off ", "blind" with "visually challenged" and "poor" with "financially **inept**".

If you work with a corporate, remember a great company never cancels any event, it's just "rescheduled". You never make a mistake, its just an "error of judgment". And calling anyone "dumb", however idiotic he may be, can cost you your job, so just stick to "**cerebrally** challenged".

Often non-verbal communication can also cause damage to some folks. For instance, an angry sports person **gesticulating** on the playground, an image or photograph displayed by an advertiser or a cartoon or **caricature** that **spites** anyone's sensibility, can all **boomerang**.

You have to be careful, a "homeless" sounds **churlish**, so better replace it by "residentially flexible"; "second-hand" must become "pre-owned". "Collateral damage" means "Civilian casualties" and a "prison" is **impertinent** so better make it a "correctional facility"!

A journalist could be sued for **libel** unless he calls an " insane" as "reality challenged", "Lazy" as "motivationally dispossessed","Murderer" as "termination specialist" and a "Nerd" as "under-attractive" !

Unless you want to be **ostracized** for being a racist, be careful to address a "black" as "african american" ," red indian" as "native american" , and a " latino " as " Hispanic ".

Police cannot "suspect" anybody anymore, they can just call him a "person of interest". No one is "unsure", it is a "conceptual conflict".

One has to be suitably **attired** for the occasion in order to be politically correct. One has to **spruce** up in a dark suit and tie for a board meeting. At a **mourning**, one has to wear a colour depending on the culture of the place. At a Hindu home, don't forget to remove your footwear before entering.

Even one's actions, positions on issues , choice of candidates one votes for and treatment of animals is closely **audited**. You have to mind your net- etiquette, and remember *public display of affection* can be either okay or **egregiously** bad depending on place and culture.

The way we refer to someone with a physical disability has changed several times in the last 30 years or so: first, the highly offensive **crippled** gave way to *handicapped*, but then that was also seen as offensive, so the preferred adjective chosen was *disabled*. But disabled is not without its critics, who dislike its focus on what a person *can't* do rather than what they can. This has led to newer expressions such as *physically challenged* and *differently abled*.

These constant changes in 'politically correct' terms have attracted a certain amount of **mockery**. Not surprisingly linguist Stephen Pinker has called this ever changing verbal landscape as a "**euphemism** treadmill "!

🐦 **Abusive**
Contextual Meaning(s) : Adjective; characterized by physical or psychological maltreatment; expressing offensive reproach
Synonyms : insulting, opprobrious, scurrilous

🐦 **Attired**
Contextual Meaning(s) : Adjective; dressed or clothed especially in fine; garments often used in combination
Synonyms : appareled, dressed, garbed

🐦 **Audited**
Contextual Meaning(s) : examined carefully for accuracy with the intent of verification
Synonyms : scrutinized

🐦 **Benign**
Contextual Meaning(s) : Adjective; pleasant and beneficial in nature or influence; kindness of disposition or manner; not dangerous to health;
Other Meaning(s) : not recurrent or progressive (especially of a tumor)
Synonyms : benignant

🐦 **Boomerang**
Contextual Meaning(s) : Verb; return to the initial position from where it came; & hit the originating source.
Other Meaning(s) : noun a curved piece of wood; when properly thrown will return to thrower; a miscalculation that recoils on its maker;
Synonyms : backfire

🐦 **Burgeoning**
Contextual Meaning(s) : Verb; growing or becoming bigger.
Synonyms : expanding, proliferating

🐦 **Cerebrally**
Contextual Meaning(s) : Adverb; in the brain; in an intellectual manner
Synonyms : intellectually

🐦 **Churlish**
Contextual Meaning(s) : Adjective; having a bad disposition; surly; rude and boorish
Synonyms : choleric

🐦 **Cloak**
Contextual Meaning(s) : Verb; hide under a false appearance
Synonyms : mask

🐦 **Crippled**
Contextual Meaning(s) : Adjective; disabled in the feet or legs
Synonyms : lame, gimpy

🐦 **Caricature**
Contextual Meaning(s) : noun; a drawing, description, or performance that exaggerates somebody's or something's characteristics for humorous or satirical effect
Synonyms : drawing, sketch

🐦 **Diplomats**
Contextual Meaning(s) : Noun; officers in a countries foreign embassy.
Synonyms : foreign officers

🐦 **Disinformation**
Contextual Meaning(s) : Noun; misinformation that is deliberately disseminated in order to influence or confuse rivals (foreign enemies or business competitors etc.)
Synonyms : deception

🐦 **Egalitarian**
Contextual Meaning(s) : Adjective; favoring social equality;
Synonyms : equalitarian, classless

🐦 **Egregiously**
Contextual Meaning(s) : Adverb; Shamelessly by (bad or civil)
Synonyms : blatantly

🐦 **Euphemism**
Contextual Meaning(s) : Noun; an inoffensive expression that is substituted for one that is considered offensive
Synonyms : political correctness

🐦 **Explicit**

Contextual Meaning(s) : Adjective; precisely and clearly expressed or readily observable; leaving nothing to implication; in accordance with fact or the primary Meaning(s) of a term
Synonyms : expressed, denotative

🐦 **Euphemism**

Contextual Meaning(s) : noun; a word or phrase used in place of a term that might be considered too direct, harsh,
Synonyms : offensive

🐦 **Genteel**

Contextual Meaning(s) : Adjective; marked by refinement in taste and manners
Synonyms : urbane, cultured, polite

🐦 **Germinated**

Contextual Meaning(s) : Verb; took birth, was originated.
Synonyms : conceived

🐦 **Gesticulating**

Contextual Meaning(s) : Adjective; making gestures (usually by hands) while speaking
Synonyms : hand movements

🐦 **Impudent**

Contextual Meaning(s) : Adjective; marked by casual disrespect; improperly forward or bold
Synonyms : insolent, impertinent, saucy

🐦 **Indisposed**

Contextual Meaning(s) : Adjective; somewhat ill or prone to illness
Other Meaning(s) : (usually followed by 'to') strongly opposed;
Synonyms : averse, unwell

🐦 **Induce**

Contextual Meaning(s) : Verb; reason or establish by induction; cause to do; cause to act in a specified manner; cause to arise; cause to occur rapidly;
Synonyms : stimulate, cause

🐦 **Inept**

Contextual Meaning(s) : Adjective; revealing lack of perceptiveness or judgment or finesse; generally incompetent and ineffectual; not elegant or graceful in expression
Synonyms : tactless, feckless, awkward, clumsy, cumbersome

🐦 **Inventory**

Contextual Meaning(s) : Noun; a detailed list of all the items in stock; (accounting) the value of a firm's current assets including raw materials and work in progress and finished goods; the merchandise that a shop has on hand; a collection of resources;
Other Meaning(s) : verb make or include in an itemized record or report
Synonyms : stock, armory

🐦 **Impertinent**

Contextual Meaning(s) : Adjective; characterized by a lightly pert and exuberant quality; improperly forward or bold; not pertinent to the matter under consideration
Synonyms : Irrelevant

🐦 **Libel**

Contextual Meaning(s) : Noun; a false and malicious publication printed for the purpose of defaming a living person;
Other Meaning(s) : noun the written statement of a plaintiff explaining the cause of action (the defamation) and any relief he seeks; verb print slanderous statements against
Synonyms : defamation

🐦 **Midget**

Contextual Meaning(s) : Adjective; very small in height; noun a person who is markedly small
Synonyms : bantam, diminutive

🐦 **Mockery**

Contextual Meaning(s) : Noun; humorous or satirical mimicry; showing your contempt by derision; a composition that imitates somebody's style in a humorous way
Synonyms : parody, lampoon, spoof, burlesque, travesty, charade, pasquinade

- **Mourning**

  Contextual Meaning(s) : Noun; state of sorrow over the death or departure of a loved one; the passionate and demonstrative activity of expressing grief
  Other Meaning(s) : Adjective; sorrowful through loss or deprivation;
  Synonyms : bereavement, lamentation

- **Novel**

  Contextual Meaning(s) : Adjective; pleasantly new or different; original and of a kind not seen before;
  Other Meaning(s) : Noun; a printed and bound book that is an extended work of fiction; a extended fictional work in prose; usually in the form of a story
  Synonyms : refreshing, fresh, new

- **Ostracized**

  Contextual Meaning(s) : Verb; exclude form a society or group.
  Synonyms : shun, exclude

- **Prejudice**

  Contextual Meaning(s) : Noun; a partiality that prevents objective consideration of an issue or situation;
  Synonyms : prepossess, bias, preconception

- **Satirical**

  Contextual Meaning(s) : Adjective; exposing human folly to ridicule
  Synonyms : lampooning

- **Spites**

  Contextual Meaning(s) : Verb; hurts someone
  Synonyms : injures

- **Sprouting**

  Contextual Meaning(s) : Noun; the process whereby seeds or spores sprout and begin to grow
  Synonyms : germination

- **Spruce**

  Contextual Meaning(s) : Verb; dress and groom with particular care, as for a special occasion; make neat, smart, or trim
  Other Meaning(s) : Adjective marked by up-to-dateness in dress and manners; noun any coniferous tree of the genus Picea; light soft moderately strong wood of spruce trees; used especially for timbers and millwork;
  Synonyms : preen

- **Succinct**

  Contextual Meaning(s) : Adjective; briefly giving the gist of something
  Synonyms : compendious, compact, summary

- **Subtler**

  Contextual Meaning(s) : Adjective; slight and not obvious
  Synonyms : understated

- **Trounced**

  Contextual Meaning(s) : Verb; Comprehensive defeat.
  Synonyms : crushed

- **Vogue**

  Contextual Meaning(s) : Noun; the popular taste at a given time; a current state of general acceptance and use
  Synonyms : trend, style, currency

ARE WE GETTING TALLER?

Anyone who has ever visited a home built around the time of the Revolutionary War along the back alleys of Philadelphia or Boston has been struck, **metaphorically** if not literally, by the characteristically low ceilings and small door frames. Even houses built in the early 1800s can make one believe that a person of those times had to be a **midget**, by today's standards. If not, it's a wonder how the original **dwellers** managed to stay conscious long enough in such houses to participate in an industrial revolution and a civil war.

If you go to the Tower of London you see small suits of armor and conclude those guys were shorter than us. Even antique beds found from that age are almost a foot shorter than beds today.

President George Washington was considered literally a giant among men in his day; he measured 6 feet, two inches. Certainly a lot shorter than a typical major league basketballer of today.

Just **promenade** down to a colonial-era **cemetery**; you will see that the tombs are very small.

Thus a strong view maintains that over the last 150 years the average height of people in the developed nations has increased approximately 10 centimeters (about four inches).

But the counter **contention** is there, too. If you go to Germany, you see suits of armor for the Black Knight and Red Knight, made for men 6'5" and that certainly suggests men were actually taller than us ,a few centuries ago.

But again, the armor suits of fighting men are unlikely to represent an unbiased sample of the population. Militaries always have had a minimum height requirements and chose to hire tall men only !

There are legends and tales about the red haired giants, but they could be **apocryphal**. There is also evidence from archaeological surveys at various locations across the world **adumbrating** that some very large sized humans existed once.

Then there are views, that say it's a bit of a myth that we were all short in ancient times. Hunter gatherers were often quite tall because of their protein rich diet. In the **neolithic** when the diet became more cereal-based we became smaller. People seemed to get shorter in medieval and later times; this was due to living a life of **deprivation** in cities that were overcrowded and unhygienic. Relatively, their ancestors were well nourished; they would have all herded animals or grown their own food. By the middle of this century as people understood nutrition and medical science, there was better life and we once again hit the heights of our bronze age ancestors !

All said and done , consensus is that the past 300 years have made us not only taller, but also **brawnier** and helped us to live longer. These changes in the human body were **sprier** than in the previous thousands of years of our evolutionary history.

The average adult man in 1850 in America stood about 5 feet 7 inches and weighed about 146 pounds; someone born then was expected to live until about 45. In the 1980s the typical adult man was about 5 feet 10 inches tall, weighed about 174 pounds and was likely to pass his 75th birthday.

Most **geneticists** believe that improvements in food production , public health and childhood nutrition have been the most important factors in allowing humans to increase in stature. Newly developed economies are observing taller average heights due to better quality of food.

The other likely factor for humans becoming taller is from the Darwinian evolutionary theory. Societies have universally found that taller people are more successful in life. A recent survey found 26 out of the last 30 American presidential contests went to the taller candidate. Our species has been **gravitating** towards choosing a tall mate. Therefore, in each generation, tall people are slightly more successful in passing on their genes; the species is getting taller by the generation. Height has another **perquisite**; it allows us more efficient **dissipation** of heat .

However if each generation **spawns** taller and taller people ,could one day our **progeny** be 16'8" tall ?

Not likely. So while humans will probably continue get a little taller for a while, there's a physical limit to this **rampant** growth, and we're probably almost there. Unless our skeletal structures also evolve. The likelihood of joint and bone problems shoots up **substantially** at this height, so do the circulation issues related to pumping blood all the way up.

We have grown to just the optimum height ,hopefully. Further growth will be **nugatory**; any taller and our food needs, housing needs and fuel needs will will grow to a level where the earth's resources won't be sufficient for all of us. And our **colonizing** of another preferably, lower-gravity planet doesn't seem **imminent** !

🖎 **Apocryphal**

Contextual Meaning(s) : adjective; probably not true, but widely believed to be true
Synonyms : fictional

🖎 **Adumbrating**

Contextual Meaning(s) : Verb; indicating or hinting
Synonyms : outlining

🖎 **Brawnier**

Contextual Meaning(s) : Adjective; more stronger or strong physically
Synonyms : heftier

🖎 **Contention**

Contextual Meaning(s) : Noun a point asserted as part of an argument; the act of competing as for profit or a prize; a contentious speech act; a dispute where there is strong disagreement
Synonyms : disputation

🖎 **Cemetery**

Contextual Meaning(s) : noun; an area of ground in which the dead are buried
Synonyms : graveyard

🖎 **Colonizing**

Contextual Meaning(s) : verb; to go to and live permanently as part of a settlement in a foreign land that was previously sparsely inhabited
Synonyms : settling

🖎 **Deprivation**

Contextual Meaning(s) : noun; act of depriving someone of food or money or rights; the disadvantage that results from losing something; a state of extreme poverty
Synonyms : privation

🖎 **Dissipation**

Contextual Meaning(s) : Noun; breaking up and scattering by dispersion
Other Meaning(s) : useless or profitless activity; using or expending or consuming thoughtlessly or carelessly; dissolute indulgence in sensual pleasure
Synonyms : discharge

🖎 **Dwellers**

Contextual Meaning(s) : Noun; the residents of a place
Synonyms : inhabitants

🖎 **Geneticists**

Contextual Meaning(s) : noun; a student or specialist in genetics
Synonyms : genetic specialist

🖎 **Gravitating**

Contextual Meaning(s) : verb; to move gradually or steadily toward something or somebody as if drawn by some force or attraction
Synonyms : inclining

🖎 **Imminent**

Contextual Meaning(s) : Adjective; close in time; about to occur
Synonyms : impending

🖎 **Midget**

Contextual Meaning(s) : Adjective; very small; noun a person who is markedly small
Synonyms : bantam

🖎 **Metaphorically**

Contextual Meaning(s) : adverb; in a metaphorical manner, e.g. She expressed herself metaphorically
Synonyms : figuratively

🖎 **Nugatory**

Contextual Meaning(s) : Adjective; of no real value
Synonyms : inconsequential

✎ *Neolithic*
Contextual Meaning(s) : noun; the latest period between about 8000 BC and 5000 BC
Synonyms : New Stone Age

✎ *Perquisite*
Contextual Meaning(s) : Noun; a right reserved exclusively by a particular person or group (especially a hereditary or official right); an incidental benefit awarded for certain types of employment (especially if it is regarded as a right)
Synonyms : privilege

✎ *Progeny*
Contextual Meaning(s) : Noun; the immediate descendants of a person
Synonyms : offspring

✎ *Promenade*
Contextual Meaning(s) : Verb; take a leisurely walk; march in a procession
Other Meaning(s) : noun; a march of all the guests at the opening of a formal dance; a square dance figure; couples march counterclockwise in a circle; a public area set aside as a pedestrian walk; a formal ball held for a school class toward the end of the academic year; a leisurely walk (usually in some public place)
Synonyms : saunter

✎ *Rampant*
Contextual Meaning(s) : Adjective; unrestrained and violent in nature
Other Meaning(s) : adjective (of a plant) having a lush and unchecked growth
Synonyms : unbridled

✎ *Spawns*
Contextual Meaning(s) : Verb; gives birth to
Synonyms : breeds

✎ *Sprier*
Contextual Meaning(s) : Verb; moving more quickly
Synonyms : nimbler

✎ *Substantially*
Contextual Meaning(s) : Adverb; in a significant manner or amount
Synonyms : considerably

PECULIAR SOCIAL CUSTOMS

Don't take **umbrage** if an old-timer in Greece spits at your baby, three times. This is a traditional way to **exorcize** evil spirits and bad luck.

Chinese generally don't make compliments. When Westerners do compliment them, the **rejoinder** is either denial, self deprecation or saying that the opposite of the compliment is true. If you say a young girl looked **captivating** it is not unusual for Chinese to say she is ugly. If you say a meal was **scrumptious**, they will say something didn't turn out right.

In Solapur, India, a yearly non-religious festival is held in which babies are thrown from a 15-meter tower. Waiting catchers hold a sheet below for the babies to land in. Nobody really knows how this tradition came about, but fortuitously they haven't lost any baby yet.

This particular **oddity** has been held for the last 200 years. On the last Monday in May, contestants stand at the top of Coopers Hill and wait for an enormous wheel of Double Gloucester cheese to be rolled. The idea is to race the cheese to the bottom of the hill. Weirdly, the cheese almost always wins, sometimes reaching speeds of over 100 km/h.

Turning the Chicago river green has been a **singular** tradition to Chicago for the past 40 year. The Chicago River is dyed green every St. Patrick's Day to kick off the weekend celebration.

Chinese consider it **brazen** to say "no" directly. A typical **commotion** is caused like this.. A Westerner takes his car to a Chinese mechanic to have it **mended**. He asks if it will be ready the next day. The mechanic says "yes" because he doesn't want to be **uncouth** and say no. The Westerners shows up the next day and is angry because his car isn't ready. The mechanic doesn't understand why the foreigner is **incensed**. The day before he was only trying to be polite and telling the Westerner what the latter wanted to hear. The Westerner should have asked, "When will my car be ready?"

In Bedouin circles, a rule while drinking tea or coffee is to give a slight shake or **jiggle** of the empty cup, while returning it, to indicate that you are done and do not want any more coffee. If you fail to shake the cup, be prepared to keep getting it refilled!

To prepare for their marriage, Scottish brides-to-be must go through a very **nauseating** pre-wedding ritual. Friends of the bride take her by surprise and cover her with eggs, spoiled milk, feathers and pretty much anything **fetid**. The blackened bride is then paraded around town. The purpose of this custom is to prepare the bride for marriage because after going through that, any marital problems will seem like nothing !

While most cultures mourn the loss of family members, women of the Dani tribe in Indonesia must suffer great physical pain in addition to emotional pain. When a family member dies, female relatives must cut off a segment of one of their fingers. This practice is performed to **gratify** ancestral ghosts. Luckily for the Dani women, this custom is rarely practiced anymore.

Most non-westerners would find the Halloween party a strange affair .October 31, Halloween is a day for parties. Children dress up as witches, ghosts or vampires, and they go from house to house playing tricks. But what's the origin of this custom? Halloween is the highest satanic holy day of the year. However, many Christians consider it **heretical** to celebrate this day.

Many African peoples have a **convention** of removing a dead body through a hole in the wall of a house, and not through the door. The reason for this seems to be that this will make it difficult (or even impossible) for the dead person to remember the way back to the living, as the puncture in the wall is immediately closed.

In south east asian countries like Indonesia, Malaysia and brunei, a person always points with his thumb as it's considered very rude to point with a forefinger.

In Thailand it's considered very **impetuous** to cross your legs in public.

Japanese children cover their tummy button when they hear thunder. Also, an **admonition** to anyone who has friends or family living in Japan. Never send red Christmas cards to anyone there. Sending red Christmas cards constitutes bad etiquette since, in Japan, funeral notices are customarily printed in red !

In the Indian subcontinent, India, Pakistan, Bangladesh and Nepal the marriages are arranged by the parents of the bride and groom through a process of meeting a number of families either through a common friend or through a matrimonial advertisement. Conventionally the criteria for selection are religion, socio-economic background, caste, and the personality of the candidates. Both the bride and the groom generally trust their parents to find the best possible **nuptial** alliance for them. But of late, courtship and dating are also gaining acceptance. Love marriages, also called self-arranged marriages have also become quite a common **covenant**. It doesn't **grate** the parents that much nowadays.

In Bulgaria, grandparents-grandchildren name continuity is a very powerful tradition. Parents name their children after their own parents as a sign of respect and gratitude.

As generations change, some of these traditions fade out, others stay depending on the view of the newer crop of human race. Some get **slaked** because they are considered politically incorrect, environment unfriendly, plain old-fashioned or unsavoury.

🖎 **Admonition**
Contextual Meaning(s) : Noun; cautionary advice about something imminent (especially imminent danger); a firm rebuke
Synonyms : reprimand, warning

🖎 **Ample**
Contextual Meaning(s) : Adjective; affording an abundant supply; more than enough in size or scope or capacity; fairly large
Synonyms : plenteous, sizeable

🖎 **Blitheness**
Contextual Meaning(s) : Noun a feeling of spontaneous good spirits
Synonyms : cheerfulness, mirth

🖎 **Boomeranged**
Contextual Meaning(s) : Verb; backfired on the originating source.
Synonyms : is a repeat

🖎 **Brazen**
Contextual Meaning(s) : Adjective; unrestrained by convention or propriety;
Other Meaning(s) : Adjective; made of or resembling brass (as in color or hardness); Verb; face with defiance or impudence
Synonyms : scamper, scurry

🖎 **Captivating**
Contextual Meaning(s) : Adjective; capturing interest as if by a spell
Synonyms : hypnotizing

🖎 **Circumvent**
Contextual Meaning(s) : Verb; avoid or try to avoid fulfilling, answering, or performing (duties, questions, or issues);
Other Meaning(s) : Verb; beat through cleverness and wit; surround so as to force to give up
Synonyms : skirt, dodge, duck,

🖎 **Commotion**
Contextual Meaning(s) : Noun; the act of making a noisy disturbance; confused movement; a disorderly outburst or tumult
Synonyms : disorder, unrest

🖎 **Countenance**
Contextual Meaning(s) : Noun; the appearance conveyed by a person's face; the human face (`kisser' and `smiler' and `mug' are informal terms for `face' and `phiz' is British); formal and explicit approval;
Synonyms : endorsement

🖎 **Convention**
Contextual Meaning(s) : Noun; orthodoxy as a consequence of being traditional
Synonyms : norm

🖎 **Covenant**
Contextual Meaning(s) : Noun; a signed written agreement between two or more parties (nations) to perform some action
Other Meaning(s) : (Bible) an agreement between God and his people in which God makes certain promises and requires certain behavior from them in return; Verb; enter into a covenant or formal agreement, enter into a covenant
Synonyms : contract

🖎 **Debase**
Contextual Meaning(s) : Verb; lower in value by increasing the base-metal content; corrupt, debase, or make impure by adding a foreign or inferior substance; often by replacing valuable ingredients with inferior ones; corrupt morally or by intemperance or sensuality
Synonyms : demoralise, profane, vitiate, deprave

🖎 **Excogitate**
Contextual Meaning(s) : Verb; reflect deeply on a subject;
Other Meaning(s) : Verb; come up with (an idea, plan, explanation, theory, or principle) after a mental effort
Synonyms : ruminate

🐚 *Exorcize*
Contextual Meaning(s) : Verb; expel through adjuration or prayers
Synonyms : expel

🐚 *Fetid*
Contextual Meaning(s) : Adjective; offensively malodorous
Synonyms : stinking

🐚 *Fickle*
Contextual Meaning(s) : Adjective; marked by erratic changeableness in affections or attachments; liable to sudden unpredictable change
Synonyms : quicksilver

🐚 *Gregariousness*
Contextual Meaning(s) : Noun; the quality of being gregarious having a dislike of being alone
Synonyms : sociability

🐚 *Heretical*
Contextual Meaning(s) : Adjective; characterized by departure from accepted beliefs or standards
Synonyms : blasphemous

🐚 *Impetuous*
Contextual Meaning(s) : Adjective; marked by violent force; characterized by undue haste and lack of thought or deliberation
Synonyms : brash

🐚 *Incessantly*
Contextual Meaning(s) : Adverb; with unflagging resolve
Synonyms : ceaselessly

🐚 *Incensed*
Contextual Meaning(s) : Adjective; angered at something unjust or wrong
Synonyms : enraged

🐚 *Jiggle*
Contextual Meaning(s) : Noun; a slight irregular shaking motion; verb move to and fro
Synonyms : wiggle

🐚 *Mended*
Contextual Meaning(s) : Verb; restored or brought back to good health or state
Synonyms : bushelled, fixed

🐚 *Nauseating*
Contextual Meaning(s) : Adjective; causing or able to cause nausea
Synonyms : sickening

🐚 *Nuptial*
Contextual Meaning(s) : Adjective; of or relating to a wedding
Synonyms : spousal

🐚 *Oddity*
Contextual Meaning(s) : Noun; a strange attitude or habit; something unusual -- perhaps worthy of collecting
Synonyms : eccentricity

🐚 *Prank*
Contextual Meaning(s) : Noun; a ludicrous or grotesque act done for fun and amusement; acting like a clown or buffoon;
Other Meaning(s) : Verb; dress up showily; dress or decorate showily or gaudily
Synonyms : caper

🐚 *Radical*
Contextual Meaning(s) : Adjective; Revolutionary
Synonyms : extreme, revolutionary

🐚 *Rejoinder*
Contextual Meaning(s) : Noun; a quick reply to a question or remark (especially a witty or critical one)
Other Meaning(s) : Noun; (law) a pleading made by a defendant in response to the plaintiff's replication
Synonyms : repartee

🐚 *Relentlessly*
Contextual Meaning(s) : Adverb; in a relentless manner
Synonyms : unrelentingly

✎ **Ruin**

Contextual Meaning(s) : Noun; failure that results in a loss of position or reputation; the process of becoming dilapidated; verb fall into ruin; reduce to ruins; destroy or cause to fail; deprive of virginity; destroy completely; damage irreparably; reduce to bankruptcy
Synonyms : dilapidation

✎ **Scramble**

Contextual Meaning(s) : Noun; an unceremonious and disorganized struggle; rushing about hastily in an undignified way
Synonyms : scamper, scurry

✎ **Scrumptious**

Contextual Meaning(s) : Adjective; extremely pleasing to the sense of taste
Synonyms : delicious

✎ **Slaked**

Contextual Meaning(s) : Adjective; allayed
Synonyms : attenuated

✎ **Supplant**

Contextual Meaning(s) : Verb; take the place or move into the position of
Synonyms : replace

✎ **Succor**

Contextual Meaning(s) : Noun; assistance in time of difficulty;
Other Meaning(s) : Verb; help in a difficult situation
Synonyms : ministration

✎ **Squander**

Contextual Meaning(s) : Verb; spend extravagantly; spend thoughtlessly; throw away
Synonyms : waste, ware, blow

✎ **Transpired**

Contextual Meaning(s) : Verb. Occurred or took place or was discussed
Synonyms : occur

✎ **Trepidation**

Contextual Meaning(s) : Noun; a feeling of alarm or dread
Synonyms : dread

✎ **Truncate**

Contextual Meaning(s) : Verb; terminating abruptly by having or as if having an end or point cut off; verb make shorter as if by cutting off; approximate by ignoring all terms beyond a chosen one;
Other Meaning(s) : Verb; replace a corner by a plane
Synonyms : prune

✎ **Umbrage**

Contextual Meaning(s) : Noun; a feeling of anger caused by being offended
Synonyms : offense, insult

✎ **Uncouth**

Contextual Meaning(s) : Ajdective; lacking refinement or cultivation or taste
Synonyms : ruffian, coarse

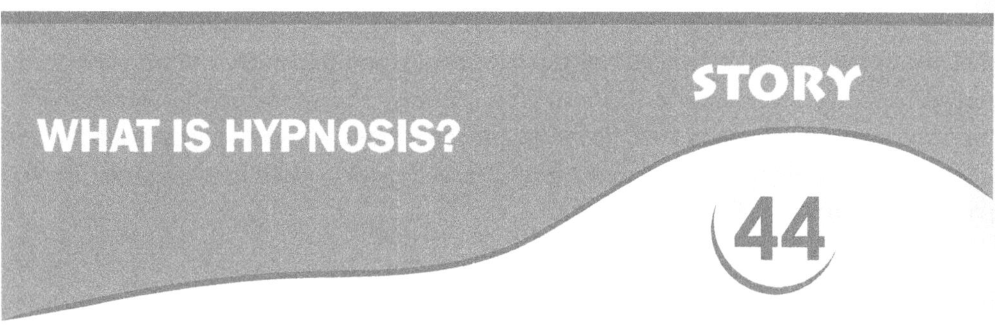

Within science, there is divergence as to whether hypnosis exists or not. Science simply has no **consensus** on what it is and how it works, although as The British Society of Clinical and Experimental Hypnosis states:

"In therapy, hypnosis usually involves the person experiencing a sense of deep relaxation with their attention narrowed down, and focused on appropriate suggestions made by the therapist."

These suggestions help people make **innate** positive changes. In a **hypnotherapy** session you are always in control and you are not made **subservient**. It is generally accepted that all hypnosis is ultimately self-hypnosis. A hypnotist merely helps to **expedite** your experience - hypnotherapy is not about being converted into a **zombie**, in fact it is the opposite, it is about empowerment. If someone tells you they can hypnotise you to be **obeisant**, ask them to hypnotise you to rob a bank, and when they can't, ask them to stop making **ludicrous** claims.

Contrary to popular belief, hypnosis is not a state of deep sleep. It does involve the induction of an **entrancement**, but when in it, the patient is actually in an enhanced state of awareness, concentrating entirely on the hypnotist's voice. In this state, the conscious mind is **smothered** and the subconscious mind is **unveiled**.

The therapist is able to suggest ideas, concepts and lifestyle adaptations to the patient, the seeds of which become firmly **embedded** inside of him.

The practice of promoting healing or positive development in any way is known as hypnotherapy. As such, hypnotherapy is a kind of psychotherapy. Hypnotherapy aims to **reinvent** patterns of behavior within the mind, enabling irrational fears, phobias, negative thoughts and **enshrouded** emotions to be overcome. As the body is released from conscious control during the relaxed **trance**-like state of hypnosis, breathing becomes slower and deeper, the pulse rate drops and the **metabolic rate** falls. Similar changes along nervous pathways and hormonal channels enable the sensation of pain to become less acute, and the awareness of unpleasant symptoms, such as nausea or indigestion, to be **mitigated**.

Hypnosis is thought to work by altering our state of consciousness in such a way that the analytical left-hand side of the brain is turned off, while the non-analytical right-hand side is made more **vigilant**. The conscious part of the mind is **sedated**, and the subconscious mind **kindled**. Since the subconscious mind is a deeper-seated, more instinctive force than the conscious mind, this is the part which has to change for the patient's behavior and physical state to alter.

For example, a patient who consciously wants to overcome their fear of spiders may try everything they consciously can ,to do it, but will still fail as long as their subconscious mind retains this terror. Hypnotic therapy is **cathartic** and helps **purge** the **ingrained** phobias .Now progress can be made by reprogramming the subconscious so that positive or neutral responses are generated instead.

The patient cannot be made to do anything they would not ordinarily do. They remain fully aware of their surroundings and situation, and are not **vulnerable** to every given command of the therapist. The important requirement is that the patient himself wants to change some behavioral habit or addiction and is highly motivated to do so. He must want the treatment to work and must establish a good clinical rapport with the therapist in order for it to do so. However the patient can learn the technique of self-hypnosis which can be practiced at home, to reinforce the usefulness of formal sessions with the therapist. This can help them counter distress and help unwind themselves.

Hypnotherapy can be applied to many psychological, emotional and physical disorders. It is used to relieve pain in surgery and dentistry and has proved to be of benefit in **obstetrics**. It can shorten the delivery stage of labour and reduce the need for painkillers. It can ease the suffering of the disabled and those facing terminal illness, and it has been shown to help people to overcome addictions such as smoking and alcoholism, and to help with **bulimia**. Children are generally easy to hypnotise and can be helped with bed wetting and chronic asthma, whilst teenagers can conquer **stammering** or blushing problems which can otherwise make their lives miserable.

Phobias of all kinds lend themselves well to hypnotherapy, and anyone suffering from panic attacks or **obsessional** compulsive behaviour, and stress-related problems like **insomnia**, may benefit. Conditions **exacerbated** by tension, such as irritable bowel syndrome, **psoriasis** and **eczema**, and excessive sweating, respond well.

Mandrake the magician whose work was based on an **instantaneous** hypnotic technique, has been a childhood comic super-hero, known to us old-timers. Mandrake gestured and **summoned** up all kinds of things his subjects were made to see.

But now its well established that hypnosis is no magic which can make the targeted person **hallucinate**. Its a **therapeutic** aid, which can help us solve our own **psychosomatic** disorders.

🖎 **Alleviated**

Contextual Meaning(s) : Adjective; (of pain or sorrow) made easier to bear
Synonyms : eased, relieved

🖎 **Aroused**

Contextual Meaning(s) : Adjective; keenly excited
Other Meaning(s) : adjective (of persons) excessively affected by emotion; aroused to action; feeling great sexual desire; brought to a state of great tension; emotionally aroused;
Synonyms : stimulated

🖎 **Bulimia**

Contextual Meaning(s) : noun; a condition in which bouts of overeating are followed by undereating, use of laxatives, or self-induced vomiting. It is associated with depression and anxiety about putting on weight.
Synonyms : compulsive eating

🖎 **Cathartic**

Contextual Meaning(s) : Adjective; emotionally cleansing.
Other Meaning(s) : strongly laxative; emotionally purging; noun a purging medicine; stimulates evacuation of the bowels
Synonyms : evacuant, purgative

🖎 **Conjured**

Contextual Meaning(s) : Verb; produced by magic
Synonyms : summoned

🖎 **Consensus**

Contextual Meaning(s) : Noun; agreement in the judgment or opinion reached by a group as a whole
Synonyms : unanimity

🖎 **Contention**

Contextual Meaning(s) : Noun; a point asserted as part of an argument; the act of competing as for profit or a prize; a contentious speech act;
Other Meaning(s) : Noun; a dispute where there is strong disagreement
Synonyms : competition

🖎 **Derisory**

Contextual Meaning(s) : Adjective; incongruous; inviting ridicule
Synonyms : preposterous, ridiculous

🖎 **Embedded**

Contextual Meaning(s) : Adjective; as an integral part of a surrounding whole; enclosed firmly in a surrounding mass
Synonyms : implanted

🖎 **Enshrouded**

Contextual Meaning(s) : Verb; hidden
Synonyms : covered

🖎 **Entrancement**

Contextual Meaning(s) : Noun; a feeling of delight at being filled with wonder and enchantment
Synonyms : ravishment

🖎 **Exacerbated**

Contextual Meaning(s) : Noun; increased the intensity of a problem
Synonyms : aggravated, vitiated

🖎 **Expedite**

Contextual Meaning(s) : Verb; process fast and efficiently; speed up the progress of; facilitate
Synonyms : hasten

🖎 **Eczema**

Contextual Meaning(s) : noun; an inflammation of the skin characterized by reddening and itching
Synonyms : rash

☙ *Hallucinate*
Contextual Meaning(s) : Verb; perceive what is not there; have illusions
Synonyms : phantasize

☙ *Hypnotherapy*
Contextual Meaning : noun; the use of hypnosis in treating illness, e.g. in dealing with physical pain or psychological problems
Synonyms : spell-casting

☙ *Ingrained*
Contextual Meaning(s) : Adjective; (used especially of ideas or principles) deeply rooted; firmly fixed or held
Synonyms : deep-rooted

☙ *Innate*
Contextual Meaning(s) : Adjective; present at birth but not necessarily hereditary; acquired during fetal development; being talented through inherited qualities; not established by conditioning or learning
Synonyms : congenital, unlearned

☙ *Insomnia*
Contextual Meaning(s) : Noun; an inability to sleep; chronic sleeplessness
Synonyms : sleeplessness

☙ *Instantaneous*
Contextual Meaning(s) : adjective; occurring immediately or almost immediately
Synonyms : immediate

☙ *Kindled*
Contextual Meaning(s) : Adjective; set a fire
Other Meaning(s) : Verb; aroused or stimulated
Synonyms : invoked

☙ *Ludicrous*
Contextual Meaning(s) : Adjective; broadly or extravagantly humorous; resembling farce; incongruous; inviting ridicule
Synonyms : laughable

☙ *Mitigated*
Contextual Meaning(s) : Adjective; made less severe or intense
Synonyms : alleviated

☙ *Metabolic rate*
Contextual Meaning(s) : noun; the speed at which the biochemical reactions of metabolism in living cells take place

☙ *Obeisant*
Contextual Meaning(s) : Adjective; slavish
Synonyms : servile, fawing

☙ *Obsessional*
Contextual Meaning(s) : Adjective; characterized by or constituting an obsession or compulsion
Synonyms : obsessive

☙ *Obstetrics*
Contextual Meaning(s) : noun; the branch of medicine that deals with the care of women during pregnancy and childbirth and for some weeks following delivery
Synonyms : medical care

☙ *Psychosomatic*
Contextual Meaning(s) : Adjective; used of illness or symptoms resulting from neurosis
Synonyms : psychoneurotic

☙ *Purge*
Contextual Meaning(s) : Noun; an act of removing by cleansing; ridding of sediment or other undesired elements; the act of clearing yourself (or another) from some stigma or charge; verb excrete or evacuate (someone's bowels or body); rid of impurities; clear of a charge; oust politically; eject the contents of the stomach through the mouth; rinse, clean, or empty with a liquid
Other Meaning(s) : make pure or free from sin or guilt
Synonyms : flush, regurgitate

☙ *Psoriasis*
Contextual Meaning(s) : noun; a skin disease usually marked by red scaly patches

🖎 **Reinvent**

Contextual Meaning(s) : Verb; create anew and make over; bring back into existence
Synonyms : recreate

🖎 **Sedated**

Contextual Meaning(s) : Adjective; under the influence of a sedative drug (sleeping pill)
Synonyms : tranquilized

🖎 **Smothered**

Contextual Meaning(s) : Adjective; held in check with difficulty; completely covered
Synonyms : blanketed

🖎 **Subservient**

Contextual Meaning(s) : Adjective; compliant and obedient to authority; abjectly submissive; characteristic of a slave or servant; serving or acting s a means or aid
Synonyms : implemental, instrumental

🖎 **Summoned**

Contextual Meaning(s) : Verb; called in an official matter, such as to attend court; asked to come; make ready for action or use
Other Meaning(s) : Verb; gathered or brought together
Synonyms : commandeered

🖎 **Stammering**

Contextual Meaning(s) : verb; to speak or say something, with many quick hesitations and repeated consonants or syllables because of a speech condition or a strong emotion

🖎 **Therapeutic**

Contextual Meaning(s) : Adjective; relating to or involved in therapy; tending to cure or restore to health; noun a medicine or therapy that cures disease or relieve pain
Synonyms : curative healing

🖎 **Trance**

Contextual Meaning(s) : Noun; a state of mind in which consciousness is fragile and voluntary action is poor or missing; a state resembling deep sleep; a psychological state induced by (or as if induced by) a magical incantation; verb attract; cause to be enamored
Synonyms : enchantment, spell

🖎 **Unveiled**

Contextual Meaning(s) : Adjective; revealed; especially by having a veil removed
Synonyms : disclosed

🖎 **Vigilant**

Contextual Meaning(s) : Adjective; carefully observant or attentive; on the lookout for possible danger
Synonyms : alert

🖎 **Vulnerable**

Contextual Meaning(s): Adjective; exposed to the possibility of being attacked or harmed, either physically or emotionally.
Synonyms : endangered, unsafe.

🖎 **Zombie**

Contextual Meaning(s) : Noun; someone who acts or responds in a mechanical or pathetic way;
Other Meaning(s) : noun several kinds of rum with fruit juice and usually apricot liqueur; a dead body that has been brought back to life by a supernatural force; a god of voodoo cults of African origin worshipped especially in West Indies; (voodooism) a spirit or supernatural force that reanimates a dead body
Synonyms : living-dead

IDIOT BOX TURNS BRAINY BEAUTY

The days of your grandpa sitting in his **recliner** with a cocktail and watching the same **irksome** channel, which hardly **aroused** you, are over. Now a days you have hundreds of channels and **paradoxically** you don't even need a television to watch most of them!

The television set was anyway not an idiot, the **indecorous** term actually referred to the people watching it! They were deemed idiots because the old TV hardly tested their intelligence and creativity.

Many of the earliest TV programs were modified versions of well-established radio shows. The '50s saw the first **flowering** of the genres that would distinguish TV from movies and radio: talk shows like *The Jack Paar Show* and sitcoms like *I Love Lucy*.

Television has changed a lot since it was created and the greatest and most **palpable** change besides its looks, is its transformation to the digital age.

Instead of the antique **unwieldy** box, the latest television is wafer thin, and promises clearer, sharper images in a wide screen format using LCD displays which are larger, flatter and clearer than the traditional cathode-ray tubes that were common in old-style TVs.

While the buzzword elsewhere in the tech market is compactness, the **redux** TV is getting bigger, brighter and thinner, with LG and Samsung weighing off against each other for the title of biggest OLED screen in the world. While both exhibited 55" screens, LG's offering had the added advantage of being 3D. Both companies were also showcasing ultra-high resolution screens, with 4 times as many pixels as the normal high definition screen. Samsung also offered up a solution to the constant need to update your set in the fast-changing world of modern tech, with a TV with an upgrade slot, allowing you to upgrade your processor with every new development. While many would consider a TV to be a luxury item designed to be regularly upgraded, perhaps this is the way forward, and a good reason to invest in a more expensive, high performing set designed for long-term use.

Many broadcasting companies have created streaming internet sites to offer their **highbrow** viewers the ability to watch television on their own schedule and with minimal commercial interruption or in some cases no commercial interruption at all. Furthermore you can access international channels and watch sports teams from other cities at home, on your computer, cell phone, or ipod and for free. So no need to rush home with incomplete shopping, just because you can't afford to miss that *Indian idol* **finale.**

Moreover, televisions are now available with browsers and all the features of a computer that make it internet **compliant.** Thus the TV and the Computer have become **symbiotic** to a large extent and their separating line is almost **diaphanous.**

It's now technically possible to order movies and TV shows to play when you want them to show so you can get on with your life and catch-up on what you've missed at your own convenience.

Internet TV is also a **purveyor** of books, movie tickets, maps, railway information as well as pizza and pickles. With the help of the **alphanumeric** remote, you can even send text messages, e-mails or chat with friends. The new TVs will let users play "Angry Birds," instantly view photos taken by multiple people and shared online, or try on virtual clothes without needing a game console or a set-top box. And they'll allow users to change the channel or search for TV shows by waving at the screen or using their voice.

Meanwhile, Bodymetrics, a London-based startup, showed off how consumers could use a Kinect-like device to turn their living room into a virtual dressing room. Users see a representation of themselves on their TV that moves in sync with them. They can select different clothes and see instantly how they fit and look.

All of these flat-panel displays look great, and most are designed to hang on a wall, so the living room remains **commodious.** Only one issue **mars** the beautiful pictures: cables to your Set Top Box, DVD Recorder, Satellite or Speakers and whatever else you connect to it. This cable **clutter** can be a real problem. This mess **heralds** the entry of television that do away with most of those cables, save for the actual electrical plug.

And finally expect the plasma screens as big as 80, a screen so sensitive to your movements that it will turn to provide you the best angle wherever in the living room you watch it from. It may become the centre piece of a future home, showing you the action in any part of your home especially the kid's room, become your front door **sentinel**, let you control devices of the entire home remotely .And all the time let you do your office applications, all of course in separate windows !

Television industry is working **sedulously** at making TV viewing more and more **toothsome** but let me warn you they may **insidiously** make couch potatoes out of you!

- **Aroused**
  Contextual Meaning(s) : Adjective; keenly excited or indicating excitement
  Other Meaning(s) : adjective; (of persons) excessively affected by emotion; aroused to action; brought to a state of great tension; emotionally aroused;
  Synonyms : excited, stimulated, stirred

- **Alphanumeric**
  Contextual Meaning(s) : adjective; consisting of or using both letters and numerals.

- **Clutter**
  Contextual Meaning(s) : Noun; a confused multitude of things;
  Other Meaning(s) : noun unwanted echoes that interfere with the observation of signals on a radar screen; verb fill a space in a disorderly way
  Synonyms : jumble, muddle, fuddle

- **Commodious**
  Contextual Meaning(s) : Adjective; large and roomy
  Synonyms : spacious

- **Compliant**
  Contextual Meaning(s) : Adjective; disposed or willing to comply
  Synonyms : docile, malleable

- **Diaphanous**
  Contextual Meaning(s) : Adjective; so thin as to transmit light
  Synonyms : filmy, gauzy, gossamer

- **Finale**
  Contextual Meaning(s) : Noun; the concluding part of any performance;
  Other Meaning(s) : noun; the closing section of a musical composition; the temporal end; the concluding time
  Synonyms : finish, conclusion

- **Flowering**
  Contextual Meaning(s) : Adjective; a developmental process

- *Other Meaning(s)* : adjective; having a flower or bloom; noun the time and process of budding and unfolding of blossoms;
  Synonyms : blossoming, unfolding

- **Heralds**
  Contextual Meaning(s) : verb; begins an era
  Synonyms : harbingers

- **Highbrow**
  Contextual Meaning(s) : Adjective; highly cultured or educated;
  Other Meaning(s) : noun a person of intellectual or erudite tastes
  Synonyms : elite

- **Indecorous**
  Contextual Meaning(s) : Adjective; lacking propriety and good taste in manners and conduct; not in keeping with accepted standards of what is right or proper in polite society
  Synonyms : indelicate, indecent, unbecoming, uncomely, unseemly, untoward

- **Insidiously**
  Contextual Meaning(s) : Adverb in a secretly harmful manner
  Synonyms : perniciously

- **Irksome**
  Contextual Meaning(s) : Adjective; so lacking in interest as to cause mental weariness
  Synonyms : boring, tedious, tiresome, wearisome

- **Mars**
  Contextual Meaning(s) : Noun; a small reddish planet that is the 4th from the sun and is periodically visible to the naked eye; minerals rich in iron cover its surface and are responsible for its characteristic color; (Roman mythology) Roman god of war and agriculture; father of Romulus and Remus; counterpart of Greek Ares
  Synonyms : a planet

☙ **Palpable**

Contextual Meaning(s) : Adjective; capable of being perceived by the senses or the mind; especially capable of being handled or touched or felt; can be felt by palpation
Synonyms : tangible

☙ **Paradoxically**

Contextual Meaning(s) : Adverb; in an illogical manner
Synonyms : illogically

☙ **Purveyor**

Contextual Meaning(s) : Noun; someone who supplies provisions or anything else
Synonyms : vendor

☙ **Recliner**

Contextual Meaning(s) : Noun; an armchair whose back can be lowered and foot can be raised to allow the sitter to recline in it
Synonyms : reclining chair, lounger

☙ **Redux**

Contextual Meaning(s) : Adjective; brought back
Synonyms : revived

☙ **Sedulously**

Contextual Meaning(s) : Adverb; in a manner involving hard work
Synonyms : industriously

☙ **Sentinel**

Contextual Meaning(s) : Noun; a security guard, a sentry
Synonyms : sentry, watchman

☙ **Symbiotic**

Contextual Meaning(s) : Adjective; Mutually beneficial
Synonyms : Interdependent, harmonious

☙ **Toothsome**

Contextual Meaning(s) : Adjective; acceptable to the taste or mind; extremely pleasing to the sense of taste
Synonyms : delectable, delicious, scrumptious, yummy

☙ **Unwieldy**

Contextual Meaning(s) : Adjective; difficult to use or handle or manage because of size or weight or shape;
Other Meaning(s) : adjective; difficult to work or manipulate; lacking grace in movement or posture
Synonyms : unmanageable, gawky, clumsy, clunky, ungainly

Evidence exists tying dogs to humans as many as 15,000 years ago. There has been an emotional bond between the two, and there are unlimited tales of their mutual care, love and affection.

Although no one knows for sure how those first bonds were **forged.** Bones and **artifacts** point to the fact that dogs and man have long shared an interdependent relationship.

Although not every dog is necessarily friendly by nature, stories emerge from time to time of a dog becoming separated from his or her family and undertaking an incredible journey toward reunion. Dogs are used in **therapy** for Alzheimer's disease and in clinical settings as comfort for the terminally ill. And **hordes** of families in all parts of world have been saved by their dogs when their homes caught fire.

A study was conducted comparing dogs, puppies, wolves and chimpanzees' ability to understand human communication methods. Since wolves have bigger brains than dogs, it was thought they would do better, and since chimpanzees are biologically closer to humans, it was thought they would do best.

The dogs surprised scientists by doing much better than wolves or chimpanzees, and even puppies as young as 9 weeks old outperformed them as well.

"Dogs have a talent for reading social **cues** in a very sophisticated way," said Hare ,who did this study.

There has also been a long standing working relationship between dogs and humans, which further cements our **symbiotic** relationship . "We know that dogs were useful for lots of things in Stone Age culture, as draft animals, in hunting, for warmth, and for protection," said Jennifer Leonard, a postdoctoral fellow at the Smithsonian Institution's National Museum of Natural History. **Herding** dogs, hunting dogs, tracking dogs and **sled** dogs have been joined by a variety of modern day working dogs. From rescue dogs to assistance dogs, from war dogs to **cadaver** dogs, our best friends have made themselves **indispensable**.

In many ways, we have become as dependent on them as they are on us.

There have been many news stories detailing the bond between dogs and humans, and tales of dog heroics enter the public consciousness, capture our imaginations, and fuel our assertions that a dog's loyalty is **unwavering**. No mere animals these, but trustworthy companions who well deserve our praise and pampering. Not surprising, I have heard some say, *to err is human, to forgive is canine !*

This begs the question, "Just how deep is the tie between humans and dogs? Did the dog know instinctively how to care for a human baby, even though she was a stray and may have had little human contact?

On the infamous 9/11, blind computer technician Omar Eduardo Rivera was at his desk on the 71st floor of the World Trade Center north tower, his guide dog "Dorado" lying under the desk. Then the plane struck. It seemed impossible to get down the stairs, so Rivera **unleashed** "Dorado" so he could escape to freedom. The dog refused to go, but soon was swept up in the tide of people and disappeared down the **stairwell**. Several minutes later, he felt the familiar lick on his left hand. Dorado had returned - fighting against the massive **exodus** - and spent the next hour guiding Rivera to safety. A very short time later the building **foundered**.

We interact with each other as social organisms. We feel for each other. We share in each others joy, and **commiserate** with each other in pain. Their feelings are hurt when we yell at them, but they cheer us up when we are down. They are **coginizant** of how we're feeling, and they let us know if they're getting **tormented** by us or if they're feeling sick. And we rush them off to the vet or the animal hospital and pray to God to help our dog. We have nurtured them from puppy to adult and they are like our own children. We weep when we bury them. And they are unbearably, heart breakingly **morose** when we are buried. It is this emotional attachment, this un-dissolvable bond, that puts dogs over the top. This is what, ultimately, makes the dog - a simple creature but not so dumb after all - man's best friend.

As well as being extremely **perspicacious**, dogs are blessed with senses much more powerful than those of humans. In particular, their sense of smell is extraordinarily well-developed.

When I drive home from work, i am told our Tibetan Lhasa comes to the door, all **agog**, even when I am about half a mile away.

Smell is the dog's dominant faculty, so much so that a huge part of its brain is devoted to analysing odours. Dogs have two giant **olfactory** bulbs attached to the brain which decode every smell they encounter. The bulbs weigh around 60 grams, four times as much as human olfactory bulbs. Since canine brains are much smaller than ours ,little wonder then that a dog's sense of smell is reckoned to be 100,000 times better than a humans.

The source of the dog's exceptional ability to smell is its wet **snout**. The moist leathery surface of the snout acts like **velcro** catching even the tiniest molecules of smells, then dissolving them so that the dog's internal, smell receptor cells can analyse them properly..

Dogs really can literally smell fear. If a dog goes into a room from where a frightened dog has just left, he will appear restless and agitated. This isn't, as many would claim, some kind of supernormal response. It's caused by a scent, an alarm pheromone, which is produced by the anal glands of frightened dogs.

Dogs can detect odours that are up to 40 feet underground. They have been used to detect leaky gas pipes. They can also smell insects hidden in the ground or in woodwork. In the United States dogs are used to sniff out termite **infestations**. Dogs can also pick up the faintest **whiff** of other creatures. Dogs can smell human fingerprints that are a week old.

Dogs can even smell electricity. While conducting an experiment, a researcher found that a dog could smell which of two compartments contained an electric current. He concluded this was because the charge resulted in the release of tiny amounts of ozone which the dog could detect.

As far as dogs are concerned, all humans have a unique smell. They can pick people out according to body and other odours they **disperse**. Scientists think the only way a dog wouldn't be able to **discern** two people apart would be if they were identical twins on identical diets. The twins would also have to remain silent.

Scientists who tested four German Shepherds discovered they track footprints by dividing the job systematically into phases. In the first two phases, they do the sniffing thoroughly but a bit slowly. Once the direction has been established, the tracking phase begin with the dog once more moving quickly.

Scientists think that simply by sniffing samples of human's breath, dogs can detect lung, breast and other cancers with an accuracy rate of between 88 and 97 percent. The accuracy rate of a multi-million-pound hospital scanner is between 85 and 90 per cent. Dogs can also be trained to alert people with heart conditions they are about to suffer a seizure. Dogs can also anticipate in advance when a person is going to have an epileptic fit. A Canadian study found that dogs who lived with children prone to epileptic episodes behaved unusually in advance of the attacks, they would lick the child's face or act protectively. Health authorities around the world are now training "seizure alert" or "seizure response" dogs, some of which can predict fits, and all of which will respond in an appropriate way when an owner does have a fit. Experts think they pick up on tiny behavioral or scent cues, or electrical activity in the owner's body.

Dogs can predict earthquakes hours before they occur by hearing the faint vibrations of the earth.

Thankfully dogs are being recognized as the amazing creatures they are and laws are being enacted to protect them from people who minimize their value. Next time you see a stray dog, think of them as just **hapless** souls living on the **margins** of society, which actually need **rehabilitation** efforts from you. For canines are the closest any species can get to humans, at least emotionally.

👁 **Agog**
Contextual Meaning(s) : Adjective; highly excited
Synonyms : agitated

👁 **Artifacts**
Contextual Meaning(s) : noun; an object made by a human being, e.g. a tool or ornament, especially one that has archaeological or cultural interest
Synonyms : antiquity

👁 **Coginizant**
Contextual Meaning(s) : Adjective; having or showing knowledge or understanding of something.
Synonyms : aware

👁 **Commiserate**
Contextual Meaning(s) : Verb; to feel or express sympathy or compassion
Synonyms : sympathize, sympathise

👁 **Cadaver**
Contextual Meaning(s) : noun; a dead body, especially one that is to be dissected
Synonyms : corpse

👁 **Cues**
Contextual Meaning(s) : Noun; a stimulus that provides information about what to do.
Synonyms : hint, clue

👁 **Discern**
Contextual Meaning(s) : Verb; detect with the senses
Synonyms : recognize, distinguish

👁 **Disperse**
Contextual Meaning(s) : Verb; distribute loosely
Other Meaning(s) : verb move away from each other; to cause to separate and go in different directions; cause to separate; cause to become widely known
Synonyms : dissipate spread, diffuse

👁 **Exodus**
Contextual Meaning(s) : Noun a journey by a large group to escape from a hostile environment;
Other Meaning(s) : the second book of the Old Testament: tells of the departure of the Israelites out of slavery in Egypt led by Moses; God gave them the Ten Commandments and the rest of Mosaic law on Mount Sinai during the Exodus
Synonyms : hegira, evacuation

👁 **Forged**
Contextual Meaning(s) : Verb; made by physical effort
Other Meaning(s) : adjective; reproduced fraudulently
Synonyms : fashioned

👁 **Foundered**
Contextual Meaning(s) : Verb; crashed or crumbled
Synonyms : collapsed

👁 **Hapless**
Contextual Meaning(s) : Adjective; deserving or inciting pity, somebody that is unfortunate.
Synonyms : pathetic, piteous, pitiable, wretched

👁 **Harrowed**
Contextual Meaning(s) : Verb; caused lot of discomfort or pain
Synonyms : tormented

👁 **Herding**
Contextual Meaning(s) : Adjective; used for driving, moving or compelling animals
Synonyms : crowding

👁 **Hordes**
Contextual Meaning(s) : noun; a large group of people
Synonyms : mob

- **Infestations**

  Contextual Meaning(s) : Noun; the state of being invaded by parasites.
  Synonyms : plague

- **Indispensable**

  Contextual Meaning(s) : adjective; extremely desirable or useful, or not to be done without
  Synonyms : crucial

- **Margins**

  Contextual Meaning(s) : Noun; area just inside the boundary, not in the mainstream
  Other Meaning(s) : The blank space around the text on a page; a permissible of difference
  Synonyms : borders

- **Morose**

  Contextual Meaning(s) : Adjective; showing a brooding ill humor
  Synonyms : sullen, melancholic

- **Narrative**

  Contextual Meaning(s) : Noun a message that tells the particulars of an act or occurrence or course of events;
  Other Meaning(s) : adjective; consisting of or characterized by the telling of a story; presented in writing or drama or cinema or as a radio or television program
  Synonyms : script

- **Olfactory**

  Contextual Meaning(s) : Adjective; of or relating to sense of small
  Synonyms : olfactive

- **Perspicacious**

  Contextual Meaning(s) : Adjective; acutely insightful and wise; mentally acute or penetratingly discerning
  Synonyms : incisive

- **Plethora**

  Contextual Meaning(s) : Noun; extreme excess in members or quantity
  Synonyms : over plus, superfluity

- **Queasy**

  Contextual Meaning(s) : Adjective; causing or fraught with or showing anxiety;
  Other Meaning(s) : adjective; feeling nausea; feeling about to vomit; causing or able to cause nausea
  Synonyms : uneasy, disquieted

- **Rehabilitation**

  Contextual Meaning(s) : Noun; the restoration of someone to a useful place in society;
  Other Meaning(s) : noun; the treatment of physical disabilities by massage and electrotherapy and exercises; vindication of a person's character and the re-establishment of that person's reputation; the conversion of wasteland into land suitable for use of habitation or cultivation
  Synonyms : reclamation, renewal

- **Sled**

  Contextual Meaning(s) : Noun; a vehicle mounted on runners and pulled by horses or dogs; for transportation over snow; verb ride (on) a sled
  Synonyms : sledge, sleigh

- **Snout**

  Contextual Meaning(s) : Noun; a long projecting or anterior elongation of an animal's head; especially the nose; beak like projection of the anterior part of the head of certain insects such as e.g. weevils; informal terms for the nose
  Synonyms : rostrum, beak

- **Symbiotic**

  Contextual Meaning(s) : Adjective; used of organisms (especially of different species) living together in a relation beneficial to each other
  Synonyms : dependent

- **Stairwell**

  Contextual Meaning(s) : noun; the vertical space in a building where stairs are located
  Synonyms : staircase

- **Therapy**

  Contextual Meaning(s) : Noun; (medicine) the act of caring for someone (as by medication or remedial training etc.)
  Synonyms : aid

- ❧ *Tormented*

  Contextual Meaning(s) : Adj.; experiencing intense pain especially mental pain; tormented or harassed by nightmares or unreasonable fears

  Synonyms : harrassed

- ❧ *Unleashed*

  Contextual Meaning(s) : Verb; to set tree

  Synonyms : release

- ❧ *Unwavering*

  Contextual Meaning(s) : Adjective; marked by firm determination or resolution; not shakable; not showing abrupt variations

  Synonyms : steadfast, unfaltering, unshakable

- ❧ *Velcro*

  Contextual Meaning(s) : verb; a trademark for a fastener consisting of two strips, one with a dense layer of tiny nylon hooks and the other of loops that interlock with them.

  Synonyms : fasten, fix

- ❧ *Whiff*

  Contextual Meaning(s) : Noun; perceive by inhaling through the nose.

  Other Meaning(s) : noun a strikeout resulting from the batter swinging at and missing the ball for the third strike; a left eye flounder found in coastal waters from New England to Brazil; a short light gust of air; noun strike out by swinging and missing the pitch charged as the third; drive or carry as if by a puff of air; smoke and exhale strongly;

  Synonyms : puff, sniff

THE HOMEMAKER ENTREPRENEUR

Underestimating the value of the homemaker can be **dreadful** to a society, a family or an individual.

Despite the advances of modern technology such as washing machines, irons and dishwashers, the home is always full of things that need doing. In most families, there is someone who is predominantly the homemaker and child carer - without her the home appears **derelict,** infact a **bedlam**. They may not be the primary income earner but their **assiduous** concern ensures that the family is fed, clothed and reaches school or work on time.

Can people see how much it would cost to hire someone to take their place, if something should happen to them. The housewife's financial worth is a lot more than most people **surmise**. Yet surprisingly the homemaker is, at times, overlooked as a value adder. Their loss or **debilitating** illness also often serves a **momentous** emotional and financial blow to the family.

Raising kids is one of the most challenging tasks that awaits you in life. There are so many sacrifices to be made, so much of emotional stress to be dealt, but it's the **rhapsodic** joy of watching your child grow up, that keeps you going. Since, child care is a full time job in itself, it would be important to decide for a couple how they are going to manage it. Mostly, the responsibility of nurturing the kids falls upon the shoulders of a woman. This is where the **fray** between stay at home moms vs. working moms comes into picture.

A housewife is today an ideological **orphan**, having no one to **champion** her case. At a time when any little **aberration** or politically incorrect slip-up becomes a **raging** controversy, it is interesting that this abnormality passes virtually unnoticed.

Even in everyday life, a woman is **fatuously** asked if she works or not, quite ignoring the fact that a typical housewife is hardly sitting and filing her nails lazily all through the day. A housewife performs an **intricate** series of tasks that span the functional, emotional and spiritual sides. She allocates fixed resources **optimally**, taking care to cover a variety of needs, both **exigent** and long term. She is **penitent** when any task gets left incomplete, she is almost **frenetic** in her commitment to home. She is referred to as a manager of the home sometimes, but this almost always in **jest**, quite forgetting that she plays precisely that role in pretty much the same way as managers elsewhere. In addition, she needs no supervision, neither does she demand a work appraisal nor a promotion. Apart from which she functions in most households as the emotional centre of the family around whom the very notion of a home is constructed. She is a manager, counsellor, accountant, provider and cheerleader rolled in one. In both form and content what she does is work. She has no set work hours and is not compensated in terms of money. She has no sundays and no leave.

Working housewives engage four to five category of manpower-babysitter (or a crèche), domestic help for cleaning, cook, school transport provider and a tutor. All of these besides putting a drain on the resources do not provide **congenial** atmosphere for the growth of the child. Working wives are getting more assertive and **egoistic** at the emotional level and dull and unromantic at home. I think the role of wife is more than fifty percent and so its monetary value far outweighs the credit she usually gets.

- **Aberration**

  Contextual Meaning(s) : Noun; state or condition markedly different from the norm
  Other Meaning(s) : an optical phenomenon resulting from the failure of a lens or mirror to produce a good image; a disorder in one's mental state;
  Synonyms : distortion, deviance

- **Anomaly**

  Contextual Meaning(s) : Noun; a person who is unusual; deviation from the normal or common order or form or rule
  Other Meaning(s) : noun (astronomy) position of a planet as defined by its angular distance from its perihelion (as observed from the sun);
  Synonyms : aberrancy

- **Assiduous**

  Contextual Meaning(s) : Adjective: marked by care and persistent effort
  Synonyms : sedulous

- **Bedlam**

  Contextual Meaning(s) : Noun; a state of extreme confusion and disorder
  Other Meaning(s) : Noun; pejorative terms for an insane asylum
  Synonyms : chaos

- **Calamitous**

  Contextual Meaning(s) : Adjective: (of events) having extremely unfortunate or dire consequences; bringing ruin
  Synonyms : black, disastrous,

- **Champion**

  Contextual Meaning(s) : Verb; protect or fight for some cause.
  Other Meaning(s) : adjective holding first place in a contest; noun someone who fights for a cause; someone who has won first place in a competition; someone who

is dazzlingly skilled in any field; a person who backs a politician or a team etc.;
Synonyms : paladin, maven

- **Chaotic**

  Contextual Meaning(s) : Adjective; lacking a visible order or organization; completely unordered and unpredictable and confusing;
  Other Meaning(s) : Adjective of or relating to a sensitive dependence on initial conditions
  Synonyms : helter-skelter, disorderly

- **Congenial**

  Contextual Meaning(s) : Adjective; suitable to one's needs or similar to one's nature
  Other Meaning(s) : adjective used of plants; capable of cross-fertilization or of being grafted;
  Synonyms : compatible, sympathetic

- **Debilitating**

  Contextual Meaning(s) : Adjective; impairing the strength and vitality
  Synonyms : disabling

- **Derelict**

  Contextual Meaning(s) : Adjective; in deplorable condition; forsaken by owner or keeper; worn and broken down by hard use;
  Other Meaning(s) : adjective failing in what duty requires; ; noun a person unable to support himself; a ship abandoned on the high seas
  Synonyms : abandoned ramshackle

- **Discern**

  Contextual Meaning(s) : Verb; detect with the senses
  Synonyms : recognize, distinguish

- **Dreadful**

  Contextual Meaning(s) : Adjective; very unpleasant; causing fear or dread or terror; exceptionally bad or displeasing
  Synonyms : repulsive, sinister

✉ *Exigent*

Contextual Meaning(s) : Adjective; requiring precise accuracy; demanding immediate attention
Synonyms : immediate, exacting

✉ *Egoistic*

Contextual Meaning(s) : adjective; pertaining to or of the nature of egoism
Synonyms : selfish, self-centred

✉ *Fatuously*

Contextual Meaning(s) : Adverb; vacuously or complacently and unconsciously foolish
Synonyms : inanely

✉ *Fray*

Contextual Meaning(s) : Noun; a noisy fight;
Other Meaning(s) : verb wear away by rubbing; cause friction
Synonyms : ruffle

✉ *Frenetic*

Contextual Meaning(s) : Adjective; excessively agitated; transported with rage or other violent emotion
Synonyms : frantic, feverish

✉ *Insipid*

Contextual Meaning(s) : Adjective; lacking interest or significance; lacking significance or impact; lacking taste or flavor or tang
Other Meaning(s) : not pleasing to the sense of taste;
Synonyms : vapid

✉ *Intricate*

Contextual Meaning(s) : Adjective; having many complexly arranged elements; elaborate
Synonyms : complex

✉ *Jest*

Contextual Meaning(s) : Noun; activity characterized by good humor; a humorous anecdote or remark intended to provoke laughter; verb act in a funny or teasing way; tell a joke; speak humorously
Synonyms : jocularly

✉ *Languidly*

Contextual Meaning(s) : Adverb; in a lazy and lethargic manner
Synonyms : lazily

✉ *Momentous*

Contextual Meaning(s) : Adjective; of very great significance
Synonyms : significant

✉ *Optimally*

Contextual Meaning(s) : Adverb; in an ideal and most desirable way
Synonyms : desirably, efficiently

✉ *Orphan*

Contextual Meaning(s) : Adjective; deprived of parents by death or desertion; child who has lost both parents; someone or something who lacks support or care or supervision;
Synonyms : abandoned

✉ *Penitent*

Contextual Meaning(s) : Adjective; feeling or expressing remorse for misdeeds;
Synonyms : repentant

✉ *Raging*

Contextual Meaning(s) : Adjective; very severe; (of the elements) as if showing violent anger; characterized by violent and forceful activity or movement; very intense
Synonyms : furious, tempestuous

✉ *Rhapsodic*

Contextual Meaning(s) : Adjective; feeling great rapture or delight
Synonyms : ecstatic, enraptured

✉ *Surmise*

Contextual Meaning(s) : verb; to conclude that something is the case on the basis of only limited evidence or intuitive feeling
Synonyms : guess, speculate

✉ *Teeming*

Contextual Meaning(s) : Adjective; abundantly filled
Synonyms : full

CHINA, THE SECOND SUPER POWER

Since the end of the Cold War, China has been pursuing a strategy that appears aimed at eventually displacing the United States as the **preponderant** global superpower. This strategy has several interlocking elements. While Beijing seeks to avoid a direct confrontation with Washington, it has been engaged in a rapid, sustained military buildup designed to prevent or if necessary defeat American efforts to project power into the Western Pacific. In fact , Beijing has been implementing an ambitious program of modernizing its Armed Forces, including space, naval and missile elements. The continuing lack of transparency of China's defense spending is alarming. This alarm grew especially after a space test in January 2007 when a Chinese **ballistic** missile destroyed a satellite in a low-earth orbit.

In practice, China's new strategy of "far sea defense" means acquiring the ability to project naval power into key ocean areas (including the Indian Ocean and Persian Gulf), while denying other naval powers the ability to operate with **impunity** in areas in **vicinity** of China.

The rapid expansion of China's naval capabilities can be considered a classic **manifestation** of great power status.

At the same time ,China has sought to use diplomacy and the growing pull of its economy to draw neighboring countries into its orbit. Beijing skillfully lifts its partners' concerns over the growth of China's economic and military capability, and persistently profiles itself as a friendly country that is trying to build a harmonious world. On the whole, even the U.S. takes a more businesslike, restrained and positive approach toward China, while the erstwhile superpower Russia's domestic political reality and international activity are often **vilified**. Moscow still ranks above Beijing if we consider the emotional **taint** of U.S. assessments.

There are at least three **reservations** worth noting in this china story. Firstly, China remains much weaker than the United States today, and it has a long way to go before it becomes a true "peer competitor." So there's no need for America to panic, just a timely and **prudent** response. China's rise should make it relatively easy for the United States to stay on good terms with its current Asian allies because of their

perceived threat from China. Many of China's neighbors are more willing than ever before to work together to maintain a balance of power that favors their interests and assures their independence, and they are looking to the United States for assistance and leadership.

Secondly, Chinese economic growth is likely to slow in the years ahead, especially as its population ages and as its emerging middle class demands additional social benefits. This situation will force Beijing to make some hard choices about domestic and international priorities and may limit the speed with which economic might is translated into military power and overseas presence. In the current global recession China, too, faces serious challenges to its continued growth, including a **ballooning** real estate bubble and (thanks to the disastrous consequences of its "one-child policy") an impending **contraction** in the supply of low-cost labor. Those who are **bullish** on America and **bearish** on China probably have it about right. China is more likely to stumble badly in the course of the coming decades than the United States is to remain **mired** in deadlock, debt and **sluggish** growth. The authoritarian regime in Beijing is going to find it difficult to **hinge** from a growth model that features massive investments in huge construction projects carried out by large, well-connected (and often state-owned) enterprises, to policies that encourage domestic consumption and genuine private entrepreneurship.

Thirdly, and most important, open war between US and china is impossible. Nuclear **deterrence** is likely to keep the competition within bounds, and **provident** and sensible diplomacy may be able to defuse or limit potential clashes of interest. Nonetheless, if China continues on the course laid out here, you should expect significant security competition between Washington and Beijing in the decades ahead.

All said and done, there are strong doubts about America's **overweening** sole superpower status lasting much longer. In most nations, the balance of opinion is that China either will replace or equal United States as the world's leading superpower. This view is especially widespread in Western Europe, where at least six-in-ten believe so. As in years past, U.S. image continues to suffer among predominantly Muslim countries.

More than half of all world's industrial goods are made in its factories. China produced half of all digital cameras and 60 per cent of microwaves, photocopiers and DVD players in the world The production and export of these goods, their prices kept low by Beijing's manipulation of the currency and labour rates, has generated the cash behind China's growing economic power. Its worker's earn hardly 10 per cent of an American worker's wage. 17 per cent of people live on less than a $1 a day. It has 16 of the world's 20 most polluted cities, but ironically half of world's emerging super tall towers, too.

Every city sports a new billion-dollar airport, but these are largely under utilised. Yet in the cities, traffic is **horrendous** and trains, the more common form of transportation are packed. The highway system is magnificent with more than 30,000 kilometres built in the last couple of years, but quite underutilized. To purchase a taxicab for example it costs $5,000, but just to drive that cab, the license alone would cost $2,500.

China's "comparative advantage" is **abetted** by its **iron-fisted** rule. Aside from the traditional advantages of low wages and low benefits, China uses the "advantage" of "low human rights" to push down the costs of the four key factors of production: labor, land, capital, and non-renewable resources.

All in all China is not ideologically admired by many. China is not a democracy, its attitude on human rights leaves a lot to be desired and the Communist Party's treatment of organised religions angers the **devoutly** religious. It's accused of practicing **crony** Capitalism. People wonder how well the masses of the Chinese people live; if they live in peace and prosperity with civil and human rights, or if they are **miserable drones** who don't dare step "out of line" for fear of imprisonment or death. Do they have decent education, food and health care, or are they brainwashed and ignorant?.

Abetted
Contextual Meaning(s) : Verb; supported, helped, is some activity.
Synonyms : assisted

Bearish
Contextual Meaning(s) : Adjective; pessimistic
Other Meaning(s) : adjective; expecting prices to fall
Synonyms : optimistic

Bullish
Contextual Meaning(s) : Adjective; optimists.
Other Meaning(s) : adjective; expecting a rise in prices
Synonyms : pessimistic

Ballistic
Contextual Meaning(s) : adjective; relating to the movements of objects propelled through the air

Ballooning
Contextual Meaning(s) : verb; to increase or rise quickly, e.g. expenses ballooning out of control
Synonyms : expand

Caveats
Contextual Meaning(s) : Noun; restrictions, qualifications or conditions with a decision or order.
Synonyms : reservations, qualifications

Contraction
Contextual Meaning(s) : Noun; the act of decreasing (something) in size or volume or quantity or scope;
Other Meaning(s) : (physiology) a shortening or tensing of a part or organ (especially of a muscle or muscle fiber); a word formed from two or more words by omitting or combining some sounds; the process or result of becoming smaller or pressed together
Synonyms : compression, condensation

Crony
Contextual Meaning(s) : Noun; a close friend who accompanies his buddies in their activities
Synonyms : buddy, sidekick

Deter
Contextual Meaning(s) : Verb try to prevent; show opposition to; turn away from by persuasion
Synonyms : discourage, dissuade

Deterrence
Contextual Meaning(s) : Noun; the act or process of discouraging actions or preventing occurrences by instilling fear or doubt or anxiety; a communication that makes you afraid to try something; a negative motivational influence
Synonyms : intimidation, disincentive

Devoutly
Contextual Meaning(s) : Adverb; in a devout and pious manner
Synonyms : piously

Drones
Contextual Meaning(s) : Noun; a stingless male bee with a slavish life.
Other Meaning(s) : noun; an aircraft with remote control.
Synonyms : laggards, dependents

Hinge
Contextual Meaning(s) : Verb; attach with something that helps growth.
Other Meaning(s) : noun a joint that holds two parts together so that one can swing relative to the other; a circumstance upon which subsequent events depend;
Synonyms : predicate

Horrendous
Contextual Meaning(s) : adjective; sufficiently unpleasant, frightening or shocking as to provoke horror
Synonyms : awful, dreadful

🖎 *Impunity*
Contextual Meaning(s) : Noun; exemption from punishment or loss
Synonyms : exemption

🖎 *Iron-fisted*
Contextual Meaning(s) : adjective; very strong or hard
Synonyms : harsh

🖎 *Manifestation*
Contextual Meaning(s) : Noun; a indication of the existence or presence or nature of some person or thing; a clear appearance; a public display of group feelings (usually of a political nature); expression without words;
Other Meaning(s) : an appearance in bodily form (as of a disembodied spirit)
Synonyms : demonstration, materialization

🖎 *Mired*
Contextual Meaning(s) : Adjective; entangled or hindered as if e.g. in mire
Synonyms : involved

🖎 *Miserable*
Contextual Meaning(s) : Adjective; characterized by physical misery; very unhappy; full of misery; contemptibly small in amount; of the most contemptible kind; deserving or inciting pity; of very poor quality or condition
Synonyms : wretched, woeful

🖎 *Overweening*
Contextual Meaning(s) : Adjective; presumptuously arrogant;
Other Meaning(s) : unrestrained, especially with regard to feelings
Synonyms : uppity

🖎 *Perceived*
Contextual Meaning(s) : Adjective; detected by means of the senses; detected by instinct or inference rather than by recognized perceptual cues
Synonyms : sensed

🖎 *Preponderant*
Contextual Meaning(s) : Adjective; having superior power and influence
Synonyms : overriding, predominant

🖎 *Provident*
Contextual Meaning(s) : Adjective; providing carefully for the future; careful in regard to one's own interests
Synonyms : cautious, thoughtful

🖎 *Prudent*
Contextual Meaning(s) : Adjective; careful and sensible; marked by sound judgment
Synonyms : judicious, circumspect

🖎 *Reservations*
Contextual Meaning(s) : Noun; an unstated doubt that prevents you from accepting something wholeheartedly
Other Meaning(s) : the act of keeping back or setting aside for some future occasion; something reserved in advance (as a hotel accommodation or a seat on a plane etc.); a statement that limits or restricts some claim; the written record or promise of an arrangement by which accommodations are secured in advance; a district that is reserved for particular purpose; the act of reserving (a place or passage) or engaging the services of (a person or group)
Synonyms : qualifications, caveats, doubts

🖎 *Sluggish*
Contextual Meaning(s) : Adjective; with little movement; very slow; slow and apathetic; (of business) not active or brisk
Synonyms : inert, torpid

🖎 *Taint*
Contextual Meaning(s) : Noun; the state of being contaminated
Other Meaning(s) : verb contaminate with a disease or microorganism; place under suspicion or cast doubt upon
Synonyms : contamination, cloud

🖎 *Vicinity*
Contextual Meaning(s) : Noun; the state of being physically near
Synonyms : neighborhood

🖎 *Vilified*
Contextual Meaning(s) : Verb; made to appear evil or bad
Synonyms : slandered, reviled

Climate change over the next 50 years is expected to **impel** a quarter of land, animals and plants into extinction, according to the first **inclusive** study into the effect of higher temperatures on the natural world.

The sheer scale of the **cataclysm** facing the planet **appalled** those involved in the research. They **reckon** that more than 1 million species will be **razed** by 2050.

The results are described as "**petrifying**" by Chris Thomas, professor of conservation biology at Leeds University, who is lead author of the research from four continents published in the magazine Nature.

Much of that **casualty** - more than one in 10 of all plants and animals. is already **irrevocable** because of the extra global warming gases already discharged into the atmosphere. But the scientists say that action to **inhibit** greenhouse gases even now could save many more from the same fate.

It took two years for the largest global collaboration of **mavens** to make the first major **appraisal** of the effect of climate change on six biologically **bounteous** regions of the world taking in 20% of the land surface.

The research in Europe, Australia, Central and South America, and South Africa, showed that species living in enormous areas had a greater chance of survival because they could simply **relocate** uphill to get cooler.

Those in flatter areas such as Brazil, Mexico and Australia, were more **assailable,** faced with the impossible task of **traversing** thousands of miles to find suitable conditions.

Birds had the greatest chance of **extricating** themselves from this **inferno**, could in theory move to a more suitable climate but the trees and other habitat they needed for survival could not keep pace and all would **perish**.

Professor Thomas said: "When scientists set about research they hope to come up with definite results, but what we found we wish we had not. It was far, far worse than we thought, and what we have discovered may even be an underestimate."

Among the more **startling** findings of the scientists was that of 24 species of butterfly studied in Australia, all but three would **vaporize** in much of their current range, and half would become extinct.

In South Africa major conservation areas such as Kruger national park **hazarded** losing up to 60% of the species under their protection.

In Europe, the continent least **perturbed** by climate change, damage is still **inchoate**, but even here under the higher estimates of climate change a quarter of the birds could become extinct, and between 11% and 17% of plant species.

One British example is the Scottish crossbill which is **extant** as yet. The future climate in Scotland will be different and the birds will be unable to survive, especially with rivals from warmer climes moving in.

The crossbill would need to move to the **gelid** Iceland, but currently there are virtually no trees and suitable food. The scientists conclude: "It seems unlikely that the species will manage to move to Iceland."

In South Africa, where many popular garden plants originate, 300 plant species were studied and more than one third were **moribund**, including South Africa's national flower, the King Protea.

"The risk of extinction increases as global warming interacts with other factors - such as landscape modification, species invasions and build-up of carbon dioxide - to disrupt communities and ecological interactions."

So many species are already destined for extinction because it takes at least 25 years for the greenhouse effect - or the trapping of the sun's rays by the carbon dioxide, methane and nitrous oxide already added to the air - to have its full effect on the planet. Deserts, grasslands and forests are already changing to make survival impossible.

The continuous discharging of more greenhouse gases, particularly by the USA, is making matters considerably worse. The research says if mankind continues to burn oil, coal and gas at the current rate, up to one third of all life forms will be finished by 2050.

Prof Thomas Gold, Emeritus Professor at Cornell University has written in his paper it was urgent to switch from fossil fuels to a non-carbon economy as quickly as possible. "It is possible to drastically reduce the output of greenhouse gases into the atmosphere and this research makes it imperative we do it as soon as possible. If we can stabilise the climate and even reverse the warming we could save these species, but we must treat this as an **exigency**".

If conservation groups want to save species they should devote at least half their energies to political campaigning to reduce global warming because that was the greatest single threat to survival of the species.

John Lanchbery, climate change campaigner for the Royal Society for the Protection of Birds, agrees: "This is a deeply depressing paper. President Bush risks having the biggest impact on wildlife since the **meteorite** that **annihilated** out the dinosaurs. At best, in 50 years, a host of wildlife will be committed to extinction because of human-induced climate change. At worst, the outcome does not bear thinking about. Drastic action to cut emissions is clearly **mandated** for everyone, but especially the USA."

🖎 **Annihilated**

Contextual Meaning(s) : Adjective; destroyed completely

Synonyms : exterminated

🖎 **Appalled**

Contextual Meaning(s) : Adjective; struck with fear, dread, or consternation

Synonyms : aghast, dismayed

🖎 **Appraisal**

Contextual Meaning(s) : Noun; the classification of someone or something with respect to its worth;

Other Meaning(s) : Noun; a document appraising the value of something (as for insurance or tax.

Synonyms : assessment

🖎 **Assailable**

Contextual Meaning(s) : Adjective; not defended or capable of being defended

Synonyms : non defendable, vulnerable

🖎 **Bounteous**

Contextual Meaning(s) : Adjective; given or giving freely

Synonyms : freehanded

🖎 **Casualty**

Contextual Meaning(s) : Noun; a decrease of military personnel or equipment; someone injured or killed or captured or missing in a military engagement;

Other Meaning(s) : Noun; someone injured or killed in an accident; an accident that causes someone to die

Synonyms : death

🖎 **Cataclysm**

Contextual Meaning(s) : Noun; a sudden violent change in the earth's surface

Other Meaning(s) : Noun; an event resulting in great loss and misfortune;

Synonyms : catastrophe, disaster

🖎 **Exigency**

Contextual Meaning(s) : Noun; a pressing or urgent situation; a sudden unforeseen crisis (usually involving danger) that requires immediate action

Synonyms : emergency, pinch

🖎 **Extant**

Contextual Meaning(s) : Adjective; still in existence; not extinct or destroyed or lost

Synonyms : existent, surviving

🖎 **Extricating**

Contextual Meaning(s) : Verb; getting out of a bad situation

Synonyms : disentangling

🖎 **Gelid**

Contextual Meaning(s) : Adjective; extremely cold

Synonyms : icy, polar

🖎 **Hazarded**

Contextual Meaning(s) : Verb; exposed to risk

Synonyms : risked

🖎 **Impel**

Contextual Meaning(s) : Verb; urge or force (a person) to an action; constrain or motivate; cause to move forward with force

Synonyms : force, propel

🖎 **Inchoate**

Contextual Meaning(s) : Adjective; imperfectly formed

Other Meaning(s) : Adjective; only partly in existence;

Synonyms : incipient

🖎 **Inclusive**

Contextual Meaning(s) : Adjective; including much or everything; and especially including stated limits

Synonyms : comprehensive

❦ *Inferno*

Contextual Meaning(s) : Noun; a very intense and uncontrolled fire; any place of pain and turmoil

Other Meaning(s) : Noun; (Christianity) the abode of Satan and the forces of evil; where sinners suffer eternal punishment;

Synonyms : perdition conflagration, hell,

❦ *Inhibit*

Contextual Meaning(s) : Verb; limit the range or extent of; to put down by force or authority

Synonyms : suppress, subdue

❦ *Irrevocable*

Contextual Meaning(s) : Adjective; incapable of being retracted or revoked

Synonyms : unalterable

❦ *Mandated*

Contextual Meaning(s) : Verb; made compulsory, required to be done as per orders

Synonyms : required, ordered

❦ *Mavens*

Contextual Meaning(s) : Noun; people who are experts at something

Synonyms : maestroes

❦ *Meteorite*

Contextual Meaning(s) : Noun; stony or metallic object tha`t is the remains of a meteoroid that has reached the earth's surface

Synonyms : meteoroid

❦ *Moribund*

Contextual Meaning(s) : Adjective; being on the point of death; breathing your last;

Other Meaning(s) : Adjective; not growing or changing; without force or vitality

Synonyms : dying, stagnant,

❦ *Perish*

Contextual Meaning(s) : Verb; pass from physical life and lose all bodily attributes and functions necessary to sustain life

Synonyms : die, decease,

❦ *Perturbed*

Contextual Meaning(s) : Adjective; thrown into a state of agitated confusion; (`rattled' is an informal term)

Synonyms : rattled

❦ *Petrifying*

Contextual Meaning(s) : Adjective; paralyzing with terror

Synonyms : frightening, paralyzing

❦ *Razed*

Contextual Meaning(s) : Adjective; torn down and broken up

Synonyms : demolished, dismantled

❦ *Reckon*

Contextual Meaning(s) : Verb; take account of; expect, believe, or suppose; make a mathematical calculation or computation; deem to be; judge to be probable; have faith or confidence in

Synonyms : regard, consider

❦ *Relocate*

Contextual Meaning(s) : Verb; move or establish in a new location; become established in a new location

Synonyms : migrate, displace

❦ *Startling*

Contextual Meaning(s) : Adjective; so remarkably different or sudden as to cause momentary shock or alarm

Synonyms : shocking

❦ *Traversing*

Contextual Meaning(s) : Verb; moving over a distance

Synonyms : spanning

❦ *Vaporize*

Contextual Meaning(s) : Verb; decrease rapidly and disappear; lose or cause to lose liquid by vaporization leaving a more concentrated residue; turn into gas; kill with or as if with a burst of gunfire or electric current or as if by shooting

Synonyms : vanish, , gasify

GOING TO THE MOVIES

There is this romantic in me, who is so hooked to the old ways of doing things that he just doesn't want to **conform** to new ways of living. I love the people, the anticipation and the **ambience** a good movie theater offers, compared to staying at home and watching movies on Television in the **everyday** surroundings. Being out with friends and enjoying the city or town is also an added **incentive** in watching movies outside home. Most of the cinema halls are nowadays part of some shopping mall or shopping centre. So one also gets to **meander** and check out the the architecture, the crowd, the stores and the **ware**, as a **fringe** benefit. Not to forget, one gets to watch a new movie the day its released and *not wait* one month for the DVD release.

The theatres let you enjoy a full on experience you can't feel anywhere else. The surround sound, the big screen and the focused atmosphere are what some people and I choose for a movie experience. Unless you have a ₹ **50,000** setup for entertainment at home, your experience at home can't match that of a good movie hall.. Besides I love having a large number of people around me tuned into the movie. When I sense (I can't really appear to be watching them, it would be rude!) strangers around me react to a scene in a movie, I get to know the average viewer's response to a movie. I enjoy laughing at the humor with 300 strangers, getting **jumpy** with them at the nervy scenes, getting collectively **mushy** at the wedding scenes, and sad at tragic moments. I have even clapped with the rest of crowd when the hero rescues the little child from the building on fire. When the detective identifies the **devious** murderer, i have been **petrified** along with the entire audience. And as the pregnant silence breaks into a well of **murmurs**, I have also been whispering out my amazement to my friends sitting alongside.

Call this strange but I confess I **eavesdrop** on the others as they walk out of the theater in order to listen to their comments on the movie. I make my own opinion but I love to know the mainstream reaction to a movie. That tells me how different is my taste from that of others in some ways while being similar in many ways. I don't rely on the media buzz, because I make my own opinion on a new flick, besides get a firsthand account of a new flick's fate based on the crowd's response right on the spot. I make full use of the ₹ 200 a ticket I paid to watch the movie in theater as compared to a **measly** ₹ 20 for the entire family on a rented DVD at home. The fact that you can get all the popcorn and coffee ready made, even delivered to your seat is another boon.

However, there is a strong **rebuttal** to my point of view, too.

Many people say it is much better to watch a movie at home than at the movie theater! When you go to the movie theater you spend a **preposterous** amount of money just to hear some guy behind you laugh like a hyena the *entire* time (even the parts that aren't that funny...). Or you'll get the seven foot tall guy who just happens to sit right in front of you, despite there being 20 other open seats in the theater. You **loathe** the ones that sit there and talk on their cell phone while the movie is on ,narrating the entire movie to their friend who could not afford to come . There is also the bunch of **obstreperous** kids who sit in the front and throw stuff at the screen the entire time and then there are the **chronic** *boo-ers* ;they are just as annoying as the people who just won't shut up during the movie. People hate to listen to screaming babies in the theater and the like. Last but not the least, the inevitable **scamper** to reach the parking lot before the others so as to get your vehicle out early.

Many would rather watch the movie **languidly** at home so that if they need to they can pause the movie for a bathroom break, get a snack, etc without missing any part of the movie. Also, they like the fact that they can sit there and watch the deleted scenes and the director's commentaries assuming they buy the Collector's Edition DVD . It also allows them to re-watch the movie if they didn't understand certain parts or if the movie was confusing as a whole. Overall the home movie watching experience is so much preferable for some that it has been **eons** since they have actually gone to the movie theater to see a movie!

Some dislike the movie halls because of irritating body odour around them, though of late the **luxuriant** theaters do have a perfume spray system to **dispel** these. Late comers can be another source of annoyance especially when they are **insolent** enough to cause a commotion about finding their seats. But there *are* the polite ones who **comport** well and reach their places without creating much racket. The noise from some section of the audience, who are **cantankerously** chattering all the way, can be disturbing, too.

Lastly, there are the spoilers, who have nothing better to do, so they watch the same movie for the second time. These guys keep foretelling the events to happen and leave no suspense for the first timers !

To each his own, one can either watch at home or be at home at the theater, depending on his taste, concept of enjoyment and the bank balance. As long as good movies are being made I really don't worry, they will be watched with or without the pause button !

🖎 **Ambience**
Contextual Meaning(s) : noun; a particular environment or surrounding influence
Synonyms : aura, atmosphere

🖎 **Cantankerously**
Contextual Meaning(s) : adverb; in a bad mood
Synonyms : boorishly, peevishly

🖎 **Chronic**
Contextual Meaning(s) : adjective; being long-lasting and recurrent or characterized by long suffering
Synonyms : habitual

🖎 **Comport**
Contextual Meaning(s) : Verb; behave in a certain manner; behave well or properly
Synonyms : conduct, carry

🖎 **Conform**
Contextual Meaning(s) : Verb; be similar, be in line with; adapt or conform oneself to new or different conditions
Synonyms : adjust, adapt

🖎 **Decorously**
Contextual Meaning(s) : Adverb; in a proper and politic manner
Synonyms : politely

🖎 **Devious**
Contextual Meaning(s) : Adjective; misleading; characterized by insincerity or deceit; evasive
Other Meaning(s) : adjective; deviating from a straight course; indirect in departing from the accepted or proper way
Synonyms : shifty

🖎 **Dispel**
Contextual Meaning(s) : verb force to go away;
Other Meaning(s) : used both with concrete and metaphoric Meaning(s); to cause to separate and go in different directions
Synonyms : disperse

🖎 **Eavesdrop**
Contextual Meaning(s) : Verb; listen without the speaker's knowledge
Synonyms : overhear

🖎 **Eons**
Contextual Meaning(s) : Noun; immeasurably long periods of time; the longest divisions of geological time
Other Meaning(s) : Noun; a divine power or nature emanating from the Supreme Being and playing various roles in the operation of the universe
Synonyms : eras

🖎 **Everyday**
Contextual Meaning(s) : Adjective; commonplace and ordinary; found in the ordinary course of events;
Other Meaning(s) : suited for everyday use
Synonyms : routine, unremarkable, casual

🖎 **Fringe**
Contextual Meaning(s) : Noun; the outside boundary or surface of something;
Other Meaning(s) : noun edging consisting of hanging threads or tassels; a social group holding marginal or extreme views; a part of the city far removed from the center; verb decorate with or as if with a surrounding fringe; adorn with a fringe
Synonyms : out skirt

🖎 **Gratification**
Contextual Meaning(s) : Noun; the act or an instance of satisfying; state of being gratified; great satisfaction
Synonyms : pleasure

🖎 **Incentive**
Contextual Meaning(s) : Noun; a positive motivational influence;
Other Meaning(s) : noun; an additional payment (or other remuneration) to employees as a means of increasing output
Synonyms : bonus

🖎 **Insolent**
Contextual Meaning(s) : Adjective; unrestrained by convention or propriety; marked by casual disrespect
Synonyms : bodacious

- *Jumpy*
  Contextual Meaning(s) : Adverb; causing or characterized by jolts and irregular movements; being in a tense state
  Synonyms : restive, edgy

- *Languidly*
  Contextual Meaning(s) : Adverb; in a lazy and lethargic manner
  Synonyms : languorous

- *Loathe*
  Contextual Meaning(s) : Verb; find repugnant or repulsive
  Synonyms : abhor, abominate, execrate

- *Luxuriant*
  Contextual Meaning(s) : Adjective; displaying luxury and furnishing gratification to the senses; marked by complexity and richness of detail
  Other Meaning(s) : adj. produced or growing in extreme abundance;
  Synonyms : lush

- *Meander*
  Contextual Meaning(s) : Noun; an aimless amble on a winding course;
  Other Meaning(s) : noun a bend or curve, as in a stream or river; verb to move or cause to move in a sinuous, spiral, or circular course
  Synonyms : ramble, thread, wander

- *Measly*
  Contextual Meaning(s) : adjective; contemptibly small in amount
  Synonyms : miserable, paltry

- *Mortified*
  Contextual Meaning(s) : Adjective; made to feel uncomfortable because of shame or wounded pride;
  Other Meaning(s) : suffering from tissue death
  Synonyms : embarrassed, humiliated.

- *Murmurs*
  Contextual Meaning(s) : Noun; whispers, hushed talk
  Other Meaning(s) : to speak softly, under one's breath
  Synonyms : mutters

- *Mushy*
  Contextual Meaning(s) : Adjective; having the consistency of mush; effusively or insincerely emotional
  Synonyms :

- *Obstreperous*
  Contextual Meaning(s) : Adjective; boisterously and noisily aggressive; noisily and stubbornly defiant
  Synonyms : defiant

- *Preposterous*
  Contextual Meaning(s) : Adjective; absurd; inviting ridicule
  Synonyms : cockeyed, ludicrous, nonsensical

- *Petrified*
  Contextual Meaning(s) : adjective; stunned or dazed with horror or fear
  Synonyms : alarmed

- *Rebuttal*
  Contextual Meaning(s) : Noun the speech or act of refuting by offering a contrary contention or argument;
  Other Meaning(s) : (law) a pleading by the defendant in reply to a plaintiff's surrejoinder
  Synonyms : contradiction

- *Scamper*
  Contextual Meaning(s) : Noun rushing about hastily in an undignified way; verb to move about or proceed hurriedly
  Synonyms : scramble, scurry

- *Uptight*
  Contextual Meaning(s) : Adjective; being in a tense state
  Synonyms : restive, nervous, fidgety

- *Voyeur*
  Contextual Meaning(s) : Noun; a viewer who enjoys seeing the private acts of others
  Synonyms : peeper

- *Ware*
  Contextual Meaning(s) : Noun; articles of the same kind or material; usually used in combination: 'silverware', 'software'; commodities offered for sale;
  Other Meaning(s) : verb spend extravagantly
  Synonyms : merchandise

Glosssary

S. No.	Words	Page No.
1	**Abandonment**	179
	Synonyms : desolation, dereliction	
2	**Aberration**	204
	Synonyms : distortion, deviance	
3	**Abetted**	210
	Synonyms : assisted	
4	**Abjured**	66
	Synonyms : retract	
5	**Abominable**	106
	Synonyms : detestable, execrable	
6	**Abort**	63
	Synonyms : terminate	
7	**abounds**	26
	Synonyms : bristles	
8	**Abstract**	77
	Synonyms : amorphous, vague	
9	**Abstruse**	160
	Synonyms : deep, recondite	
10	**Abusive**	164
	Synonyms : insulting, opprobrious, scurrilous	
11	**Abysmally**	170
	Synonyms : atrociously, awfully	
12	**Accessible**	54
	Synonyms : approachable	
13	**Accorded**	72
	Synonyms : granted	
14	**Acquiesce**	92
	Synonyms : assent, accede	
15	**Acquisition**	20
	Synonyms : attainment	
16	**Acquisitive**	172
	Synonyms : covetous	
17	**Acrimonious**	43
	Synonyms : bitter	
18	**Acrimony**	114
	Synonyms : bitterness, acerbity, jaundice, tartness, thorniness	
19	**Adapt**	118
	Synonyms : adjust	
20	**Admonition**	183
	Synonyms : reprimand, warning	
21	**Adorned**	97
	Synonyms : decorated, bedecked	
22	**Adulation**	77
	Synonyms : worship, admiration	
23	**Adulterating**	41
	Synonyms : adulterant	
24	**Adumbrating**	175
	Synonyms : outlining	
25	**Advent**	6
	Synonyms : arrival, onset	
26	**Advertent**	21
	Synonyms : attentive	
27	**Advocate**	119
	Synonyms : exponent, counsel, counselor, counsellor, counselor-at-law, pleader, preach, recommend, urge	
28	**Aesthetic**	6
	Synonyms : artistic, pleasing	
29	**Aesthetically**	8
	Synonyms : esthetically	
30	**Affirm**	50
	Synonyms : aver, avow	
31	**Aficionados**	178
	Synonyms : connoisseur	
32	**Aggravated**	171
	Synonyms : provoked	
33	**Aggregation**	1
	Synonyms : accumulation, assemblage	
34	**Agility**	73
	Synonyms : lightness, lightsomeness, nimbleness	
35	**Agog**	200
	Synonyms : agitated	
36	**Agrarian**	119
	Synonyms : agricultural, farming	

S. No.	Words	Page No.
37	**Akin**	7
	Synonyms : similar	
38	**Albatross**	119
	Synonyms : mollymawk, millstone	
39	**Allegedly**	45
	Synonyms : supposedly	
40	**Allegiance**	178
	Synonyms : fealty, commitment, loyalty, dedication	
41	**Alleviate**	218
	Synonyms : relieve, palliate, assuage	
42	**Alloying**	179
	Synonyms : debasing, adulterating	
43	**Alludes**	72
	Synonyms : touches	
44	**Alluring**	179
	Synonyms : enticing	
45	**Altercation**	41
	Synonyms : affray, fracas	
46	**Amateur**	145
	Synonyms : recreational, unpaid	
47	**Ameliorate**	106
	Synonyms : amend	
48	**Amenable**	30
	Synonyms : responsive	
49	**Amorphous**	7
	Synonyms : unstructured, formless	
50	**Ample**	72
	Synonyms : copious, plenteous, sizeable	
51	**Anachronists**	159
	Synonyms : misdated	
52	**Analogous**	186
	Synonyms : corresponding	
53	**Anchorites**	15
	Synonyms : hermits	
54	**Annihilated**	214
	Synonyms : exterminated	
55	**Anoint**	41
	Synonyms : announce, inunct,	
56	**Anomaly**	115, 122
	Synonyms : aberrancy	
57	**Anorexia**	30
	Synonyms : eating disorder	
58	**Anti**	31
	Synonyms : against	
59	**Antipathy**	88
	Synonyms : aversion, distaste	
60	**Antiquated**	119
	Synonyms : obsolete	
61	**Antithesis**	12
	Synonyms : oppositeness	
62	**Apex**	114
	Synonyms : solar apex, apex of the sun's way, vertex, peak, acme	
63	**Apologists**	50
	Synonyms : proponent, advocate	
64	**Apotheosized**	179
	Synonyms : deified	
65	**Appalled**	213
	Synonyms : aghast, dismayed	
66	**Apportioned**	154
	Synonyms : dealt out	
67	**Appraisal**	213
	Synonyms : assessment	
68	**Appraise**	2
	Synonyms : evaluate, assess	
69	**Apprehensive**	37
	Synonyms : anxious, wary	
70	**Aquiline**	3
	Synonyms : hooked	
71	**Arbitrarily**	219
	Synonyms : randomly, indiscriminately,	
72	**Arcane**	12
	Synonyms : mysterious	
73	**Archived**	159
	Synonyms : stored, filed	
74	**Armour**	128
	Synonyms : kevlar	
75	**Aroma**	98
	Synonyms : fragrance, perfume	
76	**Aroused**	195
	Synonyms : stimulated	
77	**Arrogate**	66
	Synonyms : usurps	
78	**Ascendency**	114
	Synonyms : dominance, ascendance, ascendence, ascendancy, control	

S. No.	Words	Page No.
79	**Asinine**	136
	Synonyms : mindless, vacuous	
80	**Assailable**	213
	Synonyms : undefendable, vulnerable	
81	**Assault**	58
	Synonyms : violation, outrage	
82	**Asserting**	45
	Synonyms : declarative, declaratory	
83	**Assiduous**	204
	Synonyms : sedulous	
84	**Assortment**	25
	Synonyms : miscellany, potpourri, motley	
85	**Astounded**	128
	Synonyms : astonished	
86	**Astral**	17
	Synonyms : stellar	
87	**Asynchronous**	87
	Synonyms : anachronistic	
88	**Atrocious**	50
	Synonyms : detestable	
89	**Attest**	148
	Synonyms : certify, testify	
90	**Attire**	89
	Synonyms : apparel	
91	**Attired**	165
	Synonyms : appareled, dressed, garbed	
92	**Attributes**	188
	Synonyms : features	
93	**Audited**	165
	Synonyms : scrutinized	
94	**Augmented**	25
	Synonyms : intensified	
95	**Authentic**	76
	Synonyms : unquestionable, veritable	
96	**Avalanches**	127
	Synonyms : bombardments, barrages	
97	**Aversion**	145
	Synonyms : antipathy, distaste	
98	**Babbling**	20
	Synonyms : jabbering	
99	**Balk**	38
	Synonyms : resist, jib	
100	**Banter**	114
	Synonyms : gossip, chaff	
101	**Barbarians**	12
	Synonyms : savages	
102	**Bard**	92
	Synonyms : lyric-poet	
103	**Baritone**	34
	Synonyms : voice	
104	**Barrage**	7
	Synonyms : shelling, onslaught	
105	**Battered**	98
	Synonyms : beaten-up	
106	**Bearish**	209
	Synonyms : optimistic	
107	**Bedlam**	204
	Synonyms : chaos	
108	**Bedrock**	109
	Synonyms : foundation	
109	**Begrudges**	30
	Synonyms : envies	
110	**Behemoth**	119
	Synonyms : colossus, giant, heavyweight, titan, goliath, monster	
111	**Beleaguered**	58
	Synonyms : surrounded, troubled	
112	**Belligerent**	58
	Synonyms : militant, aggressive	
113	**Bemoans**	123
	Synonyms : rafter, resist, jib	
114	**Bemusement**	218
	Synonyms : bewilderment, obfuscation, bafflement	
115	**Benign**	164
	Synonyms : benignant	
116	**Besotted**	49
	Synonyms : inebriated	
117	**Bettered**	97
	Synonyms : ameliorated	
118	**Bewilderment**	93
	Synonyms : obfuscation, bafflement	
119	**Biased**	144
	Synonyms : colored, slanted	
120	**Binge**	171
	Synonyms : splurge, gorge, overindulge	

S. No.	Words	Page No.
121	**Binges**	122
	Synonyms : indulgences	
122	**Blackballed**	155
	Synonyms : banished	
123	**Blasphemy**	155
	Synonyms : profanation, desecration, sacrilege	
124	**Bleakest**	58
	Synonyms : gloomy, dour	
125	**Blitheness**	102
	Synonyms : cheerfulness, mirth	
126	**Blunt**	62
	Synonyms : deaden	
127	**Blustery**	122
	Synonyms : stormy	
128	**Bohemians**	130
	Synonyms : gypsies	
129	**Boisterous**	131
	Synonyms : obstreperous, defiant	
130	**Bonding**	25
	Synonyms : attachment	
131	**Boomerang**	165
	Synonyms : backfire	
132	**Bounteous**	213
	Synonyms : freehanded	
133	**Bountiful**	7
	Synonyms : plentiful, liberal	
134	**Bragging**	16
	Synonyms : boasting	
135	**Brainstorm**	219
	Synonyms : insight, brainwave	
136	**Brainy**	89
	Synonyms : intellectual	
137	**Brawnier**	176
	Synonyms : heftier	
138	**Brawny**	66
	Synonyms : powerful, sinewy	
139	**Brazen**	182
	Synonyms : blatant	
140	**Breeze**	33
	Synonyms : cinch	
141	**Bridle**	115
	Synonyms : check, curb	
142	**Brokering**	144
	Synonyms : mediating, negotiating	
143	**Brooding**	136
	Synonyms : contemplative, pensiveness	
144	**Browbeat**	30
	Synonyms : bullyrag, hector	
145	**Brutally**	127
	Synonyms : viciously, savagely	
146	**Buffs**	98
	Synonyms : enthusiast	
147	**Bullish**	209
	Synonyms : pessimistic	
148	**Bump**	172
	Synonyms : knock, blow	
149	**Burgeoning**	164
	Synonyms : expanding, proliferating	
150	**Burnishing**	6
	Synonyms : buffing	
151	**Buttressing**	148
	Synonyms : bolstering	
152	**Bygone**	172
	Synonyms : departed, foregone, gone	
153	**Callow**	41
	Synonyms : fledgling, jejune	
154	**Camouflage**	148
	Synonyms : disguise	
155	**Canard**	45
	Synonyms : rumour	
156	**Cantankerously**	223
	Synonyms : boorishly, peevishly	
157	**Capitulation**	59
	Synonyms : fall, surrender	
158	**Captivating**	182
	Synonyms : hypnotizing	
159	**Casanovas**	132
	Synonyms : playboys	
160	**Casualty**	213
	Synonyms : death	
161	**Cataclysm**	213
	Synonyms : catastrophe, disaster	
162	**Catalyst**	12
	Synonyms : accelerator	
163	**Catering**	160
	Synonyms : providing, servicing	

S. No.	Words	Page No.
164	**Cathartic**	192
	Synonyms : evacuant, purgative	
165	**Caveats**	63
	Synonyms : reservations, qualifications	
166	**Celebrated**	38
	Synonyms : notable, renowned	
167	**Censured**	155
	Synonyms : condemned	
168	**Cerebrally**	165
	Synonyms : intellectually	
169	**Chafe**	171
	Synonyms : fret, fray	
170	**Chagrin**	37
	Synonyms : humiliation, mortification	
171	**Chagrined**	54
	Synonyms : abashed, embarrassed	
172	**Champion**	204
	Synonyms : paladin, maven	
173	**Chaotic**	131
	Synonyms : helter-skelter, disorderly	
174	**Chicanery**	63
	Synonyms : trickery, shenanigan	
175	**Chore**	110
	Synonyms : job, task	
176	**Chronic**	223
	Synonyms : habitual	
177	**Chronicles**	76
	Synonyms : annals	
178	**Chunk**	16
	Synonyms : lump, clump	
179	**Churlish**	165
	Synonyms : choleric	
180	**Circumscribed**	170
	Synonyms : delimited, limited	
181	**Circumvent**	102
	Synonyms : skirt, dodge, duck	
182	**Circumvents**	66
	Synonyms : eludes, skirts	
183	**Citadel**	50
	Synonyms : fortress	
184	**Cited**	122
	Synonyms : quoted	
185	**Climactic**	155
	Synonyms : culminating point	
186	**Cloak**	164
	Synonyms : mask	
187	**Closeted**	145
	Synonyms : confined	
188	**Clutter**	196
	Synonyms : jumble, muddle, fuddle	
189	**Coalesces**	34
	Synonyms : blends	
190	**Coaxes**	109
	Synonyms : palavers	
191	**Coerce**	150
	Synonyms : hale, squeeze, pressure, force	
192	**Coevals**	29
	Synonyms : contemporaries	
193	**Coginizant**	200
	Synonyms : aware	
194	**Cogitating**	115
	Synonyms : cerebrating, thinking	
195	**Coined**	25
	Synonyms : invented	
196	**Collaborative**	37
	Synonyms : cooperative	
197	**Colossal**	77
	Synonyms : prodigious, stupendous	
198	**Comatose**	11
	Synonyms : unconscious	
199	**Comely**	2
	Synonyms : pretty	
200	**Commiserate**	200
	Synonyms : sympathize, sympathise	
201	**Commodious**	196
	Synonyms : spacious	
202	**Commotion**	182
	Synonyms : disorder, unrest	
203	**Compacting**	178
	Synonyms : compressing, condensing	
204	**Compensate**	145
	Synonyms : indemnify, redress	
205	**Complacency**	141
	Synonyms : smugness	
206	**Compliant**	196
	Synonyms : docile, malleable	

S. No.	Words	Page No.
207	**Complimentary**	82
	Synonyms : free, gratuitous	
208	**Comport**	223
	Synonyms : conduct, carry	
209	**Composted**	161
	Synonyms : converted	
210	**Comprehend**	2
	Synonyms : grasp	
211	**Compunction**	123
	Synonyms : remorse, self-reproach	
212	**Conceal**	89
	Synonyms : hold back, hold in, hide	
213	**Concede**	15
	Synonyms : yield	
214	**Concierge**	186
	Synonyms : caretaker, guide	
215	**Concur**	2
	Synonyms : agree	
216	**Concurrent**	42
	Synonyms : simultaneous	
217	**Condign**	29
	Synonyms : deserved, merited	
218	**Confer**	25
	Synonyms : bring together, draw together	
219	**Confined**	76
	Synonyms : captive, imprisoned, jailed	
220	**Conform**	222
	Synonyms : adjust, adapt	
221	**Confrontation**	72
	Synonyms : encounter, showdown,	
222	**Congenial**	205
	Synonyms : compatible, sympathetic	
223	**Congregate**	219
	Synonyms : assemble	
224	**Congruous**	38
	Synonyms : appropriate, matching	
225	**Conjecture**	144
	Synonyms : guess, speculation	
226	**Conjure**	41
	Synonyms : raise, invoke	
227	**Connoisseurs**	41
	Synonyms : buffs, enthusiasts	
228	**Conscientious**	130
	Synonyms : painstaking, scrupulous	
229	**Consensus**	191
	Synonyms : unanimity	
230	**Conspiracy**	93
	Synonyms : cabal, confederacy	
231	**Constrained**	114
	Synonyms : encumbered	
232	**Construed**	149
	Synonyms : deconstructed	
233	**Consummate**	73
	Synonyms : masterful, virtuoso,	
234	**Consummating**	186
	Synonyms : realizing	
235	**Contemplating**	98
	Synonyms : considering	
236	**Contemporary**	41
	Synonyms : contemporaneous	
237	**Contended**	38
	Synonyms : argued	
238	**Contention**	175
	Synonyms : disputation	
239	**Contingency**	159
	Synonyms : eventuality, contingence	
240	**Contingents**	82
	Synonyms : delegations, crews	
241	**Contraction**	209
	Synonyms : compression, condensation	
242	**Contraptions**	188
	Synonyms : devices	
243	**Contrite**	30
	Synonyms : remorseful	
244	**Convention**	183
	Synonyms : norm	
245	**Convoluted**	67
	Synonyms : Byzantine, tortuous	
246	**Cornucopia**	156
	Synonyms : profuseness, richness	
247	**Corpulent**	89, 132
	Synonyms : fat, rotund	
248	**Corroborate**	148
	Synonyms : substantiate, validate	

S. No.	Words	Page No.
249	**Cosseted**	114
	Synonyms : mollycoddled, pampered	
250	**Countenance**	102
	Synonyms : visages	
251	**Countenance**	102
	Synonyms : endorsement	
252	**Countenances**	2
	Synonyms : visages	
253	**Court**	50
	Synonyms : romance, solicit, woo	
254	**Covenant**	183
	Synonyms : contract	
255	**Covet**	29
	Synonyms : envy	
256	**Credence**	93
	Synonyms : acceptance, credenza	
257	**Credibility**	109
	Synonyms : credibleness, believability	
258	**Credible**	33
	Synonyms : believable	
259	**Creditor**	217
	Synonyms : lender, loaner	
260	**Crippled**	166
	Synonyms : lame, gimpy	
261	**Crony**	210
	Synonyms : buddy, sidekick	
262	**Crumbs**	2
	Synonyms : Morsel	
263	**Crusade**	42
	Synonyms : campaign	
264	**Cues**	199
	Synonyms : indications, prompts	
265	**Cuisine**	131
	Synonyms : culinary art	
266	**Culminating**	97
	Synonyms : Resulting	
267	**Cumbersome**	54
	Synonyms : awkward, clumsy	
268	**Curiously**	92
	Synonyms : oddly, peculiarly	
269	**Cynics**	17
	Synonyms : faultfinders	
270	**Dandy**	66
	Synonyms : gallant, smashing	
271	**Dawn**	25
	Synonyms : daybreak,	
272	**Dearer**	54
	Synonyms : costlier	
273	**Dearth**	170
	Synonyms : paucity, famine, shortage	
274	**Debacle**	67
	Synonyms : fiasco	
275	**Debase**	102
	Synonyms : demoralise, profane, vitiate, deprave,	
276	**Debilitating**	204
	Synonyms : disabling	
277	**Debonair**	136
	Synonyms : debonaire, suave	
278	**Debunked**	2
	Synonyms : expose	
279	**Deceived**	37
	Synonyms : cheated, tricked	
280	**Decimated**	11
	Synonyms : destroyed	
281	**Deconstruct**	12
	Synonyms : interpret	
282	**Deconstructing**	148
	Synonyms : perceiving	
283	**Degenerates**	21
	Synonyms : deteriorate	
284	**Deleterious**	140
	Synonyms : hazardous	
285	**Delineated**	77
	Synonyms : represented, outlined	
286	**Delinquency**	29
	Synonyms : dereliction	
287	**Deluged**	218
	Synonyms : submerged	
288	**Delusion**	20
	Synonyms : misconception	
289	**Delved**	73
	Synonyms : dug	
290	**Demise**	161
	Synonyms : dug	
291	**Demographic**	7
	Synonyms : death, dying	

S. No.	Words	Page No.
292	**Demoted**	97
	Synonyms : population-statististic	
293	**Demur**	21
	Synonyms : disagree	
294	**Demystified**	179
	Synonyms : demysted	
295	**Deplorable**	58
	Synonyms : lamentable, woeful	
296	**Deploy**	118
	Synonyms : marshal	
297	**Deployed**	89
	Synonyms : positioned	
298	**Deprecating**	160
	Synonyms : belittling, slighting	
299	**Deprivation**	21, 176
	Synonyms : privation, neediness	
300	**Deracinate**	12
	Synonyms : uproot, , displace	
301	**Derelict**	204
	Synonyms : abandoned ramshackle	
302	**Derisory**	187
	Synonyms : nonsensical	
303	**Descry**	73
	Synonyms : spot, espy, spy	
304	**Desecration**	41
	Synonyms : profanation, sacrilege	
305	**Desiccated**	12
	Synonyms : arid	
306	**Despicable**	30
	Synonyms : detestable	
307	**Detente**	155
	Synonyms : ceasefire	
308	**Deter**	127
	Synonyms : discourage, dissuade	
309	**Deterrence**	209
	Synonyms : intimidation, disincentive	
310	**Detracts**	159
	Synonyms : misleads	
311	**Devious**	222
	Synonyms : shifty	
312	**Devour**	188
	Synonyms : glutton, raven	
313	**Devoutly**	210
	Synonyms : piously	
314	**Dexterity**	73
	Synonyms : sleight	
315	**Dialect**	21
	Synonyms : idiom	
316	**Diaphanous**	196
	Synonyms : filmy, gauzy, gossamer	
317	**Dilettante**	159
	Synonyms : dabbler	
318	**Diminution**	178
	Synonyms : decrease, reduction, step-down, decline	
319	**Diminutive**	6
	Synonyms : bantam, tiny	
320	**Diplomats**	164
	Synonyms : foreign officers	
321	**Dire**	126
	Synonyms : awful, horrific, desperate	
322	**Disabused**	20
	Synonyms : correct	
323	**Discern**	201
	Synonyms : recognize, distinguish	
324	**Discriminatory**	114
	Synonyms : preferential, invidious, prejudiced, discriminative	
325	**Disdain**	55
	Synonyms : contempt, scorn	
326	**Disenchanted**	33
	Synonyms : crestfallen	
327	**Disenthrallment**	58
	Synonyms : disenchantment	
328	**Disillusionment**	114
	Synonyms : disillusion	
329	**Disinformation'**	165
	Synonyms : deception	
330	**Dismantle**	7
	Synonyms : disassemble	
331	**Disparate**	217
	Synonyms : different, dissimilar	
332	**Dispel**	223
	Synonyms : disperse	
333	**Disperse**	201
	Synonyms : dissipate spread, diffuse	
334	**Dispersive**	66
	Synonyms : diffusing, scattering, spreading	

S. No.	Words	Page No.
335	**Disposable**	141
	Synonyms : dispensable	
336	**Disputatious**	122
	Synonyms : contentious, litigious	
337	**Disseminate**	68
	Synonyms : circulate, broadcast	
338	**Dissertation**	38
	Synonyms : thesis	
339	**Dissipation**	176
	Synonyms : discharge	
340	**Dissuade**	45
	Synonyms : deters	
341	**Distended**	155
	Synonyms : bloated, turgid	
342	**Distinguish**	73
	Synonyms : differentiate, discern,	
343	**Distracting**	68
	Synonyms : perturbing	
344	**Dithery**	30
	Synonyms : indecisive	
345	**Diurnally**	118
	Synonyms : day time-active	
346	**Diva**	110
	Synonyms : prima donna	
347	**Divergent**	149
	Synonyms : diverging	
348	**Dodgy**	127
	Synonyms : crafty, cunning, foxy, dicey	
349	**Dogma**	114
	Synonyms : tenet	
350	**Dole**	83
	Synonyms : pogy, charity	
351	**Dormant**	46
	Synonyms : inactive, hibernating, torpid	
352	**Downsides**	145
	Synonyms : demerits	
353	**Dreadful**	204
	Synonyms : repulsive, sinister	
354	**Drones**	210
	Synonyms : laggards, dependents	
355	**Dubious**	62
	Synonyms : doubtful	
356	**Duck**	54
	Synonyms : dodge, sidestep	
357	**Dwarf**	17
	Synonyms : overshadow	
358	**Dwellers**	175
	Synonyms : inhabitants	
359	**Dysfunctional**	81
	Synonyms : nonadaptive	
360	**Earnestly**	38
	Synonyms : seriously	
361	**Eavesdrop**	222
	Synonyms : overhear	
362	**Ebbing**	3
	Synonyms : declining, receding	
363	**Ebullient**	109
	Synonyms : exuberant	
364	**Echelons**	114
	Synonyms : garrisons, regiments	
365	**Eclectic**	130
	Synonyms : eclecticist	
366	**Eclipsed**	16
	Synonyms : occulted	
367	**Ecstatic**	123
	Synonyms : enraptured, rapturous, rapt	
368	**Edifying**	178
	Synonyms : enlightening	
369	**Effeminate**	136
	Synonyms : emasculate, cissy,	
370	**Efficacious**	114
	Synonyms : effective, effectual	
371	**Efficacy**	118
	Synonyms : effectiveness, potency	
372	**Egalitarian**	164
	Synonyms : equalitarian, classless	
373	**Egregiously**	165
	Synonyms : blatantly	
374	**Elevates**	123
	Synonyms : raise	
375	**Elicited**	46
	Synonyms : evoked	
376	**Elitism**	171
	Synonyms : aristocracy	
377	**Elucidatory**	67
	Synonyms : enlightening	
378	**Emanates**	50
	Synonyms : radiates, emits	

S. No.	Words	Page No.
379	**Embark**	171
	Synonyms : enter, ship, venture	
380	**Embedded**	191
	Synonyms : implanted	
381	**Embellish**	34
	Synonyms : fancify, grace,deck	
382	**Emblem**	155
	Synonyms : allegory	
383	**Embrace**	217
	Synonyms : espouse, adopt	
384	**Embracing**	145
	Synonyms : hugging	
385	**Embryonic**	33
	Synonyms : budding	
386	**Empowered**	179
	Synonyms : sceptered, sceptred	
387	**Enamored**	109
	Synonyms : crazy, dotty, gaga, infatuated, in love, smitten, soft on, taken with	
388	**Encapsulate**	34
	Synonyms : capsulise	
389	**Encomiums**	115
	Synonyms : paeans, panegyrics	
390	**Encompassing**	38
	Synonyms : covering, including	
391	**Endemic**	25
	Synonyms : indigenous	
392	**Endorse**	154
	Synonyms : indorse, certify	
393	**Endorsed**	45
	Synonyms : approved	
394	**Endowed**	67
	Synonyms : gifted	
395	**Endurance**	127
	Synonyms : survival	
396	**Enduring**	77
	Synonyms : abiding, imperishable	
397	**Engulfing**	97
	Synonyms : consuming, absorbing	
398	**Enigma**	76
	Synonyms : mystery, conundrum	
399	**Enshrouded**	191
	Synonyms : covered	
400	**Ensuant**	118
	Synonyms : consequent	
401	**Enticed**	135
	Synonyms : tempted	
402	**Entrancement**	191
	Synonyms : ravishment	
403	**Entreating**	83
	Synonyms : beseeching	
404	**Entrenched**	119
	Synonyms : implanted	
405	**Enumerate**	109
	Synonyms : count	
406	**Envisage**	34
	Synonyms : visualize	
407	**Eons**	223
	Synonyms : eras	
408	**Epicurean**	171
	Synonyms : hedonic, sybaritic	
409	**Epitome**	76
	Synonyms : prototype, paradigm	
410	**Epitomize**	73
	Synonyms : typify,	
411	**Epitomizes**	188
	Synonyms : exemplifies	
412	**Erection**	16
	Synonyms : building	
413	**Erratic**	118
	Synonyms : mercurial, temperamental	
414	**Escalate**	82
	Synonyms : intensify	
415	**Escalated**	122
	Synonyms : incremented	
416	**Eschew**	25
	Synonyms : shun	
417	**Espionage**	156
	Synonyms : spying	
418	**Espouse**	148
	Synonyms : embrace, adopt	
419	**Essayed**	136
	Synonyms : attempted	
420	**Eternal**	130
	Synonyms : ageless, perpetual	
421	**Eulogized**	93
	Synonyms : extolled, panegyrized	

S. No.	Words	Page No.
422	**Euphemism**	164
	Synonyms : political correctness	
423	**Euphoria**	15
	Synonyms : ecstacy	
424	**Evacuated**	217
	Synonyms : emptied, removed	
425	**Evacuation**	17
	Synonyms : emptying	
426	**Evade**	54
	Synonyms : hedge, fudge	
427	**Everyday**	222
	Synonyms : routine, unremarkable, casual	
428	**Evolving**	178
	Synonyms : developing	
429	**Exacerbated**	192
	Synonyms : worsened	
430	**Exacting**	128
	Synonyms : exigent, stern, strict, fastidious	
431	**Exaggeration**	81
	Synonyms : overstatement, hyperbole	
432	**Exasperates**	41
	Synonyms : frustrates	
433	**Excogitate**	102
	Synonyms : ruminate	
434	**Excruciating**	159
	Synonyms : agonizing, torture-some	
435	**Exculpate**	144
	Synonyms : exonerate, acquit	
436	**Exhilaration**	54
	Synonyms : excitement	
437	**Exhorted**	38
	Synonyms : motivated, forced	
438	**Exigency'**	214
	Synonyms : emergency, pinch	
439	**Exigent**	204
	Synonyms : immediate, exacting	
440	**Exodus**	200
	Synonyms : hegira, evacuation	
441	**Exogenous**	82
	Synonyms : exogenic	
442	**Expansive**	6
	Synonyms : grand	
443	**Exorcize**	182
	Synonyms : expel	
444	**Expansive**	6
	Synonyms : grand	
445	**Expedite**	191
	Synonyms : hasten	
446	**Expiate**	12
	Synonyms : atone	
447	**Expletives**	160
	Synonyms : swearword	
448	**Explicit**	164
	Synonyms : expressed, denotative	
449	**Exploits**	135
	Synonyms : feats	
450	**Exponents**	92
	Synonyms : advocates, proponents	
451	**Exposure**	16
	Synonyms : publicity	
452	**Extant**	214
	Synonyms : existent, surviving	
453	**Extirpate**	140
	Synonyms : uproot	
454	**Extirpation**	12
	Synonyms : excision, ablation, cutting out	
455	**Extolling**	109
	Synonyms : exalt	
456	**Extraneous**	25
	Synonyms : foreign, external	
457	**Extrapolate**	41
	Synonyms : generalize, infer	
458	**Extricating**	213
	Synonyms : disentangling	
459	**Extroverted**	130
	Synonyms : outgoing	
460	**Exude**	136
	Synonyms : transude, ooze	
461	**Exudes**	109
	Synonyms : transmits	
462	**Facet**	73
	Synonyms : aspect	
463	**Face-value**	148
	Synonyms : par value, nominal value	

S. No.	Words	Page No.
464	**Facile**	72
	Synonyms : eloquent, fluent	
465	**Factitious**	45
	Synonyms : fake, unauthentic	
466	**Fallout**	77
	Synonyms : side- effect	
467	**Fallow**	46
	Synonyms : uncultivated, barren	
468	**Fancy**	6
	Synonyms : envision, project	
469	**Fastidious**	77
	Synonyms : squeamish	
470	**Fatal**	12, 49
	Synonyms : mortal	
471	**Fatuously**	204
	Synonyms : inanely	
472	**Feckless**	73
	Synonyms : inept	
473	**Fecund**	26
	Synonyms : fertile, prolific	
474	**Felons**	132
	Synonyms : criminals, crooks	
475	**Feral**	21
	Synonyms : ferine, savage	
476	**Ferreting**	156
	Synonyms : hound	
477	**Fervently**	114
	Synonyms : fierily, fervidly	
478	**Fetid**	183
	Synonyms : stinking	
479	**Feuds**	63
	Synonyms : altercations	
480	**Fickle**	110
	Synonyms : quicksilver	
481	**Fictional**	156
	Synonyms : fabricated, invented	
482	**Fidelity**	110
	Synonyms : dedication	
483	**Fidget**	88
	Synonyms : fidgetiness, restlessness	
484	**Figurative**	72
	Synonyms : non-literal, figural	
485	**Fillip**	122
	Synonyms : boost	
486	**Finale**	196
	Synonyms : finish, conclusion	
487	**Finesse**	106
	Synonyms : finish	
488	**Fissure**	155
	Synonyms : cleft, crevice	
489	**Flamboyant**	41
	Synonyms : brilliant	
490	**Flapping**	50
	Synonyms : beating	
491	**Flatter**	187
	Synonyms : blandish	
492	**Flaunt**	7
	Synonyms : ostentate, swank	
493	**Flip**	88
	Synonyms : reverse, back	
494	**Flippant**	20
	Synonyms : dismissive	
495	**Floundering**	83
	Synonyms : falter, waver	
496	**Flowering**	195
	Synonyms : blossoming, unfolding	
497	**Fluff**	37
	Synonyms : frivolity	
498	**Flummoxing**	140
	Synonyms : confounding	
499	**Flurry**	66
	Synonyms : bustle, hustle	
500	**Footprint**	172
	Synonyms : footmark, influence	
501	**Forays**	55
	Synonyms : adventures	
502	**Forestall**	171
	Synonyms : prevent, foreclose	
503	**Foretell**	186
	Synonyms : auspicate, presage, augur, herald	
504	**Forged**	199
	Synonyms : fashioned	
505	**Former**	149
	Synonyms : previous	
506	**Formidable**	58
	Synonyms : redoubtable, unnerving	

S. No.	Words	Page No.
507	**Fortification**	156
	Synonyms : munition	
508	**Fostered**	76
	Synonyms : nourished	
509	**Foundered**	200
	Synonyms : collapsed	
510	**Fragile**	110
	Synonyms : delicate, frail, flimsy	
511	**Franchise**	135
	Synonyms : dealership, licencee	
512	**Frantic**	16
	Synonyms : rabid	
513	**Fraught**	114
	Synonyms : pregnant	
514	**Fray**	204
	Synonyms : ruffle	
515	**Frenetic**	205
	Synonyms : frantic, feverish	
516	**Frenetically**	178
	Synonyms : demoniacally	
517	**Fringe**	222
	Synonyms : out skirt	
518	**Frivolous**	159
	Synonyms : flighty	
519	**Frivolously**	114
	Synonyms : farivolous	
520	**Frosty**	26
	Synonyms : crisp, frozen	
521	**Fruition**	12, 33
	Synonyms : realization	
522	**Fudged**	148
	Synonyms : tweaked	
523	**Fuelled**	41
	Synonyms : fired	
524	**Fugacious**	140
	Synonyms : ephemeral, transient, transitory	
525	**Furor**	17
	Synonyms : rage	
526	**Furore**	26
	Synonyms : cult, rage	
527	**Futile**	188
	Synonyms : unavailing fruitless, vain	
528	**Fuzzy**	97
	Synonyms : bleary, foggy	
529	**Gaffes**	160
	Synonyms : blunders	
530	**Gainsaid**	92
	Synonyms : disputed, challenged	
531	**Garish**	114
	Synonyms : ostentatious, gaudy	
532	**Geezer**	136
	Synonyms : bloke, man	
533	**Gelid**	11, 214
	Synonyms : icy, polar	
534	**Genteel**	164
	Synonyms : urbane, cultured, polite	
535	**Germane**	144
	Synonyms : related	
536	**Germinated**	164
	Synonyms : conceived	
537	**Gesticulating**	165
	Synonyms : hand movements	
538	**Ghettoes**	93
	Synonyms : slum	
539	**Gigantic**	12
	Synonyms : gargantuan	
540	**Gingerly**	17
	Synonyms : charily	
541	**Glaring**	188
	Synonyms : crying, gross, rank	
542	**Glimpse**	6
	Synonyms : glance	
543	**Gossip**	93
	Synonyms : scuttlebutt, gab	
544	**Gourmet**	171
	Synonyms : epicure, gastronome, foodie	
545	**Grappling**	122
	Synonyms : wrestling, rassling	
546	**Grate**	183
	Synonyms : satisfaction	
547	**Gratification**	171
	Synonyms : satisfaction, delight	
548	**Gratify**	183
	Synonyms : pleasure	
549	**Grave**	145
	Synonyms : sociability	
550	**Gregariousness**	102
	Synonyms : sociability	

S. No.	Words	Page No.
551	**Grim**	41

Synonyms : harsh

552	**Grittier**	137

Synonyms : pluckier

553	**Grooming**	110

Synonyms : dressing, training, preparation

554	**Groovy**	109

Synonyms : swagger, bang-up, bully, corking, cracking, dandy, great, keen, neat, nifty, not bad, peachy, slap-up, swell, smashing

555	**Grossing**	98

Synonyms : collecting

556	**Guileful**	149

Synonyms : crafty, cunning, dodgy, foxy, wily

557	**Gullible**	62

Synonyms : fleeceable, green

558	**Gushing**	6

Synonyms : pouring, effusive

559	**Haggling**	154

Synonyms : wrangling

560	**Hallucinate**	192

Synonyms : phantasize

561	**Handy**	179

Synonyms : convenient

562	**Handicap**	82

Synonyms : disable, invalid, incapacitate

563	**Hapless**	201

Synonyms : pathetic, piteous, pitiable, wretched

564	**Harbinger**	156

Synonyms : announce

565	**Harnessed**	110

Synonyms : exploit, convert

566	**Harrowed**	67

Synonyms : distressed

567	**Harvest**	119

Synonyms : crop, reap

568	**Haywire**	159

Synonyms : awry, whacky

569	**Hazard**	107

Synonyms : jeopardy, peril

S. No.	Words	Page No.
570	**Hazarded**	214

Synonyms : risked

571	**Hecklers**	42

Synonyms : badgerer

572	**Hectoring**	132

Synonyms : bullying

573	**Hegemony**	219

Synonyms : domination

574	**Heinous**	59

Synonyms : atrocious, flagitious,

575	**Heist**	42

Synonyms : robbery, caper

576	**Helm**	42

Synonyms : command

577	**Heralds**	196

Synonyms : harbingers

578	**Herding**	199

Synonyms : crowding

579	**Hereditary**	3

Synonyms : inherited, genetic

580	**Heretical**	183

Synonyms : blasphemous

581	**Hiatus**	135

Synonyms : respite, reprieve

582	**Highbrow**	196

Synonyms : elite

583	**Hindrances**	98

Synonyms : encumbrances, handicaps

584	**Hindsight**	42

Synonyms : retrospectively

585	**Hinge**	209

Synonyms : predicate

586	**Hoarded**	123

Synonyms : accumulated

587	**Hoist**	109

Synonyms : lift, wind,

588	**Hone**	218

Synonyms : polish

589	**Honorific**	94

Synonyms : title

590	**Horizon**	178

Synonyms : skyline, vision

591	**Hurling**	97

Synonyms : throwing

S. No.	Words	Page No.
592	**Hybrid**	67
	Synonyms : intercrossed	
593	**Hypothesize**	114
	Synonyms : speculate, theorize, theorise, conjecture, hypothesise, hypothecate, suppose	
594	**Iconic**	15
	Synonyms : symbolic	
595	**Ideated**	26
	Synonyms : conceptualised, formulated	
596	**Libel**	38
	Synonyms : calumny, slander	
597	**Ilk**	12
	Synonyms : type	
598	**Illicit**	126
	Synonyms : illegitimate, outlaw, outlawed, unlawful	
599	**Illusions suffice**	98
	Synonyms : famed,redoubtable, respected	
600	**Illustrious**	73
	Synonyms : famed, glorious, redoubtable	
601	**Imminent**	58, 176
	Synonyms : impendent	
602	**Immured**	59
	Synonyms : incarcerated, jailed	
603	**Impair**	122
	Synonyms : vitiates	
604	**Impeccably**	188
	Synonyms : perfectly	
605	**Impeded**	106
	Synonyms : occlude, block	
606	**Impediment**	54
	Synonyms : ruction, handicap	
607	**Impediments**	187
	Synonyms : blockages	
608	**Impel**	213
	Synonyms : force, propel	
609	**Impersonating**	33
	Synonyms : pose	
610	**Impertinent**	165
	Synonyms : Irrelevant	
611	**Impervious**	140
	Synonyms : imperviable	
612	**Impetuous**	183
	Synonyms : brash	
613	**Implements**	67
	Synonyms : tools	
614	**Imports**	76
	Synonyms : implications	
615	**Importunes**	29
	Synonyms : beseeches	
616	**Impregnable**	140
	Synonyms : inviolable	
617	**Improvisation**	62
	Synonyms : extemporization	
618	**Impunity**	208
	Synonyms : exemption	
619	**Improvisations**	106
	Synonyms : extemporizations	
620	**Impunity**	208
	Synonyms : exemption	
621	**Inborn**	72
	Synonyms : inbred, innate	
622	**Incarcerated**	126
	Synonyms : interned, immured	
623	**Incarnation**	97
	Synonyms : personification, embodiment, avatar	
624	**Incendiary**	62
	Synonyms : inflammatory, instigative	
625	**Incensed**	182
	Synonyms : enraged	
626	**Incentive**	222
	Synonyms : bonus	
627	**Inception**	126
	Synonyms : origin, origination	
628	**Incessantly**	102
	Synonyms : ceaselessly	
629	**Inchoate**	214
	Synonyms : incipient	
630	**Incinerate**	187
	Synonyms : burn	
631	**Incipient**	122
	Synonyms : inchoate	
632	**Incisive**	93
	Synonyms : discriminating, penetrating,	
633	**Incite**	67
	Synonyms : instigate	

S. No.	Words	Page No.
634	**Inclusive**	213
	Synonyms : comprehensive	
635	**Incompetent**	148
	Synonyms : incapable, bungling, clumsy, fumbling	
636	**Incorrigible**	62
	Synonyms : unreformable	
637	**Incurred**	127
	Synonyms : undergone	
638	**Incredible**	68
	Synonyms : implausible, unbelievable	
639	**Incredulous**	122
	Synonyms : skeptical	
640	**Increment**	45
	Synonyms : increase, growth	
641	**Indebted**	145
	Synonyms : grateful	
642	**Indecorous**	195
	Synonyms : indelicate, indecent, unbecoming, uncomely, unseemly, untoward	
643	**Indifference**	218
	Synonyms : apathy, phlegm, stolidity	
644	**Indigent**	30
	Synonyms : impoverished, necessitous	
645	**Indignation**	38
	Synonyms : outrage	
646	**Indiscretion**	160
	Synonyms : peccadillo, injudiciousness	
647	**Indispensable**	102
	Synonyms : essential	
648	**Indisposed**	165
	Synonyms : averse, unwell	
649	**Indolent**	131
	Synonyms : slothful, work-shy	
650	**Induce**	164
	Synonyms : stimulate, cause	
651	**Industriously**	63
	Synonyms : energetically	
652	**Inebriated**	123
	Synonyms : intoxicated, drunk	
653	**Inept**	165
	Synonyms : tactless, feckless, awkward, clumsy, cumbersome	
654	**Infallible**	29
	Synonyms : unerring, foolproof	
655	**Infamous**	59
	Synonyms : ill-famed, notorious	
656	**Infamy**	127
	Synonyms : opprobrium	
657	**Infatuation**	15
	Synonyms : crush	
658	**Inferno**	213
	Synonyms : perdition conflagration, hell	
659	**Infestations**	201
	Synonyms : plague	
660	**Inflated**	62
	Synonyms : exaggerated, hyperbolic	
661	**Inflicted**	106
	Synonyms : wreaked	
662	**Infuriated**	127
	Synonyms : angered, enraged, furious, maddened	
663	**Infused**	136
	Synonyms : instilled	
664	**Ingenious**	131
	Synonyms : adroit, imaginative, inventive	
665	**Ingest**	141
	Synonyms : devour	
666	**Ingests**	109
	Synonyms : consume	
667	**Ingrained**	192
	Synonyms : deep-rooted	
668	**Ingratiating**	54
	Synonyms : insinuating, ingratiatory	
669	**Inhibit**	213
	Synonyms : suppress, subdue	
670	**Iniquitous**	42
	Synonyms : sinful, unfair	
671	**Innate**	191
	Synonyms : congenital, unlearned	
672	**Innocuous**	140
	Synonyms : harmless	
673	**Innuendo**	45
	Synonyms : insinuation	

S. No.	Words	Page No.
674	**Insalubrious**	30
	Synonyms : unhealthful, unhealthy	
675	**Insatiable**	66
	Synonyms : unquenchable	
676	**Insidiously**	196
	Synonyms : perniciously	
677	**Insight**	218
	Synonyms : perceptiveness, perceptivity, penetration	
678	**Insipid**	218
	Synonyms : jejune, bland, savourless,	
679	**Insolent**	223
	Synonyms : bodacious	
680	**Insolvency**	81
	Synonyms : bankruptcy	
681	**Insomnia**	192
	Synonyms : sleeplessness	
682	**Instinctive**	62
	Synonyms : impossible, unacceptable	
683	**Insufferable**	136
	Synonyms : uncountable	
684	**Intangibles**	76
	Synonyms : unity, wholeness	
685	**Integrity**	63
	Synonyms : prohibition , edict	
686	**Interdicting**	140
	Synonyms : resourceful, clever	
687	**Intimate**	62
	Synonyms : cozy, inner	
688	**Intimated**	89
	Synonyms : informed	
689	**Intonation**	33
	Synonyms : cantillation	
690	**Intoxicated**	149
	Synonyms : drunk, inebriated,	
691	**Intrepid**	130
	Synonyms : valiant	
692	**Intricacies**	7
	Synonyms : elaborations	
693	**Intricate**	204
	Synonyms : complex	
694	**Intrigue**	156
	Synonyms : machination, scheme	
695	**Intrinsic**	77
	Synonyms : intrinsical	
696	**Intrinsically**	62
	Synonyms : basically	
697	**Intrusion**	160
	Synonyms : trespass, encroachment, usurpation, invasion	
698	**Inundated**	178
	Synonyms : afloat, awash, flooded, overflowing	
699	**Inveigle**	109
	Synonyms : wheedle, cajole, palaver, blarney, coax, sweet-talk	
700	**Inventory**	87, 165
	Synonyms : stock, armory	
701	**Inveterate**	154
	Synonyms : confirmed, habitual	
702	**Involunatarily**	132
	Synonyms : forced	
703	**Irate**	41
	Synonyms : livid	
704	**Irksome**	195
	Synonyms : boring, tedious, tiresome, wearisome	
705	**Ironic**	219
	Synonyms : dry, wry	
706	**Ironically**	106
	Synonyms : wryly	
707	**Irony**	114
	Synonyms : sarcasm, satire, caustic remark	
708	**Irrevocable**	213
	Synonyms : unalterable	
709	**Jest**	205
	Synonyms : jocularly	
710	**Jiggle**	182
	Synonyms : wiggle	
711	**Jingoism**	42
	Synonyms : chauvinism, super-patriotism	
712	**Jogging**	45
	Synonyms : activating	
713	**Jostling**	6
	Synonyms : shoving	
714	**Juggernaut**	219
	Synonyms : steamroller	

S. No.	Words	Page No.
715	**Jumpy**	222
	Synonyms : restive, edgy	
716	**Kindled**	192
	Synonyms : invoked	
717	**Knavish**	148
	Synonyms : sly, tricksy, tricky, wily	
718	**Knell**	82
	Synonyms : ring	
719	**Knotty**	49
	Synonyms : complex	
720	**Labyrinthine**	49
	Synonyms : serpentine	
721	**Lamentable**	115
	Synonyms : distressing, pitiful	
722	**Languidly**	223
	Synonyms : languorous	
723	**Lance**	128
	Synonyms : spear	
724	**Latter**	149
	Synonyms : second	
725	**Laudation**	115
	Synonyms : appreciation	
726	**Leapfrogged**	76
	Synonyms : jumped	
727	**Leapfrogging**	118
	Synonyms : jumping	
728	**Leery**	155
	Synonyms : mistrustful	
729	**Legacy**	81
	Synonyms : bequest	
730	**Legend**	45
	Synonyms : fable, caption	
731	**Lethal**	58
	Synonyms : baleful	
732	**Libel**	38, 165
	Synonyms : defamation	
733	**Lilliputians**	12
	Synonyms : pigmies	
734	**Lingua**	20
	Synonyms : tongue	
735	**Lionized**	155
	Synonyms : glorified	
736	**Lissomeness**	21
	Synonyms : nimbleness, agility	
737	**Litheness**	21
	Synonyms : suppleness	
738	**Littering**	141
	Synonyms : strewing	
739	**Loathe**	223
	Synonyms : abhor, abominate, execrate	
740	**Ludicrous**	191
	Synonyms : laughable	
741	**Luminaries**	110
	Synonyms : celebrities	
742	**Lure**	63
	Synonyms : enticement	
743	**Luxuriant**	223
	Synonyms : lush	
744	**Magnet**	7
	Synonyms : attraction	
745	**Maiden**	135
	Synonyms : inaugural, first	
746	**Makeshift**	68
	Synonyms : stopgap, improvised	
747	**Malaise**	122
	Synonyms : unease, uneasiness	
748	**Malingering**	145
	Synonyms : skulking	
749	**Malleable**	20
	Synonyms : pliable	
750	**Mandated**	214
	Synonyms : required, authorized	
751	**Mandatory**	66
	Synonyms : compulsory, required	
752	**Manicured**	6
	Synonyms : groomed	
753	**Manifest**	114
	Synonyms : attest, certify, demonstrate, evidence, apparent, evident, patent, plain, unmistakable	
754	**Manifestation**	208
	Synonyms : demonstration, materialization	
755	**Manipulated**	63
	Synonyms : tampered	
756	**Manipulative**	50
	Synonyms : scheming	
757	**Margins**	201
	Synonyms : borders	

S. No.	Words	Page No.
758	**Mars**	196
	Synonyms : a planet	
759	**Mask**	38
	Synonyms : dissemble, cloak	
760	**Masquerades**	63
	Synonyms : disguises	
761	**Maturation**	20
	Synonyms : ripening suppuration	
762	**Mavens**	213
	Synonyms : maestros	
763	**Maverick**	42
	Synonyms : rebel, irregular, unorthodox	
764	**Meander**	222
	Synonyms : ramble, thread, wander	
765	**Measly**	223
	Synonyms : miserable, paltry	
766	**Mediocre**	178
	Synonyms : second-rate, average, fair, middling	
767	**Megalomaniac**	154
	Synonyms : pathological-egotist	
768	**Memoirs**	144
	Synonyms : autobiographies	
769	**Menace**	97
	Synonyms : peril	
770	**Mended**	182
	Synonyms : bushelled, fixed	
771	**Merchandise**	54
	Synonyms : ware, trade	
772	**Mercurial**	50
	Synonyms : temperamental	
773	**Mess**	68
	Synonyms : disorderliness	
774	**Meteorite**	214
	Synonyms : meteoroid	
775	**Meticulously**	66
	Synonyms : punctiliously	
776	**Middling**	118
	Synonyms : mediocre	
777	**Midget**	175
	Synonyms : bantam, diminutive	
778	**Mingling**	3
	Synonyms : blending, merging	
779	**Minuscule**	109
	Synonyms : miniscule, minuscular, small letter, lowercase, lower-case letter, little, small	
780	**Mired**	209
	Synonyms : involved	
781	**Miserable**	210
	Synonyms : wretched, woeful	
782	**Misgiving**	145
	Synonyms : scruple, qualm	
783	**Misgivings**	171
	Synonyms : reservations	
784	**Mitigated**	191
	Synonyms : alleviated	
785	**Mockery**	166
	Synonyms : parody, lampoon, spoof, burlesque, travesty, charade, pasquinade	
786	**Modicum**	154
	Synonyms : iota	
787	**Modulation**	33
	Synonyms : inflection	
788	**Momentous**	204
	Synonyms : significant	
789	**Moneyed**	92
	Synonyms : affluent, , wealthy	
790	**Moniker**	93
	Synonyms : nickname, cognomen, sobriquet,	
791	**Monumental**	11
	Synonyms : massive, monolithic	
792	**Moot**	41
	Synonyms : consider, debate	
793	**Moribund**	214
	Synonyms : dying, stagnant,	
794	**Morose**	200
	Synonyms : sullen, melancholic	
795	**Morphed**	188
	Synonyms : transformed	
796	**Mortified**	62
	Synonyms : embarrassed, humiliated,	
797	**Motif**	122
	Synonyms : motive, theme	
798	**Motley**	20
	Synonyms : smorgasbord, potpourri	

S. No.	Words	Page No.
799	**Mourning**	165
	Synonyms : bereavement, lamentation	
800	**Mundane**	110
	Synonyms : quotidian, routine, workaday	
801	**Murmurs**	222
	Synonyms : mutters	
802	**Mushy**	222
	Synonyms :	
803	**Mutilation**	49
	Synonyms : injury	
804	**Myriad**	161
	Synonyms : countless	
805	**Mystical**	144
	Synonyms : recondite, orphic	
806	**Myth**	45
	Synonyms : legend	
807	**Narrative**	62
	Synonyms : story, tale	
808	**Nascent**	29
	Synonyms : incipient	
809	**Nauseating**	183
	Synonyms : sickening	
810	**Nebulous**	66
	Synonyms : vague	
811	**Nemesis**	97
	Synonyms : bane, curse, scourge	
812	**Neural**	66
	Synonyms : nervous	
813	**Niche**	160
	Synonyms : recess, corner	
814	**Nightmare**	42
	Synonyms : incubus	
815	**Nocturnally**	118
	Synonyms : nightly	
816	**Nondescript**	82
	Synonyms : characterless	
817	**Noted**	15
	Synonyms : renowned	
818	**Notional**	41
	Synonyms : speculative, imaginary,	
819	**Notorious**	178
	Synonyms : ill-famed, infamous	
820	**Novel**	164
	Synonyms : refreshing, fresh, new	
821	**Noxious**	115
	Synonyms : baneful, pernicious	
822	**Nuances**	62
	Synonyms : shades, fineries	
823	**Nugatory**	176
	Synonyms : inconsequential	
824	**Nuptial**	183
	Synonyms : spousal	
825	**Obeisant**	191
	Synonyms : servile, fawing	
826	**Obese**	29
	Synonyms : corpulent, rotund	
827	**Obituary**	161
	Synonyms : obit, necrology	
828	**Objurgated**	110
	Synonyms : chastened, excoriated	
829	**Obligation**	141
	Synonyms : indebtedness	
830	**Obligatory**	171
	Synonyms : compulsory	
831	**Oblivion**	6
	Synonyms : limbo	
832	**Obscure**	148
	Synonyms : bedim, veil, befog, becloud,	
833	**Obsessed**	41
	Synonyms : haunted, preoccupied	
834	**Obsessional**	192
	Synonyms : obsessive	
835	**Obsolete**	119
	Synonyms : superannuated, disused	
836	**Obstinate**	179
	Synonyms : stubbornness, bullheadedness, obstinacy, pigheadedness, self-will, mulishness	
837	**Obstreperous**	223
	Synonyms : defiant	
838	**Obviate**	119
	Synonyms : deflect, avert	
839	**Occlusion**	49
	Synonyms : obstructing	
840	**Oddity**	182
	Synonyms : eccentricity	
841	**Odious**	67
	Synonyms : detestable, execrable	

S. No.	Words	Page No.
842	**Olfactory**	200
	Synonyms : olfactive	
843	**Ominous**	160
	Synonyms : inauspicious, threatening	
844	**Onerous**	11
	Synonyms : burdensome, taxing	
845	**One-upmanship**	16
	Synonyms : outdoing	
846	**Onus**	82
	Synonyms : load, encumbrance	
847	**Opaque**	89
	Synonyms : obscuring, hiding	
848	**Opining**	106
	Synonyms : animadverting	
849	**Optimally**	204
	Synonyms : desirably , efficiently	
850	**Ornithologist**	135
	Synonyms : bird-watcher	
851	**Orphan**	204
	Synonyms : abandoned	
852	**Ostracized**	29, 165
	Synonyms : excommunicate	
853	**Otiose**	188
	Synonyms : pointless, superfluous	
854	**Outlandish**	68
	Synonyms : bizarre, freakish	
855	**Outnumbers**	118
	Synonyms : beat	
856	**Outspoken**	29
	Synonyms : forthright, candid	
857	**Overweening**	209
	Synonyms : uppity	
858	**Oxymoron**	81
	Synonyms : trope	
859	**palliate**	84
	Synonyms : relieve, extenuate	
860	**Palpable**	195
	Synonyms : tangible	
861	**Paradigm**	118
	Synonyms : standard	
862	**Paradoxically**	195
	Synonyms : contradictorily	
863	**Paranoia**	155
	Synonyms : psychosis	
864	**Parlance**	107
	Synonyms : idiom	
865	**Parsimoniously**	82
	Synonyms : cheaply, miserly	
866	**Partisan**	144
	Synonyms : zealot, denominational	
867	**Parturition**	82
	Synonyms : birthing	
868	**Pedestal**	188
	Synonyms : stand	
869	**Pejorative**	114
	Synonyms : dyslogistic, expletive	
870	**Pellucid**	2
	Synonyms : luculent, crystalline, transparent	
871	**Pelted**	62
	Synonyms : bombarded, hit	
872	**Penitent**	204
	Synonyms : repentant	
873	**Perceived**	209
	Synonyms : sensed	
874	**Perched**	102
	Synonyms : roosted	
875	**Perennially**	26
	Synonyms : incessantly	
876	**Perilous**	83
	Synonyms : precarious	
877	**Peripheral**	94
	Synonyms : superficial, marginal	
878	**Perish**	213
	Synonyms : die, decease	
879	**Perked**	109
	Synonyms : energised	
880	**Permeated**	137
	Synonyms : percolated	
881	**Perquisite**	176
	Synonyms : privilege	
882	**Perseverance**	123
	Synonyms : tenacity, pertinacity	
883	**Perspicacious**	200
	Synonyms : incisive	
884	**Perspicacity**	144
	Synonyms : shrewdness, astuteness	
885	**Persuasive**	93
	Synonyms : cogent, compelling	

S. No.	Words	Page No.
886	**Pertinent**	20
	Synonyms : appropriate	
887	**Pertinently**	97
	Synonyms : fittingly, appropriately	
888	**Perturbed**	214
	Synonyms : rattled	
889	**Petrifying**	213
	Synonyms : frightening, paralyzing	
890	**Phenomenal**	38
	Synonyms : fantastic	
891	**Phlegmatic**	130
	Synonyms : apathetic, stoic	
892	**Pilfer**	188
	Synonyms : cabbage, purloin	
893	**Pillories**	83
	Synonyms : crucifies, harangues	
894	**Pioneers**	128
	Synonyms : trailblazing	
895	**Piquant**	38, 122
	Synonyms : salty, savory	
896	**Pitch**	115
	Synonyms : promote	
897	**Pithily**	160
	Synonyms : sententiously	
898	**Pivotal**	76
	Synonyms : polar	
899	**Placate**	218
	Synonyms : pacify, conciliate, gruntle	
900	**Placidly**	46
	Synonyms : calmly, quietly	
901	**Platter**	26
	Synonyms : plate	
902	**Plebeian**	7
	Synonyms : common, pedestrian	
903	**Plethora**	115
	Synonyms : overplus, superfluity	
904	**Pliability**	128
	Synonyms : ductility	
905	**Pointed**	21
	Synonyms : targeted	
906	**Poised**	77
	Synonyms : collected, equanimous	
907	**Polygamous**	130
	Synonyms : heteroicous, polyoicous	
908	**Pontifical**	137
	Synonyms : grandiloquent, pompous,	
909	**Poodle**	87
	Synonyms : dog-breed	
910	**Posterity**	159
	Synonyms : descendants	
911	**Postulates**	7
	Synonyms : diktat	
912	**Postulation**	20
	Synonyms : supposition	
913	**Pragmatic**	187
	Synonyms : hardheaded, hard-nosed, practical	
914	**Prank**	102
	Synonyms : caper	
915	**Precise**	73
	Synonyms : accurate, exact	
916	**Precision**	110
	Synonyms : preciseness	
917	**Precocious**	63
	Synonyms : prodigious	
918	**Precursor**	62
	Synonyms : forerunner, harbinger, herald	
919	**Predate**	11
	Synonyms : antedate, precede,	
920	**Predated**	118
	Synonyms : preceded	
921	**Predating**	20
	Synonyms : antedating	
922	**Predators**	55
	Synonyms : marauders	
923	**Predisposed**	144
	Synonyms : prejudiced	
924	**Prejudice**	148
	Synonyms : prepossess, bias, preconception	
925	**Prejudices**	132
	Synonyms : biases	
926	**Premium**	7
	Synonyms : superior, bounty	
927	**Preponderant**	208
	Synonyms : overriding, predominant	

S. No.	Words	Page No.
928	**Preposterous**	223
	Synonyms : derisory, nonsensical	
929	**Pretentious**	63
	Synonyms : ostentatious, kitsch	
930	**Prevail**	77
	Synonyms : triumph, persist	
931	**Pristine**	141
	Synonyms : pure	
932	**Probe**	148
	Synonyms : investigation, examine	
933	**Proclaimed**	15
	Synonyms : announced	
934	**Prodded**	122
	Synonyms : pushed	
935	**Prodigal**	123
	Synonyms : profligate, spendthrift	
936	**Proffered**	186
	Synonyms : offered	
937	**Profligate**	123
	Synonyms : prodigal, squanderer, rake, spendthrift	
938	**Profound**	72
	Synonyms : deep	
939	**Progeny**	176
	Synonyms : offspring	
940	**Prognosis**	159
	Synonyms : medical projection, forecast	
941	**Proliferation**	118
	Synonyms : escalation	
942	**Prolific**	38
	Synonyms : fertile, fecund	
943	**Promenade**	175
	Synonyms : saunter	
944	**Propaganda**	154
	Synonyms : publicity	
945	**Propelling**	33
	Synonyms : driving	
946	**Prophecy**	114
	Synonyms : prognostication, vaticination, divination	
947	**Prophesied**	98
	Synonyms : presaged	
948	**Prophylactic**	109
	Synonyms : sulubrious, preventive	
949	**Proponents**	98
	Synonyms : champion, protagonist	
950	**Propriety**	144
	Synonyms : properness, correctitude	
951	**Prosaic**	188
	Synonyms : banal	
952	**Proscribe**	128
	Synonyms : forbid, disallow	
953	**Proscription**	141
	Synonyms : banishment	
954	**Protracted**	156
	Synonyms : lengthy, prolonged	
955	**Protracted**	58
	Synonyms : extended, lengthy, prolonged	
956	**Providence**	154
	Synonyms : prudence	
957	**Provident**	209
	Synonyms : cautious, thoughtful	
958	**Proximity**	25
	Synonyms : propinquity	
959	**Proxy**	154
	Synonyms : placeholder, procurator	
960	**Prudent**	209
	Synonyms : judicious, circumspect	
961	**Psephology**	159
	Synonyms : election-study	
962	**Psychic**	45
	Synonyms : clairvoyant	
963	**Psychosomatic**	192
	Synonyms : psychoneurotic	
964	**Puberty**	21
	Synonyms : pubescence	
965	**Puckish**	109
	Synonyms : impish, mischievous,	
966	**Pugnacity**	119
	Synonyms : aggressiveness, belligerence	
967	**Puissance**	136
	Synonyms : power, strength	
968	**Pulchritude**	1
	Synonyms : beauty	
969	**Pulpit**	30
	Synonyms : dais, podium, rostrum	
970	**Pundits**	7
	Synonyms : experts, savants	

S. No.	Words	Page No.
971	**Purge**	192
	Synonyms : flush, regurgitate	
972	**Purported**	187
	Synonyms : putative, supposed	
973	**Purveyor**	196
	Synonyms : vendor	
974	**Quacks**	45
	Synonyms : charlatan, mountebank	
975	**Qualms**	131
	Synonyms : scruples	
976	**Quandary**	72
	Synonyms : dilemma, predicament	
977	**Queasy**	115
	Synonyms : anxious, uneasy	
978	**Quipped**	81
	Synonyms : gagged	
979	**Quixotic**	41
	Synonyms : romantic, wild-eyed	
980	**Quotidian**	62
	Synonyms : routine, unremarkable	
981	**Rabid**	170
	Synonyms : overzealous	
982	**Raconteurs**	98
	Synonyms : anecdotists	
983	**Radical**	103
	Synonyms : extreme, revolutionary	
984	**Raging**	204
	Synonyms : furious, tempestuous	
985	**Raiment**	89
	Synonyms : regalia, apparel	
986	**Rallied**	58
	Synonyms : mobilized, gathered	
987	**Ramifications**	140
	Synonyms : complications	
988	**Rampant**	176
	Synonyms : unbridled	
989	**Ranting**	6
	Synonyms : harangue, rant	
990	**Rapture**	179
	Synonyms : ecstasy, transport, exaltation	
991	**Rarefied**	15
	Synonyms : lofty	
992	**Rationale**	145
	Synonyms : principle	
993	**Raunchy**	93
	Synonyms : obscene, salacious	
994	**Ravenous**	141
	Synonyms : edacious	
995	**Razed**	213
	Synonyms : demolished, dismantled	
996	**Realm**	72
	Synonyms : region	
997	**Reap**	119
	Synonyms : harvest, glean, draw	
998	**Rebooted**	135
	Synonyms : regard, consider	
999	**Rebuffed**	58
	Synonyms : snubbed, rejected	
1000	**Rebuttal**	223
	Synonyms : contradiction	
1001	**Recidivism**	123
	Synonyms : retrogression	
1002	**Recipe**	110
	Synonyms : formula	
1003	**Reckon**	213
	Synonyms : regard, consider	
1004	**Reciprocal**	154
	Synonyms : mutual,	
1005	**Recliner**	195
	Synonyms : reclining chair, lounger	
1006	**Reclusive**	178
	Synonyms : cloistered, sequestered	
1007	**Recompense**	46
	Synonyms : compensation, compensate, indemnify	
1008	**Recondite**	21
	Synonyms : esoteric	
1009	**Recounts**	114
	Synonyms : recites	
1010	**Redolent**	131
	Synonyms : aromatic, evocative,	
1011	**Redux**	195
	Synonyms : revived	
1012	**Reeled**	217
	Synonyms : lurched, careened	
1013	**Refrain**	30
	Synonyms : abstain, desist	

S. No.	Words	Page No.
1014	**Rehabilitation**	201
	Synonyms : reclamation, renewal	
1015	**Reign**	187
	Synonyms : sovereignty	
1016	**Reinforcement**	20
	Synonyms : strengthener	
1017	**Reinvent**	191
	Synonyms : recreate	
1018	**Rejoinder**	182
	Synonyms : repartee	
1019	**Relapse**	123
	Synonyms : recidivate, regress	
1020	**Relegate**	217
	Synonyms : demote, bump, banish, bar	
1021	**Relegated**	41
	Synonyms : demoted	
1022	**Relentlessly**	102
	Synonyms : unrelentingly	
1023	**Relic**	159
	Synonyms : souvenir, token	
1024	**Relinquish**	66
	Synonyms : surrender, forgo	
1025	**Relocate**	213
	Synonyms : migrate, displace	
1026	**Reminisced**	6
	Synonyms : recalled	
1027	**Remiss**	131
	Synonyms : delinquent, neglectful	
1028	**Render**	6
	Synonyms : deliver, return	
1029	**Renegades**	29
	Synonyms : deserters, apostates.	
1030	**Repast**	88
	Synonyms : meal	
1031	**Replenishes**	89
	Synonyms : refills	
1032	**Repository**	188
	Synonyms : monument depository, museum	
1033	**Repudiate**	148
	Synonyms : renounce	
1034	**Repudiated**	30
	Synonyms : disowned	
1035	**Reservations**	208
	Synonyms : qualifications, caveats, doubts	
1036	**Reservoir**	45
	Synonyms : answerer	
1037	**Resurgence**	25
	Synonyms : revival, revivification	
1038	**Revelry**	25
	Synonyms : partying	
1039	**Reveres**	66
	Synonyms : worships	
1040	**Reverts**	88
	Synonyms : regresses, returns	
1041	**Rhapsodic**	204
	Synonyms : ecstatic, enraptured	
1042	**Riches**	123
	Synonyms : wealth	
1043	**Rigmarole**	171
	Synonyms : rigamarole,	
1044	**Ritual**	25
	Synonyms : rite	
1045	**Ritualized**	123
	Synonyms : traditionalized	
1046	**Robust**	178
	Synonyms : full-bodied, racy, rich	
1047	**Rookie**	114
	Synonyms : beginner, greenhorn	
1048	**Rudimentary**	106
	Synonyms : elementary	
1049	**Ruffled**	218
	Synonyms : frilled, rippled	
1050	**Ruin**	59
	Synonyms : dilapidation, ramshackle	
1051	**Ruined**	92
	Synonyms : finished, undone	
1052	**Ruminate**	41
	Synonyms : excogitate, mull	
1053	**Rustic**	92
	Synonyms : bucolic, pastoral	
1054	**Sacrilegious**	29
	Synonyms : profane	
1055	**Sagging**	83
	Synonyms : drooping, droopy	
1056	**Salubrious**	148
	Synonyms : healthful	

S. No.	Words	Page No.
1057	**Salvation**	84
	Synonyms : redemption	
1058	**Sanctimonious**	30
	Synonyms : pietistic, pharisaic, self-righteous	
1059	**Sanctum**	49
	Synonyms : holy-place	
1060	**Sapience**	148
	Synonyms : sagacity	
1061	**Satirical**	164
	Synonyms : lampooning	
1062	**Saturnine**	107
	Synonyms : morose, doleful	
1063	**Savior**	107
	Synonyms : Redeemer, Deliverer	
1064	**Savory**	25
	Synonyms : piquant, spicy	
1065	**Scamper**	223
	Synonyms : scramble, scurry	
1066	**Scathed**	2
	Synonyms : hurt	
1067	**Scintilla**	161
	Synonyms : shred iota	
1068	**Scores**	171
	Synonyms : tons, dozens	
1069	**Scourge**	97
	Synonyms : terror, bane, curse	
1070	**Scramble**	102
	Synonyms : scamper, scurry,	
1071	**Scrumptious**	182
	Synonyms : delicious	
1072	**Scrupulously**	21
	Synonyms : conscientiously, religiously	
1073	**Secluded**	145
	Synonyms : cloistered, sequestered	
1074	**Sedated**	192
	Synonyms : ranquilized	
1075	**Sedulously**	196
	Synonyms : industriously	
1076	**Sedulousness**	45
	Synonyms : diligence	
1077	**Segregating**	171
	Synonyms : discriminating	
1078	**Semantics**	148
	Synonyms : linguistics	
1079	**Semetic**	58
	Synonyms : jewish	
1080	**Seminal**	87
	Synonyms : germinal, originative	
1081	**Sentence**	144
	Synonyms : condemnation	
1082	**Sentinel**	196
	Synonyms : sentry, watchman	
1083	**Sequel**	42
	Synonyms : continuation, subsequence	
1084	**Serene**	122
	Synonyms : unagitated, tranquil	
1085	**Shallow**	97
	Synonyms : shoal	
1086	**Shards**	127
	Synonyms : fragments, pieces	
1087	**Shibboleths**	45
	Synonyms : slogans, catchwords	
1088	**Shipped**	26
	Synonyms : transported	
1089	**Shoddy**	66
	Synonyms : tawdry	
1090	**Shoving**	6
	Synonyms : thrusting	
1091	**Shun**	25
	Synonyms : eschew	
1092	**Sidestep**	54
	Synonyms : hedge, fudge	
1093	**Siege**	59
	Synonyms : military-blockade, occupation	
1094	**Sift**	144
	Synonyms : sieve, strain	
1095	**Simulated**	33
	Synonyms : imitated	
1096	**Sinful**	187
	Synonyms : extraordinary, extravagant	
1097	**Singular**	182
	Synonyms : unique, curious, remarkable	
1098	**Sinister**	68
	Synonyms : minacious, dark	
1099	**Sired**	106
	Synonyms : begot	
1100	**Sketchy**	94
	Synonyms : unelaborated, vague	

S. No.	Words	Page No.
1101	**Skinny**	6
	Synonyms : boney	
1102	**Skirting**	25
	Synonyms : encircling	
1103	**Slaked**	183
	Synonyms : attenuated	
1104	**Slander**	38
	Synonyms : aspersion, defamation, denigration	
1105	**Slant**	150
	Synonyms : tilt, lean, tip	
1106	**Slashing**	54
	Synonyms : Adjective	
1107	**Slated**	73
	Synonyms : planned	
1108	**Sled**	199
	Synonyms : sledge, sleigh	
1109	**Sleuth**	109
	Synonyms : stag, snoop	
1110	**Slew**	188
	Synonyms : flock, wad	
1111	**Sluggish**	209
	Synonyms : inert, torpid	
1112	**Slyly**	110
	Synonyms : craftily, cunningly, foxily, knavishly, trickily, artfully	
1113	**Smothered**	191
	Synonyms : blanketed	
1114	**Snappy**	178
	Synonyms : jaunty, spruce, crisp	
1115	**Sneered**	114
	Synonyms : leers	
1116	**Snitched**	110
	Synonyms : informed	
1117	**Snout**	200
	Synonyms : rostrum, beak	
1118	**Snowballs**	29
	Synonyms : expand	
1119	**Soaring**	15
	Synonyms : towering	
1120	**Solace**	171
	Synonyms : consolation, comfort	
1121	**Sourced**	26
	Synonyms : obtained	
1122	**Souvenirs**	84
	Synonyms : memorabilia, mementos	
1123	**Spawns**	176
	Synonyms : breeds	
1124	**Speck**	144
	Synonyms : tinge, soupcon	
1125	**Speculation**	38
	Synonyms : conjecture surmise	
1126	**Spike**	66
	Synonyms : surge	
1127	**Spites**	165
	Synonyms : injures	
1128	**Splurges**	122
	Synonyms : wastes	
1129	**Spouse**	3
	Synonyms : mate	
1130	**Sprawl**	16
	Synonyms : conurbation	
1131	**Spree**	123
	Synonyms : fling	
1132	**Sprier**	176
	Synonyms : nimbler	
1133	**Sprouted**	41
	Synonyms : mushroomed	
1134	**Sprouting**	14
	Synonyms : germination	
1135	**Spruce**	165
	Synonyms : preen	
1136	**Spurious**	145
	Synonyms : inauthentic, specious	
1137	**Squander**	103
	Synonyms : waste, ware, blow	
1138	**Squandered**	188
	Synonyms : wasted	
1139	**Squandering**	46
	Synonyms : wasting	
1140	**Squelched**	128
	Synonyms : quelled, quenched	
1141	**Staggering**	140
	Synonyms : astounding	
1142	**Stagnated**	118
	Synonyms : idle, laze	
1143	**Stampedes**	17
	Synonyms : panic	

S. No.	Words	Page No.
1144	**Staple**	187
	Synonyms : necessity	
1145	**Startling**	213
	Synonyms : shocking	
1146	**Steeped**	17
	Synonyms : soaked, drenched	
1147	**Stellar**	37
	Synonyms : astral, leading	
1148	**Stigmatized**	155
	Synonyms : branded, denounced	
1149	**Stimulation**	20
	Synonyms : arousal	
1150	**Stingy**	131
	Synonyms : scrimpy	
1151	**Strident**	77
	Synonyms : shrill, raucous,	
1152	**Strife**	156
	Synonyms : discord, unrest	
1153	**Stringent**	62
	Synonyms : rigorous, tight	
1154	**Stroll**	178
	Synonyms : saunter, amble, promenade, perambulation	
1155	**Suave**	136
	Synonyms : debonair	
1156	**Subservient**	191
	Synonyms : obsequious, servile	
1157	**Substance**	6
	Synonyms : kernel, content	
1158	**Substantial**	126
	Synonyms : significant, solid, hearty	
1159	**Substantially**	176
	Synonyms : considerably	
1160	**Substantive**	219
	Synonyms : essential, substantial, meaty	
1161	**Succinct**	165
	Synonyms : compendious, compact, summary	
1162	**Subversive**	156
	Synonyms : seditious	
1163	**Succor**	102
	Synonyms : ministration	
1164	**Suffice**	98
	Synonyms : do, serve	
1165	**Sullied**	119
	Synonyms : besmirched, stained, tainted	
1166	**Summoned**	192
	Synonyms : commandeered	
1167	**Sundry**	144
	Synonyms : assorted, miscellaneous, mixed	
1168	**Supercilious**	131
	Synonyms : snide, haughty	
1169	**Supplant**	102
	Synonyms : replace	
1170	**Surge**	92
	Synonyms : billow, zoom	
1171	**Swankier**	170
	Synonyms : flashier	
1172	**Swapped**	67
	Synonyms : exchanged	
1173	**Swears**	109
	Synonyms : vows	
1174	**Synergy**	219
	Synonyms : interdependence	
1175	**Symbiotic**	196
	Synonyms : dependent	
1176	**Synergy**	219
	Synonyms : interdependence	
1177	**Tactile**	87
	Synonyms : tactual, haptic	
1178	**Taint**	208
	Synonyms : contamination, cloud	
1179	**Tainted**	42
	Synonyms : besmirched, tarnished	
1180	**Tampering**	145
	Synonyms : meddling	
1181	**Tangible**	219
	Synonyms : touchable, real, palpable	
1182	**Tarnished**	110
	Synonyms : besmirched, sullied	
1183	**Tatters**	154
	Synonyms : swarming	
1184	**Teeming**	26
	Synonyms : full	
1185	**Teleported**	170
	Synonyms : transported	

S. No.	Words	Page No.
1186	**Tenable**	33
	Synonyms : viable	
1187	**Tendering**	54
	Synonyms : servicing	
1188	**Therapeutic**	192
	Synonyms : curative healing	
1189	**Therapy**	199
	Synonyms : aid	
1190	**Thrall**	178
	Synonyms : bondage, slavery, thralldom, thraldom	
1191	**Thrive**	119
	Synonyms : prosper, fly high, flourish, boom, get ahead, expand	
1192	**Thriving**	37
	Synonyms : flourishing, booming	
1193	**Throttle**	114
	Synonyms : choke, restrict, restrain, trammel,	
1194	**Tickling**	15
	Synonyms : tingling	
1195	**Timbre**	33
	Synonyms : tone	
1196	**Timorous**	38
	Synonyms : fearful, trepid	
1197	**Titanic**	118
	Synonyms : titane	
1198	**Toddler**	20
	Synonyms : yearling, bambino	
1199	**Toil**	109
	Synonyms : travail, grind, drudge	
1200	**Toothsome**	196
	Synonyms : delectable, delicious, scrumptious, yummy	
1201	**Tormented**	200
	Synonyms : harrassed	
1202	**Totalitarian**	154
	Synonyms : autocratic	
1203	**Trait**	191
	Synonyms : characterstic	
1204	**Trampled**	114
	Synonyms : trodden	
1205	**Trance**	50
	Synonyms : enchantment, spell	
1206	**Tranquil**	50
	Synonyms : serene, placid, calm	
1207	**Transcendence**	26
	Synonyms : transcendency, superiority	
1208	**Transgression**	38
	Synonyms : breach, overstepping, violation	
1209	**Transition**	97
	Synonyms : passage, conversion, changeover	
1210	**Transpired**	102
	Synonyms : happened	
1211	**Transpiring**	188
	Synonyms : happening	
1212	**Traumatized**	42
	Synonyms : shock	
1213	**Traversing**	213
	Synonyms : spanning	
1214	**Treasured**	140
	Synonyms : cherished	
1215	**Trepidation**	103
	Synonyms : dread	
1216	**Trivial**	109
	Synonyms : picayune	
1217	**Trivialize**	149
	Synonyms : minimalize	
1218	**Trounced**	164
	Synonyms : crushed	
1219	**Truancy**	29
	Synonyms : hooky	
1220	**Truncate**	103
	Synonyms : prune	
1221	**Tumble**	128
	Synonyms : collapse	
1222	**Tumultuous**	97
	Synonyms : riotous, troubled	
1223	**Turbulence**	82
	Synonyms : upheaval	
1224	**Turpitude**	110
	Synonyms : depravity	
1225	**Twilight**	29
	Synonyms : dusk ,nightfall	
1226	**Ubiquitous**	29, 76
	Synonyms : omnipresent	

S. No.	Words	Page No.
1227	**Umbrage**	182
	Synonyms : offense, insult	
1228	**Unanimous**	217
	Synonyms : consentient	
1229	**Unbiased**	130
	Synonyms : fair	
1230	**Uncongenial**	25
	Synonyms : incompatible, hostile, unfriendly	
1231	**Uncouth**	182
	Synonyms : ruffian, coarse	
1232	**Underpinning**	115
	Synonyms : buttressing, bolstering	
1233	**Unexampled**	58
	Synonyms : unprecedented	
1234	**Unflagging**	58
	Synonyms : indefatigable, tireless	
1235	**Unleashed**	200
	Synonyms : release	
1236	**Unpalatable**	76, 83
	Synonyms : inedible, distasteful	
1237	**Unprecedented**	219
	Synonyms : unexampled, historic	
1238	**Unremmitingly**	82
	Synonyms : ceaselessly, incessantly	
1239	**Unscrupulous**	145
	Synonyms : dissolute	
1240	**Unsolicited**	178
	Synonyms : unasked	
1241	**Unveiled**	191
	Synonyms : disclosed	
1242	**Unwavering**	200
	Synonyms : steadfast, unfaltering, unshakable	
1243	**Unwieldy**	195
	Synonyms : unmanageable, gawky, clumsy, clunky, ungainly	
1244	**Upshot**	122
	Synonyms : consequence	
1245	**Uptight**	114
	Synonyms : restive, nervous, fidgety	
1246	**Ushered**	186
	Synonyms : introduced, announced	
1247	**Utilitarian**	140
	Synonyms : useful	
1248	**Vacillating**	41
	Synonyms : wavering	
1249	**Vacuous**	128
	Synonyms : inane, asinine, mindless	
1250	**Vanguard**	77
	Synonyms : forefront,	
1251	**Vanity**	2
	Synonyms : vainglory	
1252	**Vanquished**	76
	Synonyms : defeaed	
1253	**Vantage**	6
	Synonyms : advantage	
1254	**Vapid**	21
	Synonyms : bland, savourless	
1255	**Vaporize**	213
	Synonyms : vanish, , gasify	
1256	**Vaporizes**	159
	Synonyms : disappears, vanishes	
1257	**Veracious**	148
	Synonyms : honest	
1258	**Veracity**	62
	Synonyms : truthfulness	
1259	**Verdant**	73
	Synonyms : luxuriant	
1260	**Verisimilitude**	188
	Synonyms : semblance	
1261	**Veritable**	186
	Synonyms : unquestionable	
1262	**Vernacular**	76
	Synonyms : common, local	
1263	**Viable**	11
	Synonyms : feasible, workable	
1264	**Vibrant**	25
	Synonyms : vivacious	
1265	**Vicinity**	208
	Synonyms : neighborhood	
1266	**Vigilant**	192
	Synonyms : alert	
1267	**Vigilantly**	89
	Synonyms : watchfully	
1268	**Vile**	68
	Synonyms : despicable	
1269	**Vilified**	208
	Synonyms : slandered, reviled	

S. No.	Words	Page No.
1270	**Vilify**	148
	Synonyms : revile, vituperate, rail	
1271	**Virile**	136
	Synonyms : manly, potent	
1272	**Virtue**	145
	Synonyms : virtuousness, merit	
1273	**Visages**	3
	Synonyms : faces	
1274	**Vitality**	58
	Synonyms : verve, vim	
1275	**Vitiating**	122
	Synonyms : harms, hurts, damages	
1276	**Vogue**	164
	Synonyms : trend, style, currency	
1277	**Volatile**	94
	Synonyms : fickle, explosive	
1278	**Voyeurism**	62
	Synonyms : scopophilia	
1279	**Vulnerability**	17
	Synonyms : susceptibility	
1280	**Vulnerable**	192
	Synonyms : exposed	
1281	**Waivers**	63
	Synonyms : concessions	
1282	**Wallow**	123
	Synonyms : rejoice, triumph, welter, billow	
1283	**Waning**	25
	Synonyms : reducing	
1284	**Ware**	222
	Synonyms : merchandise	
1285	**Waxing**	98
	Synonyms : enlarging	
1286	**Weed**	76
	Synonyms : grass	
1287	**Wherewithal**	12, 106
	Synonyms : means	
1288	**Whiff**	201
	Synonyms : puff, sniff	
1289	**Whir**	217
	Synonyms : whiz	
1290	**Wick**	161
	Synonyms : taper	
1291	**Wield**	218
	Synonyms : handle, exert, maintain	
1292	**Winnow**	145
	Synonyms : sifting, fan	
1293	**Winsome**	1
	Synonyms : charming	
1294	**Wizards**	49
	Synonyms : virtuoso, ace	
1295	**Wooing**	62
	Synonyms : courting	
1296	**Wordsmith**	73
	Synonyms : author	
1297	**Wrangle**	135
	Synonyms : haggle, quarrel	
1298	**Wrath**	123
	Synonyms : anger, ire	
1299	**Wrecks**	187
	Synonyms : crashes	
1300	**Yearning**	66
	Synonyms : longing	
1301	**Zenith**	76
	Synonyms : vertex	
1302	**Zilch**	170
	Synonyms : nil, zero	
1303	**Zips**	6
	Synonyms : rushes	
1304	**Zombie**	191
	Synonyms : living-dead	

The number of words covered in the book are **1304** (through stories) besides **1850+** unique words (as their synonyms) which comes to a total of **3100+** unique words.

www.ingramcontent.com/pod-product-compliance
Lightning Source LLC
Chambersburg PA
CBHW081934160726
47999CB00008B/2385